North–South:

A programme for survival

Report of the Independent Commission on
International Development Issues

Willy Brandt

Abdlatif Y. Al-Hamad	(Kuwait)
Rodrigo Botero Montoya	(Colombia)
Antoine Kipsa Dakouré	(Upper Volta)
Eduardo Frei Montalva	(Chile)
Katharine Graham	(USA)
Edward Heath	(UK)
Amir H. Jamal	(Tanzania)
Lakshmi Kant Jha	(India)
Khatijah Ahmad	(Malaysia)
Adam Malik	(Indonesia)
Haruki Mori	(Japan)
Joe Morris	(Canada)
Olof Palme	(Sweden)
Peter G. Peterson	(USA)
Edgard Pisani	(France)
Shridath Ramphal	(Guyana)
Layachi Yaker	(Algeria)

Ex officio Members
Jan Pronk	(Netherlands)
Goran Ohlin	(Sweden)
Dragoslav Avramović	(Yugoslavia)

The MIT Press
Cambridge, Massachusetts

The map on the front cover is based upon the Peters Projection
rather than the more familiar Mercator Projection.

The Peters Projection introduces several innovative characteristics:
an accurate rendition of the proportion of the land surface area;
graphical representation of the entire world surface, including the
polar regions; the Equator is placed at the centre of the map; the
usual grid of 180 Meridians (East and West) and 90 Meridians each
(North and South) is replaced by a decimal degree network dividing
the earth both East and West and North and South into 100 fields
each; angle accuracy in the main North–South, East–West directions.

The surface distortions that do appear are distributed at the Equator
and the poles; the more densely settled earth zones, it is claimed,
appear in proper proportion to each other. This projection represents
an important step away from the prevailing Eurocentric geographical
and cultural concept of the world.

The map is printed by courtesy of Dr Arno Peters of the University
of Bremen.

Fifth printing, October 1980
Fourth printing, July 1980
Third printing, June 1980
Second printing, April 1980
First MIT Press paperback edition, 1980
First published 1980 by Pan Books Ltd,
Cavaye Place, London SW10 9PG
© The Independent Commission on International Development Issues 1980
ISBN 0 − 262 − 52059 − 1
Library of Congress catalogue number:
    80 − 50086.
Printed and bound in the United States of America

Contents

Abbreviations

The following are the main abbreviations used in the text:

CIEC	Conference on International Economic Cooperation
CMEA	Council for Mutual Economic Assistance (also known as Comecon)
EEC	European Economic Community
FAO	Food and Agriculture Organization of the United Nations
GATT	General Agreement on Tariffs and Trade
GSP	Generalized System of Preferences
IBRD	International Bank for Reconstruction and Development (also known as the World Bank)
IDA	International Development Association
ILO	International Labour Office/Organization
IMF	International Monetary Fund
ODA	Official Development Assistance
OECD	Organization for Economic Cooperation and Development
OPEC	Organization of Petroleum Exporting Countries
UNCTAD	United Nations Conference on Trade and Development
UNDP	United Nations Development Programme
UNEP	United Nations Environment Programme
UNESCO	United Nations Educational, Scientific and Cultural Organization
UNIDO	United Nations Industrial Development Organization
WHO	World Health Organization
WIPO	World Intellectual Property Organization

Staff of the Commission

A Plea for Change: Peace, Justice, Jobs

An Introduction by Willy Brandt

In the summer of 1978, half a year after we had started our work, a friend and distinguished African leader sent me an encouraging message: our Commission, he said, could 'contribute to the development of worldwide moral values'.

It is not for me to judge if and how far we have been able to meet that high expectation, but this Report, in any case, deals with some of the world's needs of the 1980s. It discusses North–South relations as the great social challenge of our time. We want to emphasize our belief that the two decades ahead of us may be fateful for mankind. We want responsible world citizens everywhere to realize that many global issues will come to a head during this period. But we also raise problems to be dealt with at once, long before we have come to the end of the century.

This Report deals with great risks, but it does not accept any kind of fatalism. It sets out to demonstrate that the mortal dangers threatening our children and grandchildren can be averted; and that we have a chance – whether we are living in the North or South, East or West – if we are determined to do so, to shape the world's future in peace and welfare, in solidarity and dignity.

The invitation to bring together this Independent Commission was the beginning of an exciting experience. For me, as for others, it has been an unforgettable education as well. It has been our advantage not to be preoccupied with national prestige, not to be under instructions from anywhere. We did not intend to take the place of governments or international institutions. But we tried to support decision-makers, and to appeal to the public on whom they rely.

We came not only from many parts of the world, but also carried with us differing convictions and different sums of experience, resulting from various fields of responsibility in political and economic life. As we discussed and argued over specifics, we found that we had gradually come to share a common vision of the kind of world we hoped for, and of some of the major problems to be overcome if our hopes were to be realized. This was remarkable – consensus became a reality.

When we first met near Bonn in December 1977, we regarded it as our task (as we said in our terms of reference) 'to study the grave global issues arising from the economic and social disparities of the world community'. And we promised 'to suggest ways of promoting adequate solutions to the problems involved in development and in attacking absolute poverty'.

When we came to discuss our conclusions, there was an even stronger feeling that reshaping worldwide North–South relations had become a crucial commitment to the future of mankind. Equal in importance to counteracting the dangers of the arms race, we believed this to be the greatest challenge to mankind for the remainder of this century. We were aware of the fact that the concept of global responsibility for economic and social development is comparatively new – in state-to-state terms it does not go back much more than one generation. It was the concept of the United Nations which – in 1945, at the end of the Second World War – created hopes (and illusions) about a world of equity and justice.

Over a period of two years, and in a number of intensive meetings, we have discussed and debated a great number of issues, agreed on many proposals, differed on some. Our Report is not meant to be a technical document. On the main thrust of our recommendations and the programme of priorities in our last chapter we are in unanimous agreement. The other chapters are also the result of our common thinking, though perhaps not every one of us may associate himself fully with each particular sentence in them.

Before speaking for my colleagues, to whom I owe much, I want to make some remarks on my own behalf. When someone asked about my right to chair a Commission of this kind, I was not surprised. In all frankness, my own record did not necessarily qualify me for the job. But learning from one's own shortcomings sometimes helps in addressing one's fellow citizens.

As a young journalist opposing dictatorship, I was not blind to the problems of colonialism and the fight for independence. During the Second World War, I also gave thought to problems of decolonization and development in terms of a new world order. I met Nehru, Nasser, Tito, and other leaders, at a time when most people, at least in my part of the world, had not even heard about a

Third World or the beginning of a non-aligned movement. Reading, travel and talks did tell me something about Asia and Latin America, Africa and the Middle East. I had not forgotten the problem of decolonization and development when, in 1971, I expressed my gratitude for the award of the Nobel Peace Prize, nor when I spoke to the General Assembly after my country had joined the United Nations, or on other occasions. But it is nonetheless true that, as a head of government, other priorities took up most of my time and kept me from realizing the full importance of North–South issues. I certainly did not give enough attention to those of my colleagues who at that time advocated a reappraisal of our priorities.

I kept in contact with the new approach to development problems. In 1974 and 1975, the Presidents of Algeria and Mexico told me about their important initiatives in calling for a new international order. But those who urged me to take on the task of forming and chairing this Commission probably recalled my contribution to what had become known as *Ostpolitik*. The problem then was: could sterile and dangerous confrontation between parts of Europe be replaced at least partially by realistic cooperation? Could one discover areas of common interest under the heavy load of irreconcilable ideological controversies?

The results have been strengthened peace and cooperation in Europe although very little has been achieved in the field of arms limitation up to now. The lesson I learned nonetheless was that one can move things by achieving practical and confidence-building agreements, so that old conflicts do not lead to new ones, and thus one can improve the political climate. In certain circumstances one may even be in a position to change the nature of a conflict. This indeed was the experience which I thought to bring to bear on our studies of North–South problems.

How to Change Attitudes

There has been much talk about a North–South dialogue. And there have been serious contributions to it. But there has also been a tremendous waste of opportunities and goodwill. The difficult and controversial subjects which divide richer and poorer countries will certainly not be solved by prejudices, nor by wishful thinking. They must be approached with a will to overcome dangerous tensions and to produce significant and useful results for nations and regions – but, first and foremost, for human beings – in all parts of the world.

I repeat: in *all* parts of the world. The Commission neither wanted to lose itself in polemics, nor to shirk difficult subjects. In the interest of global needs and universal efforts, it does advocate the greater involvement of the Soviet Union and its allies. No less important, the People's Republic of China should be invited to cooperate more intensively and – in doing so – let others benefit from its experience as by far the largest developing country. High level contacts with these countries and expert talks in some of their capitals underlined the Commission's endeavour to move a step further than the Pearson Commission found it possible to do a decade ago.

The Commission agreed on the necessity for a thorough rethinking to create a new type of relationship which could accommodate all nations. Such change can be brought about within the remainder of this century if governments of both developed and developing countries are convinced of the need to act. One should not give up the hope that problems created by men can also be solved by men.

This calls for understanding, commitment and solidarity – between peoples and nations. But they can come about only with a feeling for realities and a grasp of intertwined interests, even if these are not identical. It also calls for courage, for a vision of the future without which no great task has ever been completed. Such endeavours must be guided by mutual respect, open-mindedness and honesty, with a willingness not only to offer criticism but also to listen to it.

Change and reform cannot take place in a one-way street: they must be supported by governments and people in both industrialized and developing countries. If we are honest and want to promote international understanding, we should not avoid any serious exchange of views. Waste and corruption, oppression and violence, are unfortunately to be found in many parts of the world. The work for a new international order cannot wait until these and other evils have been overcome. We in the South *and* the North should frankly discuss abuses of power by élites, the outburst of fanaticism, the misery of millions of refugees, or other violations of human rights which harm the cause of justice and solidarity, at home and abroad.

This Report will be formally presented to the Secretary-General of the United Nations, and through him to governments and international organizations. But at the same time we hope to reach open-minded, responsible women and men all over the world. It is our ambition to enable ordinary people to see more clearly how their jobs and their daily lives are interlocked with those of communities at the other end of the world. We are asking them to think things over, to be sensible and act humanely and thus help secure a common future.

In our terms of reference we said the Commission would strive above all to convince decision-makers and public opinion 'that profound changes are required in international relations, particularly international economic relations'. We also promised to 'pay careful attention to the UN resolutions on development problems and other issues explored in international fora in recent years'.

Most people know that the existing system of international institutions was established at the end of the Second World War, thirty-five years ago, and that the South – mostly as latecomers on the international scene – faces numerous disadvantages which need fundamental correction. Hence the demand for a new international economic order. Fundamental change, of course, is not the result of paperwork but part of a historical process, of what is developing or foreshadowed in people's minds.

We expect much of those among the young generations who will soon carry major political responsibility. We hope that their insistence on dealing with human beings rather than bloodless abstractions or self-serving institutions grows stronger. We also hope that they are more concerned with human values than with bureaucratic regulations and technocratic constraints. And we are convinced of the great role education has to play: a better knowledge of international, and not least North–South, affairs will widen our views and foster concern for the fate of other nations, even distant ones, and for problems of common interest. The Commission feels that schools all over the world should pay more attention to international problems so that young people will see more clearly the dangers they are facing, their own responsibilities and the opportunities of cooperation – globally and regionally as well as within their own neighbourhood.

There is a real danger that in the year 2000 a large part of the world's population will still be living in poverty. The world may become overpopulated and will certainly be overurbanized. Mass starvation and the dangers of destruction may be growing steadily – if a new major war has not already shaken the foundations of what we call world civilization.

Shaping Order from Contradictions

We are aware that this Report is being published at a time when rich countries are deeply worried by the prospects of prolonged 'recession' and the diminishing stability of international relations.

We believe that these difficulties are more serious than those of past recessions and economic crises. It would be dangerous and insincere to suggest that they can be overcome with the conventional tools of previous decades.

Many people in government, and elsewhere, may consider this to be the worst possible moment for advocating radical changes. How can industrial nations preoccupied with grave problems of their own be expected to make far-reaching and bold moves to intensify cooperation with the developing world? But we believe that it is precisely in this time of crisis that basic world issues must be faced and bold initiatives taken.

We see signs of a new awareness that mankind is becoming a single community; but so far they have not been strong enough to stem the drift. In the short period since our Commission first met, in December 1977, the international situation has gone from bad to worse. It is no exaggeration to say that the future of the world can rarely have seemed so endangered. But it would be an illusion to reduce all the problems of the world to the conflict between North and South. Our world has many more facets, and world development is not merely an economic process. As one of our Commissioners remarked towards the end of our deliberations, the new generations of the world need not only economic solutions, they need ideas to inspire them, hopes to encourage them, and first steps to implement them. They need a belief in man, in human dignity, in basic human rights; a belief in the values of justice, freedom, peace, mutual respect, in love and generosity, in reason rather than force.

While the struggle continues for a new structure of international relations, non-economic considerations are being taken more seriously: religious and ethnic factors, education and public opinion. Peace is the aim of all religions, beliefs, philosophies. It is the great desire of all races, nations and creeds. Is it impossible to derive from this desire a *common* passion for peace as the emotional and moral driving force of our enterprises? But even here there should be no illusions. Peace, conciliation and other common values do not develop automatically. Development in the broad sense of a quest for peace may enable us to identify conflicts and handle them in ways that will no longer result in military or economic wars. There must be room for the idea of a global community, or at least a global responsibility evolving from the experience of regional communities.

It seems to be a permanent task for man to shape order out of contradictions. Efforts to restructure international relations receive invaluable support wherever they can be based on similar values. The impulses from churches and religious communities as well as from humanism can strengthen worldwide solidarity and thus help resolve North–South problems.

Destruction or Development?

Our Report is based on what appears to be the simplest common interest: that mankind wants to survive, and one might even add has the moral obligation to survive. This not only raises the traditional questions of peace and war, but also of how to overcome world hunger, mass misery and alarming disparities between the living conditions of rich and poor.

If reduced to a simple denominator, this Report deals with peace. War is often thought of in terms of military conflict, or even annihilation. But there is a growing awareness that an equal danger might be chaos – as a result of mass hunger, economic disaster, environmental catastrophes, and terrorism. So we should not think only of reducing the traditional threats to peace, but also of the need for change from chaos to order.

At the beginning of a new decade, only twenty years short of the millennium, we must try to lift ourselves above day-to-day quarrels (or negotiations) to see the menacing long-term problems. We see a world in which poverty and hunger still prevail in many huge regions, in which resources are squandered without consideration of their renewal; in which more armaments are made and sold than ever before; and where a destructive capacity has been accumulated to blow up our planet several times over.

There is no reasonable alternative to a policy of reducing tensions and bringing about a higher degree of cooperation. Quick solutions are an illusion; what is of paramount importance is the need to build up more confidence and to curb the mounting spiral of sophisticated and expensive weaponry. Antagonism in power politics and ideology can lead to dangerous armed conflicts. Efforts have been made to ease tensions in the most crucial areas of East–West relations. But the production and sale of arms keeps growing and can easily get out of hand. We may already be arming ourselves to death.

The relationship between armament and development is still very

13

much in the dark. The prospects which might open up if only part of the unproductive arms spending were turned to productive expenditure on development are only slowly dawning on people. The annual military bill is now approaching 450 billion US dollars, while official development aid accounts for less than 5 per cent of this figure. Four examples:

1 The military expenditure of only half a day would suffice to finance the whole malaria eradication programme of the World Health Organization, and less would be needed to conquer river-blindness, which is still the scourge of millions.

2 A modern tank costs about one million dollars; that amount could improve storage facilities for 100,000 tons of rice and thus save 4000 tons or more annually: one person can live on just over a pound of rice a day. The same sum of money could provide 1000 classrooms for 30,000 children.

3 For the price of one jet fighter (20 million dollars) one could set up about 40,000 village pharmacies.

4 One-half of one per cent of one year's world military expenditure would pay for all the farm equipment needed to increase food production and approach self-sufficiency in food-deficit low-income countries by 1990.

Could one be content to call something a 'new world economic order' if it did not include major progress towards disarmament? Arrangements on the limitation of intercontinental destruction machines are to be welcomed, but they cannot replace disarmament.

The past thirty years have seen peace in the northern hemisphere, against a background of military blocs controlling sophisticated arms, while the southern half of this earth has suffered outbreaks of violent unrest and military clashes. Some Third World countries have substantially boosted their armaments, sometimes to protect their legitimate or understandable security interests, but sometimes also for prestige purposes and sometimes encouraged by arms-producing countries. Business has been rewarding for both old and new arms suppliers who have spread an incredible destructive capability over the globe. It is a terrible irony that the most dynamic and rapid transfer of highly sophisticated equipment and technology from rich to poor countries has been in the machinery of death.

The involvement of so-called great powers, especially the nuclear superpowers, in the conflicts of other continents entails the risk of escalation. We join with those who warn against interventionism; there certainly is no military solution to the problems of energy or commodities.

On the other hand, manifest disrespect for international law and rules of conduct will certainly not make it easier to settle bilateral disputes or problems of a multilateral character. North–South relations should be seen for what they are, a historic dimension for the active pursuit of peace. Instead the tensions between North and South are complicating East–West antagonism, and Third World countries could easily become theatres of conflict between nuclear world powers.

Such tensions not only endanger peace but also disturb the development of reasonable economic relations and retard the growth of prosperity. That is one reason for asking: when will the arms-producing countries be prepared – in the framework of the United Nations or directly – to agree on certain rules of conduct? These might range from the disclosure of exports, both of arms and of the capacity to produce arms, to a non-discriminating arrangement barring certain types of weapons from export or preventing arms deliveries to certain areas. But it should be realized, of course, that by now arms exports are not coming exclusively from the North.

Peace can be consolidated by developing systematic cooperation with defined goals, by building confidence, by checking and reducing armaments, and by jettisoning ideological deadweight. People must be made aware of the relationship between problems of disarmament and development. The motives of power, influence and commerce – and, absurdly, prestige – that lie behind the arms trade must be harnessed to development, which would be a source of legitimate pride.

There is much in favour of a 'programme of survival' with common and unifying objectives: we must aim at a global community based on contract rather than status, on consensus rather than compulsion.

An End to Poverty and Hunger

It is a matter of humanity to conquer hunger and disease on our way to the next millennium – to prove wrong those forecasters who say we will have to face the distress of hundreds of millions of people suffering from starvation and preventable diseases at the turn of the twenty-first century.

The United Nations Children's Fund (UNICEF) estimated that in 1978 alone more than 12 million children under the age of five died of hunger. And although the United Nations declared 1979 the Year of the Child these devastating figures will not have changed for the better.

History has taught us that wars produce hunger, but we are less aware that mass poverty can lead to war or end in chaos. While hunger rules peace cannot prevail. He who wants to ban war must also ban mass poverty. Morally it makes no difference whether a human being is killed in war or is condemned to starve to death because of the indifference of others.

Mankind has never before had such ample technical and financial resources for coping with hunger and poverty. The immense task can be tackled once the necessary collective will is mobilized. What is necessary can be done, and must be done, in order to provide the conditions by which the poor can be saved from starvation as well as destructive confrontation.

Solidarity among men must go beyond national boundaries; we cannot allow it to be reduced to a meaningless phrase. International solidarity must stem both from strong mutual interests in cooperation *and* from compassion for the hungry.

The elimination of hunger is the most basic of human needs. Therefore we attach great importance to the increase of international food production and to the promotion of agriculture in many parts of the world which have become precariously dependent on imports.

The quality of life is almost meaningless without health, which depends on proper nutrition and a healthy environment. This also demands more research and operational funds devoted to combating the diseases of people in poor countries. Health care, social development and economic progress must advance interdependently if we are to attain our objectives for the year 2000.

Illiteracy too is a tremendous waste of human potential. Literacy – which goes beyond just being able to read and write – arouses people's consciousness and helps them participate in community life. Thus it is also a prerequisite for fighting hunger and disease.

We emphasize that human needs can only be met by the productive efforts of the society which strives to meet those needs. The only way to make this possible for developing countries, particularly the poorest ones, is to enable them to build up and develop their own productive capability. Therefore, we support additional and immediate measures for these countries. In our Report we suggest that such endeavours should, amongst others, include health, reforestation, river-basin projects, energy development, mineral exploration. These priority programmes constitute another important set of tasks to be achieved by the year 2000.

Leaders in the South shoulder the bulk of responsibilities. They should also be aware how important it is that public opinion in the North is convinced that measures of international reform which need support will really affect the living conditions of their people as a whole.

It would be unrealistic indeed to expect justice and welfare to be brought about by international resolutions any more easily than by national decisions. The work for international and national order and reforms must belong together. The greatest compliment we can pay to a friend is to be candid with him; our experience in this Commission, speaking in a friendly way from different viewpoints, has given us new insights.

To diminish the distance between 'rich' and 'poor' nations, to do away with discrimination, to approach equality of opportunities step by step, is not only a matter of striving for justice, which in itself would be important. It is also sound self-interest, not only for the poor and very poor nations but for the better-off as well.

New Responsibilities

Indeed, a new epoch in man's history began when the majority of nations now in existence achieved their political independence in the period following the Second World War. As a result of decolonization in most parts of what came to be called the Third World, long-established power structures crumbled or collapsed, leaving vacuums and giving birth to new political and economic groupings. At the same time we witness the revitalization of old cultures. And the end of false superiority-complexes.

All of us on the Commission considered it most deplorable that the process of decolonization is still not complete. And that thus, especially in Africa, valuable human potential continues to be fettered. We want this to be brought to a rational and productive end.

The countries which were released from colonial dependence, which became new or reborn nations, have been struggling to gain equality of opportunity in their development, and to be their own masters, not only politically but also economically and culturally. The new countries made it clear that they want control over their own resources. They were making efforts to increase their share in the international production of goods and in the world's trade. And they pleaded for beneficial cooperation, assistance and transfer of resources – financial grants, low-interest loans, goods and technologies – in order to overcome their poverty and to achieve equality of opportunity.

There has been a substantial change in the international debate since the 1950s. In those years, people in the industrialized countries and elsewhere saw the problem as one of enlightened charity. And those speaking on behalf of the Third World were essentially right in pointing out that their people, with their own resources, were responsible for the lion's share of their achievements, for which aid-givers sometimes claimed more credit than was really due.

There will always be room for humanitarian aid, I believe, even in the most perfect social system imaginable – and, of course, even more so in a world with immense distress to overcome. But the international debate on development, at the threshold of the 1980s, deals not just with 'assistance' and 'aid' but with new structures. What is now on the agenda is a rearrangement of international relations, the building of a new order and a new kind of comprehensive approach to the problems of development.

Such a process of restructuring and renewal has to be guided by the principle of equal rights and opportunities: it should aim at fair compromise to overcome grave injustice, to reduce useless controversies, and to promote the interlocked welfare of nations. Experience has shown that much determination and purposeful effort will be required to produce structural changes with a fair balance and for mutual benefit.

A right to share in decision-making processes will be essential if the developing countries are to accept their proper share of responsibility for international political and economic affairs. It is this right which nourishes the aspirations of developing countries for a new international order, and these aspirations will have to materialize if relations are to be placed on a new basis of confidence and trust in international cooperation.

On our road towards a new international order, we certainly cannot ignore one of the most tragic consequences of current conflicts and tensions: millions of refugees whose lives have been uprooted and often desperately impoverished. Speaking perhaps undiplomatically: since the death camps in Europe and the Hiroshima bomb, mankind has never been so humiliated as in Indochina recently, and especially in Cambodia.

The whole international community must take responsibility for the conditions of fellow human beings who become victims of intolerance and brutality. The burdens of countries who are close neighbours to regimes which cause an exodus of refugees should be shared in a spirit of solidarity by others who are better off.

Towards a Globalization of Policies

We are increasingly confronted, whether we like it or not, with more and more problems which affect mankind as a whole, so that solutions to these problems are inevitably internationalized. The globalization of dangers and challenges – war, chaos, self-destruction – calls for a domestic policy which goes much beyond parochial or even national items. Yet this is happening at a snail's pace. A rather defensive pragmatism still prevails, when what we need are new perspectives and bold leadership for the real interests of people and mankind. The 'international community' is still too cut off from the experience of ordinary people, and vice versa.

Quite a number of problems are becoming common to societies with differing political regimes. They could be called system-bridging: ranging from energy to ecology, from arms limitation to redistribution of employment, from micro-electronics to new scientific options which today are only faintly outlined. Whether these matters are discussed in Boston or Moscow, in Rio or Bombay, everywhere there are people who see their whole planet involved, at a breathtaking pace, in the same problems of energy shortage, urbanization with environmental pollution, and highly sophisticated technology which threatens to ignore human values and which people may not be able to handle adequately.

Communications and understanding have not caught up. In fact we face a situation where in the North technological innovations and material changes are more advanced than most people realize whereas in the South the consciousness and aspirations of many people seem to be ahead of material reality. To them we owe a new awareness of the environmental and ecological dangers to our planet.

In the crucial field of fuel energy mankind still behaves as if all these resources – up to now so abundantly wasted – were renewable. The oil stock of our planet has been built up in a long process over millions of years, and is being blown 'up the chimney' within only a few generations. Exhaustion of these resources is foreseeable but their replacement by alternative fuels is not. Pollution and exploitation are all-embracing, whether of the atmosphere or soil, or of seas which are being overfished with little regard to replenishment. Are we to leave our successors a scorched planet of advancing deserts, impoverished landscapes and ailing environments?

The grave consequences of increasing soil erosion and desertification should also concern all of us. Unchecked deforestation at its present rate would halve the stock of usable wood by the end of this century (and deprive more than one billion poor people of their essential fuel for cooking). The 'absorptive capacity' of trees, which checks carbon dioxide pollution, would be reduced to a dangerous level. It is not just a risk to the environment, it is a plundering of our planet, without regard for the generations to come.

The interest in preserving peace and abolishing hunger needs no further reasoning. But the interest in mutual survival *must* also be linked to the overriding issues of energy and the environment and the risk of self-destruction.

In the Mutual Interest

It would be dishonest to gloss over different convictions, and foolish to disguise conflicts of interest. But it would also be extremely unwise if we failed to balance and link interests wherever a common denominator can be found. North and South have more interests in common on a medium- and long-term basis than many have so far been able to recognize. And experience shows that durable solutions are often found only after confrontation has been brought to an end.

In this Report we stick to the thesis that there *are* growing mutual interests. These require a change in the character of cooperation. We are becoming more aware that a quickened pace of development in the South also serves people in the North.

The mutuality of interests can be spelled out clearly in the areas of energy, commodities and trade, food and agriculture, monetary solutions and inflation control, financing of projects and programmes, technological innovations, ground and space communications. The depletion of renewable and non-renewable resources, throughout the planet, the ecological and environmental problems, the exploitation of the oceans, not to forget the unbridled arms race, which both drains resources and threatens mankind – all of these also create problems which affect peace and will grow more serious in the absence of a global vision.

Perhaps one can illustrate part of the problem from the development of some of the present industrialized countries in the nineteenth and early twentieth centuries. A long and assiduous learning process was necessary until it was generally accepted that higher wages for workers increased purchasing power sufficiently to move the economy as a whole. Industrialized countries now need to be interested in the expansion of markets in the developing world. This will decisively affect job opportunities in the 1980s and 1990s and the prospect of employment.

Whoever wants a bigger slice of an international economic cake cannot seriously want it to become smaller. Developing countries cannot ignore the economic health of industrialized countries, which not only affects their readiness to import but also increases their willingness to participate in a more constructive transfer of resources. Most industrialized countries, even during the biggest boom in human history, have not tried hard enough to get near the minimum aid target to which most of them had solemnly agreed. That record is not only disappointing but also reminds us that, had the target been met, several developing countries would now be importing more goods and services, thus mitigating economic difficulties of the North.

A steady and secure supply of raw materials can only be obtained if the developing countries still want to supply them, free from compulsion and at their own discretion, because they get fair and stable prices and substantially better opportunities for processing at home. That, too, is what 'mutual interests' means.

An enormous challenge derives from the millions of unemployed in the North, but still more from the far greater number in the South. Protectionism certainly leads in the wrong direction for it helps to maintain at considerable cost structures that are becoming obsolete. It stops people from adapting to new forms of the international division of labour and postpones essential decisions. To avoid too sudden changes, which create abrupt frictions and severe social setbacks, new rules on adjustment must be mutually accepted.

It is extremely important to refute the notion that competitive newcomers from the Third World are intruders and 'enemies of the system'. By calling them 'newly industrializing countries', we cannot imply that the older industrialized countries have any priority rights among the nations of the world. People in the industrialized countries will have to realize faster and more comprehensively that the division of labour that was imposed or structured in colonial times cannot be cemented. The interrelationship between exports and imports will become much stronger than people are aware of. Only if the North provides better access to its own markets can it expect to export more.

Development loans will only increase the debt burden on Third World countries if they are geared to set up industries in those countries without creating the means of repayment. But not everything depends on North–South relations. Cooperation *between* developing countries will assume growing importance: there is a vast potential for special economic relations, exchange of knowhow, and reduction of dependence. Wider regional cooperation could enable smaller states to become parts of larger economic areas and to broaden their relations with the outside world. There also is a vast need for research and scientific cooperation in the South.

It is our conviction that we will have to face more seriously the need for a transfer of funds, especially in favour of the most handicapped developing countries, with a certain degree of automaticity and predictability disconnected from the uncertainties of national budgets and their underlying constraints. What is at stake are various possible forms of international levies.

Why should it be unrealistic to entertain the idea of imposing a suitable form of taxation on a sliding scale according to countries' ability? There could be even a small levy on international trade, or a heavier tax on arms exports. Additional revenues could be raised on the international commons, such as sea-bed minerals. While advancing such ideas, which are already under discussion in various circles, the Commission was aware of possible reservations. But – after an intensive exchange of views – we felt that new thinking is necessary to overcome the shortcomings of the present system of development assistance and at the same time strengthen the notion of universal, collective burden-sharing.

One might argue that it is hard to imagine international taxation without international government. But we believe that certain elements of what might be called international government are already called for to meet both mutual and national interests, and that by the end of this century the world will probably not be able to function without some practicable form of international taxation; and a decision-making process which goes a good deal beyond existing procedures. The survival of mankind, in justice and dignity, will make it necessary to use new methods to open new roads. But communications must be made widespread so that ordinary people know what is happening, and why.

None of the important problems between industrialized and developing countries can effectively be solved by confrontation: sensible solutions can only result from dialogue and cooperation. This demands a new perception of mutual dependence of states and people, to use the words of one of our colleagues. He added: development means interdependence, and both are preconditions of human survival.

There are many aspects of this interdependence: all nations will benefit from a strengthened global economy, reduced inflation and an improved climate for growth and investment. All nations will benefit from better management of the world's finite resources (and from a stabilization of the world's population). All nations – industrialized and developing, market or centrally planned economies – have a clear interest in greater security, and in improved political capability and leadership to manage global problems. But new vision will not end hard bargaining.

A historical process is not determined by resolutions or books, and privileged groups have seldom changed their attitudes wholly voluntarily. Arguments do play a role; words can be weapons. Nevertheless, a higher degree of intercommunication does not necessarily lead to better understanding. Reasoning in terms of ideologies and power-politics too often leads us away from, not closer to, a 'common language'. In spite of even deep-rooted controversies, we must seek agreement on content in order to arrive at common notions with the same meaning for all parties involved. This is a difficult but necessary task if one is to foster durable understanding. International resolutions are worded so ambiguously and can have so many different meanings that they sound artificial. Indeed, very often only the participants know how specific compromise formulations came about. Such resolutions should be made understandable and given appeal to people since they must get a chance to identify themselves with the work done on an international level.

What Does Development Mean?

This Commission did not try to redefine development, but we agreed (among other things) that the focus has to be not on machines or institutions but on people. A refusal to accept alien models unquestioningly is in fact a second phase of decolonization. We must not surrender to the idea that the whole world should copy the models of highly industrialized countries.

One must avoid the persistent confusion of growth with development, and we strongly emphasize that the prime objective of development is to lead to self-fulfilment and creative partnership in the use of a nation's productive forces and its full human potential. We must do away with the idea that our problems exist only because there are 'developed' countries and countries which *want* to be 'developed'. After all, the technological and economic development process in the North has not yet come to an end, and there is fierce discussion about how to progress from here – with different technologies, with a less wasteful way of life. Ideologies of growth in the North (and not only in the West of the North) have had too little concern for the *quality* of growth.

A people aware of their cultural identity can adopt and adapt elements true to their value-system and can thus support an appropriate economic development. There is no uniform approach; there are different and appropriate answers depending on history and cultural heritage, religious traditions, human and economic resources, climatic and geographic conditions, and political patterns of nations. But there is a common notion that cultural identity gives people dignity.

Over recent years experts and international observers have become aware that development strategies which used to aim at increasing production as a whole will have to be modified and supplemented in order to achieve a fairer distribution of incomes taking into account the essential needs of the poorest strata and the urgency of providing employment for them. It certainly makes no sense to impose methods of production in developing countries that leave their labour force largely unused, and there are now indications that new technologies might further reduce job opportunities in the North *and* the South unless reasonable employment and social justice are made essential objectives.

These strategies will not meet with an adequate response in the Third World as long as the industrialized countries stick to a guiding philosophy which is predominantly materialistic and based on a belief in the automatic growth of the gross national product and of what they regard as living standards.

One must beware of false hopes of general solutions when so many individual and national aspirations have to be brought together. It is also a vain hope that solutions will come automatically or that an automatic process will improve the lives of the unprivileged. The hope that faster economic growth in developing countries by itself would benefit the broad masses of poor people has not been fulfilled.

In many countries there are people excluded from economic growth as well as from participation in shaping their own environment; they live in conditions of absolute poverty and misery unworthy of mankind. Only if governments are committed to enabling the poor to benefit from increasing growth can the plea for increased international assistance and cooperation command moral strength.

We take it for granted that all cultures deserve equal respect, protection and promotion. The more the process of modernization is reduced to a merely technical matter, the more important conservation of cultural identity and independence becomes. We know that serious tensions arise from adaptation to the requirements of modern technology, the use of which cannot be avoided in combating the still-growing problems of hunger and poverty. It is imperative to find a balance between the chances offered by modern technology and the existence of individual peoples and regions which do not want to, and must not, lose their individuality. The solutions to these problems cannot be uniform.

The dangers of 'cultural' imperialism should not be overlooked. Solidarity among nations has to be based on a mutual recognition of values. Nonetheless, a technologically based world civilization may require a common social and work ethos. Better living conditions will hardly be achieved without a sense of responsibility for the fate of fellow human beings and without a humane motivation to work and production. Focusing on questions of historical guilt will not provide answers to the crucial problem of self-responsibility on which alone mutual respect can build. Self-righteousness will neither create jobs nor feed hungry mouths.

International social justice should take into account the growing awareness of a fundamental equality and dignity among all men and women. Scientific, technological and economic opportunities should be developed to allow a more humane social and economic order for all people. Strong efforts should be made to further a growing recognition of human rights and of the rights of labour and international conventions for protecting them.

This Report aims to point out some of the immense risks threatening mankind and to show that the legitimate self-interests of nations often merge into well-understood common interests. We also want to make it manifest that mankind is faced with very critical issues. They are not hopeless, if decision-makers of the world lend their weight to the solutions. Situations are seldom hopeless if they are not accepted as such. And hope itself is the most important element in overcoming obstacles which might otherwise seem insurmountable.

Summit for Survival

What, then, shall be done in terms of international negotiations? Too often the discussion is 'a dialogue of the deaf'.The air is thick with alibis for inaction. This applies to all sides. We judge ourselves by our good points and the other side by their failings. The result is frustration and deadlock.

In our opinion there are good reasons to propose and organize as rapidly as possible – after thorough preparation – an international meeting at the highest level, perhaps to be followed by others, to discuss North–South emergency matters and, if possible, to reach agreements, as concrete as possible, on how to turn certain mutual interests into creative partnerships, immediately and for the longer term.

We want to make it quite clear that North and South cannot proceed with 'business as usual' only adding a few bits here and there. What is required is intellectual reorientation, serious steps towards structural change, increased practical cooperation. A more relaxed climate of negotiations should do away with rhetorical warfare and unjustified expressions of distrust.

While we discussed 'summitry', a statesman from the Caribbean raised the question whether one could 'create a more productive negotiating environment under the umbrella of the UN system'. This is something on which we suggest urgent and serious consultations, all the more since the Non-Aligned countries at their meeting in Havana in the summer of 1979 also emphasized the need for global negotiations with a priority agenda.

The United Nations system should of course be developed and reviewed. Its shortcomings are well known and hard to surmount. Yet it is the only system we have got. International cooperation in the monetary and financial areas should become more universal and every effort must be made to include those countries still on the outside. (Member countries have tolerated the excessive growth of the international bureaucracy, and only they can reverse the trend. But their difficulties in containing the growth of their own bureaucracies is not reassuring. There is not only a need to review the state of international organizations; in some areas the existing ones may need to be supplemented to meet emerging concerns.)

A summit conference might substantially advance the efforts of the international community to solve the most urgent problems. This should include joint responsibility in the fields of energy and commodities, of finance and jobs, but also a global enterprise to overcome the worst aspects of world hunger and malnutrition by the year 2000.

Such a summit meeting should be in close contact with the UN, but it would have to include only a limited number of heads of states or governments. It should after consultation reflect regional and other main groupings, so as to allow discussions to take place between a manageable number of heads of states or governments (each preferably with only one adviser, and behind closed doors). There are, of course, world conferences which need a great number of participants and depend upon much publicity, but serious deliberations cannot take place at meetings with thousands of people participating.

The agenda for this kind of summit would include those items which – in a broader sense – come under mutual interests in the field of peace, justice and jobs. The views expressed at such a conference could not commit the international community. But decisions could be prepared and an adequate composition could provide the necessary climate for binding decisions in other fora.

Global questions require global answers; since there is now a risk of mankind destroying itself, this risk must be met by new methods.

An Appeal to the World

Finally, I wish to speak frankly to the leaders of certain states and groups of countries.

First to the United States. I do not believe that the American people could be indifferent to poverty and starvation anywhere in the world, and US organizations have indeed shown that they are concerned and ready to help. Yet the United States, which in the early 1960s was a leader in this field, has substantially reduced its international development efforts. As a proportion of its GNP, its foreign aid has dropped to a very low level. I understand many of the reasons for the dwindling US commitment but I sincerely hope that they do not reflect unchangeable aspects of American political life. I also hope that negative experiences with one or two countries will not affect American attitudes to the developing countries as a whole. When the nations of the world join in an enterprise to enhance the chances of world survival and promote global prosperity, the most powerful and wealthy nation cannot be content to play a marginal role, and no one else would want it to.

The Soviet Union has done much, in a few generations, to conquer poverty within its own boundaries. But the countries of the East have shown little readiness to share responsibilities in favour of the poor countries. However, I have been assured by Soviet leaders and those of East European countries that they view mankind's common problems with great seriousness. There certainly is a capability to participate in analysing these problems; and there is an awareness that their mutual relationships – to use another word for dependence – will continue to grow in the future. But there is still a missing logical step towards establishing global development criteria which can be quantified. Such a step would also be in the interest of the eastern countries themselves.

In the past, cooperation with the Third World has often turned into an arena of ideological conflict and controversy. If unchecked, East–West rivalry in this matter will be a great threat to world *détente*. All countries involved in East–West tensions will have to cooperate on agreements or even rules to prevent the transfer of their rivalries to the South. This would also reduce the temptation to exploit those rivalries.

In my own part of the world I find a wide range of attitudes to world development issues. Some of the smaller countries of Western or Northern Europe have been stirred by the magnitude of world needs to make a generous and progressive response. Others have been more reserved: they have not been over-generous in their cooperation and have tended to resist suggestions that the world economy needs to be reformed. The European Community has developed its own approach in some ways imaginatively, but its programme too is modest. In some individual countries there has lately been retrenchment in aid programmes and withdrawal from international responsibilities, while others have decided to increase their assistance. I hope my fellow Europeans will be convinced that their future lies in strengthening, not weakening, their positive ties with the Third World.

Japan is in a position to understand the problems of development especially well, having herself moved so quickly into the position of being a leading industrial nation. Many of us have been impressed by Japan's forward planning and active adjustment policies. I think other countries can learn from this experience. Japan has also announced a substantial increase in its development aid and is playing an important role in the dynamic changes in her part of the world. I hope she will continue to recognize the responsibility for the world economy at large that her great economic power confers on her.

I do not underestimate the difficulties, but I believe that the areas of universal cooperation must be successfully broadened. It is only natural that such cooperation must include the People's Republic of China with its great potential in many fields of international cooperation.

As for most of the developing countries, the work of our Commission has deepened my understanding of the difficult tasks faced by them and their leaders. Undoubtedly, the major share of the burden for effectively attacking poverty lies with them, their peoples and their governments. The awareness is gaining ground that egalitarian reforms and increased participation by all sections of their population can substantially improve conditions for more rapid and stable growth.

The developing countries understandably want greater influence in world affairs. But more power may already have passed from North to South than is generally appreciated, and in the years to come they will have to bear an increasing share of the responsibility for the preservation of world peace, without which all the rest of our endeavours will come to nothing.

Together with my colleagues I believe that the nations of this world not only have to but are able to live together in peace. We think that the task is to free mankind from dependence and oppression, from hunger and distress. New links must be developed which substantially increase the chances of achieving freedom, justice and solidarity for all. This is a great task for both the present generation and for the next.

The shaping of our common future is much too important to be left to governments and experts alone. Therefore, our appeal goes to youth, to women's and labour movements; to political, intellectual and religious leaders; to scientists and educators; to technicians and managers; to members of the rural and business communities. May they all try to understand and to conduct their affairs in the light of this new challenge.

Bonn/Geneva, 20 December 1979

1 North–South: The Setting

The crisis through which international relations and the world economy are now passing presents great dangers, and they appear to be growing more serious. We believe that the gap which separates rich and poor countries – a gap so wide that at the extremes people seem to live in different worlds – has not been sufficiently recognized as a major factor in this crisis. It is a great contradiction of our age that these disparities exist – and are in some respects widening – just when human society is beginning to have a clearer perception of how it is interrelated and of how North and South depend on each other in a single world economy. Yet all the efforts of international organizations and the meetings of the major powers have not been able to give hope to developing countries of escaping from poverty, or to reshape and revive the international economy to make it more responsive to the needs of both developing and industrialized countries. The dialogue between North and South will not by itself solve all the world's current problems, many of which are political rather than economic; but we are satisfied that the world community can have no real stability until it faces up to this basic challenge.

The North–South dialogue is not only an essential task in itself: it is also a wider call for action. It can make global action more probable by demonstrating that countries and continents can overcome their differences and resolve the contradictions between their self-interest and their joint interests. Now that both North and South are increasingly aware of their interdependence, they need to revitalize the dialogue to achieve specific goals, in a spirit of partnership and mutual interest rather than of inequality and charity. The dialogue must aim to give every society a full opportunity to develop as it wishes and satisfy the essential needs of its people at an acceptable pace; and to create a dynamic world in which every country can achieve its own development, each respecting the other and respecting also the imperatives of a shared planet. Leaders of public opinion everywhere must develop new insights into the historical forces which have for too long dominated and divided the international community; they must help the world to escape them and to break the vicious circle of shrill protest and mute response by tackling the causes rather than the symptoms of global problems.

We came to these problems separated widely by our experience and our positions on the political spectrum. But we have all come to agree that fundamental changes are essential, whether in trade, finance, energy, or other fields, if we are to avoid a serious breakdown of the world economy in the decades of the eighties and the nineties, and to give it instead a new stimulus to function in the interest of all the world's people.

The North–South Divide

There are obvious objections to a simplified view of the world as being divided into two camps. The 'North' includes two rich industrialized countries south of the equator, Australia and New Zealand. The 'South' ranges from a booming half-industrial nation like Brazil to poor landlocked or island countries such as Chad or the Maldives. A few southern countries – mostly oil-exporters – have higher *per capita* incomes than some of the northern countries. But in general terms, and although neither is a uniform or permanent grouping, 'North' and 'South' are broadly synonymous with 'rich' and 'poor', 'developed' and 'developing'.

Most of the North–South dialogue has been between the developing countries and the market-economy industrialized countries, which is how we will usually interpret the 'North' in this Report. But many of our observations also apply to the industrialized countries of Eastern Europe, which do not want to be lumped together with the West, or to be contrasted with the South in a division which they see as the consequences of colonial history. When we speak of the 'South' we also usually exclude China, which has not formally joined the grouping of the developing countries, though it commonly identifies itself with them. But we attach great importance to the participation of the East European countries and China in the international economic system and institutions.

Predicament of the South

The nations of the South see themselves as sharing a common

predicament. Their solidarity in global negotiations stems from the awareness of being dependent on the North, and unequal with it; and a great many of them are bound together by their colonial experience. The North including Eastern Europe has a quarter of the world's population and four-fifths of its income; the South including China has three billion people – three-quarters of the world's population but living on one-fifth of the world's income. In the North, the average person can expect to live for more than seventy years; he or she will rarely be hungry, and will be educated at least up to secondary level. In the countries of the South the great majority of people have a life expectancy of closer to fifty years; in the poorest countries one out of every four children dies before the age of five; one-fifth or more of all the people in the South suffer from hunger and malnutrition; fifty per cent have no chance to become literate.

Behind these differences lies the fundamental inequality of economic strength. It is not just that the North is so much richer than the South. Over 90 per cent of the world's manufacturing industry is in the North. Most patents and new technology are the property of multinational corporations of the North, which conduct a large share of world investment and world trade in raw materials and manufactures. Because of this economic power northern countries dominate the international economic system – its rules and regulations, and its international institutions of trade, money and finance. Some developing countries have swum against this tide, taking the opportunities which exist and overcoming many obstacles; but most of them find the currents too strong for them. In the world as in nations, economic forces left entirely to themselves tend to produce growing inequality. Within nations public policy has to protect the weaker partners. The time has come to apply this precept to relations between nations within the world community.

From Aid to Interdependence

To help conquer poverty and hunger and to create a more just and a more effective international economic system, fundamental structural changes must be made in the markets in which developing countries are suppliers – of commodities, of manufactures, of labour – and in which they are customers – for capital and technology. Such changes are also required in the mechanisms and institutions which generate and distribute international finance, investment and liquidity. The issue today is not only, or even mainly, one of aid; rather of basic changes in the world economy to help developing countries pay their own way. And the countries of the North, given their increasing interdependence with the South, themselves need international economic reform to ensure their own future prosperity.

The North–South debate is often described as if the rich were being asked to make sacrifices in response to the demands of the poor. We reject this view. The world is now a fragile and interlocking system, whether for its people, its ecology or its resources. Many individual societies have settled their inner conflicts by accommodation, to protect the weak and to promote principles of justice, becoming stronger as a result. The world too can become stronger by becoming a just and humane society. If it fails in this, it will move towards its own destruction.

Mutual Interests in Growth

While the international system has become much more complicated, with more independent nations, more institutions and more centres of influence, it has also become much more interdependent. More and more local problems can only be solved through international solutions – including the environment, energy, and the coordination of economic activity, money and trade. Above all, the achievement of economic growth in one country depends increasingly on the performance of others. The South cannot grow adequately without the North. The North cannot prosper or improve its situation unless there is greater progress in the South.

Many people in the North have questioned whether it is feasible, and even desirable, to maintain high rates of growth. It is undoubtedly true that past growth has been associated with heavy inroads on exhaustible resources and damage to the environment. But it can be argued that it is not growth, as such, but particular technologies, lifestyles and industries which have made a heavy impact on environment and resources; and these can and should be controlled by selective intervention. Indeed, many forms of environmental protection are assisted by growth and the public resources which growth can provide. The quality of growth will command increasing attention; but it is unlikely that industrialized societies will reject growth itself, which since 1950 has permitted a reduction of about one-third in lifetime working hours and considerable improvements in standards of well-being.

The Scourge of Unemployment

Only economic growth can provide the means for more jobs and incomes, whether in North or South. All countries are troubled by rising unemployment. But for the South it is a question not just of stability but of survival. Raising employment levels in the South is acutely difficult. The numbers for whom jobs have to be provided are much greater than in the North, and resources for investment much more modest. It has been estimated that in India alone eight million jobs must be created every year between now and the year 2000 to cope with population growth – even though it is slowing down – and the past backlog of unemployment. With 600 million people, India has a GNP two-fifths the size of that of the United Kingdom, which has 55 million people. This story can be retold for many other countries, especially those of sub-Saharan Africa, where productive capacity is lower and labour force growth even faster than in South Asia. To increase employment at a reasonable rate, and to avoid social and economic disaster in the Third World, calls for a tremendous effort both of national management and international collaboration.

Only with considerable increases in their resources for investment, and with more effective employment creation putting incomes in the hands of the poor, can these countries hope to increase the desperately slow pace of improvement of living conditions. Yet for the North to contribute to those resources – by expanding trade with the Third World, by changing the Third World's disadvantageous position in world markets, by increasing financial assistance – and also to solve its own problems – growth is a political necessity. Rising unemployment in the North is therefore from every point of view a cause for alarm. Part of it is due to technological change and new investment which substitutes capital for labour. But there are more important factors, primarily declining demand, and also more women workers and more jobs overseas, particularly through investments by multinational corporations. Imports from developing countries have not been a major factor – indeed, as we discuss in Chapters 3 and 11, as many jobs have been created in recent years through selling to these countries as have been lost through competitive imports.

The Necessity for Restructuring

Even though population is ceasing to grow in some northern countries, the labour force in most of them will continue to increase for some time. The growth in output required to absorb the labour force growth between 1980 and 1985, with productivity increasing, has been estimated at 3 to 5 per cent. Virtually all countries will require active employment policies, to cope with the past backlog of the jobless, and because foreseeable economic growth will not generate full employment. Industrial countries face a major challenge: solving their own employment problems, including the 'restructuring' of production to meet their domestic needs and the needs of the international economy.

Restructuring is a continuous process in efficient economies, through which more productive activities replace less productive ones – as in leather goods, shoes, textiles or ships, whose production has increasingly moved to the Third World. The switch in the North to other activities is sometimes resisted and protection is demanded. In an expanding economy the call for protectionist measures, including subsidies, is less likely as economic growth provides many opportunities for alternatives employing labour and capital more efficiently. Restructuring is always needed as nations change their relative competitiveness, but it is also required for domestic economic efficiency. It should be a positive process. Future jobs in the North are thus related to both domestic and international policies to expand the northern economies. A significant proportion of jobs in the North depend on trade with the South. There will be difficult conflicts within the North between those who have to change their employment and those who do not. But if the North fails to adjust, it will be more difficult for everybody.

We are convinced that many of the world's problems can be solved in the mutual interest of North and South. The South has called for a new regime to protect the commodities which they export against price-falls and fluctuations. The North has only slowly moved towards this, while being concerned about future supplies of raw materials and low investment in minerals, which cannot improve without remunerative and more stable prices. The South wants access to the markets of the North for its manufacturing, which raises problems for specific industries in the the North – but overall the North can expand employment by a balanced increase in its trade with the South. The South needs to buy from the North, and to repay its debts, but for that it must earn foreign currency in the North by selling its goods there. The South wants a code to provide more harmonious relations with multinational corporations – but both sides can benefit if these corporations can invest confidently in the South, and if the South can have more confidence in the multinationals' behaviour; future mineral investment in the South depends on such arrangements. Above all, we believe that a large-scale transfer of resources to the South can make a major impact on growth in both the South and the North and help to revive the flagging world economy.

After the Second World War: A Historical Note

The current crisis can only be understood in the perspective of the postwar decades, and in the context of the world institutions that grew up at that time. At the end of the Second World War, the United Nations was established with its headquarters in New York. It aimed to achieve universal membership and was built on the principle of one vote for each country – with a veto right for major powers in the Security Council. In 1946 the UN still had only 55 members. After 1947, when India gained independence, a succession of countries achieved nationhood in Africa, Asia, the Caribbean and the Pacific until by 1979 the UN had 152 members, so that the South outnumbered both the West and the East.

When the war ended the United States emerged as the dominant western power, and together with Britain took the lead in shaping the new institutions to provide the framework for world finance and trade. While the western powers were committed to intervention in their home economies, they were determined to avoid the protectionism and 'beggar thy neighbour' policies of the 1930s, by creating a strong free-trade system; it was a combination of Keynes at home, and Adam Smith abroad. In 1944, when they met at Bretton Woods in New Hampshire, they established two central instruments for international financial and monetary cooperation: the International Bank for Reconstruction and Development (IBRD), known as the World Bank, to provide loans to assist the reconstruction of Europe and Japan, and for the developing world; and the International Monetary Fund (IMF) to be the regulator of currencies, promoting stable exchange rates and providing liquidity for the freer flow of trade.

International Institutions

The Bretton Woods system was originally intended to include an International Trade Organization which was negotiated and agreed in Havana in 1948; but the Havana charter was never ratified by the US Congress. Some of its commercial provisions were incorporated in the less ambitious General Agreement on Tariffs and Trade (GATT) of 1948, which was intended as an interim arrangement, but became a mechanism which has served as the principal forum for multinational trade negotiation. The wider aims, including steps towards organizing commodity markets, were never implemented.

The World Bank and the IMF were established in Washington in 1945, where they have remained – working in adjoining buildings (though with separate staffs and different objectives). They were open to all countries, though the major industrial countries controlled them through votes weighted by contributions. The United States, which at first raised most of the Bank's funds, retained a strong influence. India and Latin America were represented at Bretton Woods but most of the Third World were still dependencies in 1944, and the views and the needs of the South were not in the forefront of the negotiations. Both the Soviet Union and China took part in the Bretton Woods conference. The Soviet Union chose not to join the institutions; and after the revolution of 1949, mainland China was not represented.

The West and the East soon established their own economic alliances. In 1947 the United States initiated the Marshall Plan for the economic recovery of Europe. It insisted that the European countries should cooperate in the allocation of US funds, and the Organization for European Economic Cooperation (OEEC) was established for this purpose: in 1960 it became the Organization for Economic Cooperation and Development (OECD), with the United States, Canada and eventually most western industrialized countries as members. In 1949 a conference in Moscow led to the Council for Mutual Economic Assistance, or CMEA – also known as Comecon – comprising Bulgaria, Czechoslovakia, Hungary, Poland, Romania and the USSR, with the German Democratic Republic joining in the following year. They developed a separate international monetary system, and their trade was governed by long-term agreements related to five-year plans. As their economic system took shape, these countries had at first only modest relations with the rest of the world economy. Later on the Mongolian People's Republic, Cuba and Vietnam joined the CMEA as developing country members; while Albania, which had joined later, left it.

The UN Agencies and the Bretton Woods Institutions

The United Nations became the principal forum for the South. The many new nations which emerged from the historic changes in the postwar years saw development issues as critical to their relations with the rest of the world, and their nation-building, which was often turbulent, depended on economic and social development. As the UN and its related agencies expanded, including the World Health Organization (WHO), the International Labour Organization (ILO), the United Nations Development Programme (UNDP), the Food and Agriculture Organization (FAO), the United Nations Educational, Scientific and Cultural Organization (UNESCO), they became instruments of development which brought the issues of international poverty more prominently to the notice of the North. The World Bank and the IMF, though increasingly concerned with the problems of development, tended to follow a more conservative approach. Between the Bretton Woods and the United Nations institutions, each with their own language and assumptions, there remained a difference of orientation, and of power. The South had majority votes in the General Assembly which gave assurance of passing resolutions; but the North's position in the World Bank and IMF gave it control over key areas of money and finance.

In the two and a half decades following the Second World War the world economy was transformed. With a liberalized trading regime and relatively stable currencies, dominated by the American dollar, the industrialized world experienced economic growth and an expansion of trade without parallel in history, which contributed to growth in some parts of the Third World. The World Bank, the IMF and GATT had to adapt themselves to the needs of developing countries. In 1960 the World Bank was augmented by the International Development Association (IDA) which provided a lending facility or 'window' for loans on much easier concessional terms to developing countries; the IMF increased and broadened its financing to assist them; while GATT attracted more members from developing countries and partly exempted them, at least in principle, from its rule of reciprocity, by which a member country seeking concessions must offer equivalent concessions to other members.

Changing Attitudes to Aid

At first the western governments saw development largely in terms of aid. The US initiated its development aid programme in 1949 and the UN began its programme of technical assistance at the beginning of the 1950s. At first aid grew very rapidly: by 1951 western countries were lending 8 billion dollars a year, almost one per cent of their gross national product, though aid loans of the eastern countries were much more restricted. In 1967 the World Bank suggested a grand assize which would 'study the consequences of twenty years of development assistance, assess the results, clarify the errors and propose the policies which will work better in the future'. This led to the formation in 1968 of a Commission chaired by Lester B. Pearson, former Prime Minister of Canada. When in 1969 the Pearson Commission published its findings, aid questions occupied much of its attention, which reflected the prevailing philosophy in development circles, as well as the fact that its recommendations were mainly addressed to the Bretton Woods institutions and to aid-giving governments.

But there was also growing interest in the fundamental problems of development – many of them, such as land reform, of a domestic nature, others related to foreign trade and investment. In the 1950s many studies suggested that developing countries' trade with industrial countries was on unequal terms and that this seriously hindered their development. The Non-Aligned countries, who had been brought together by anti-colonialism and a desire to stand apart from the Cold War, began to press for fairer conditions of trade. And when the first UN Conference on Trade and Development (UNCTAD) was held in 1964, the Group of 77 (which now includes well over 100 members) was formed, by which the developing counties sought to promote their economic interests jointly. This group included a wide range, from semi-industrialized countries in Latin America to extremely poor countries in Africa and Asia, but they were determined to maintain a unified bargaining front in the face of the richer countries of the North, and this profoundly influenced the subsequent course of North South relations.

New Trends in the 1970s

By the early 1970s the focus of debate had shifted away from aid to the structure of the world economic system. While the developing countries had benefited from the evolution of the international institutions, they wanted it to go much further. They maintained that the rules of the GATT were not sufficiently relevant to their special needs. They complained that the origins and initial power-structure of the Bretton Woods institutions limited the capacity for change, and they asked for a restructuring of the international financial system. In trade, finance and technology they were looking for reform and innovation.

But in UNCTAD and elsewhere the Group of 77 faced an uphill

task. At successive meetings they put forward proposals for international economic reform, but the North either did not like them or was not ready for them. The North has also argued that the South often makes inflexible demands which allow little room for negotiation. On the other hand, while some countries have made positive proposals, the North as a group has tended to react passively to those put forward by the South rather than present a constructive position of its own.

At the beginning of the 1970s the world economy suffered a modest recession; though it recovered rapidly in 1972 there was high inflation in several countries, and prices of grains and capital goods rose considerably. The monetary system had already weakened when the dollar was divorced from gold in August 1971; the postwar rules for the management of exchange rates were abandoned early in 1973. Major countries had to cope simultaneously with problems of inflation, unemployment and the balance of payments, and their domestic restraints were holding back international trade. The Bretton Woods system had already begun to crumble.

A decisive change occurred with the increase in the price of oil in late 1973, which marked a major turning point in North–South relations. The oil-exporting countries, organized since 1960 in OPEC, the Organization of Petroleum Exporting Countries, announced a series of increases which quadrupled the price of crude oil in 1973–4. With hindsight it might seem inevitable, as the real price of oil had been falling for some time and did not reflect the future scarcity of energy resources. But the price change gave a substantial shock to the world economy in which the flows of oil were already playing a major part. A few oil-exporting countries found themselves with large financial surpluses, while oil-importing countries suffered sudden deterioration in their balance of payments. The results were serious in the industrialized countries, and – together with other price increases and the effects of global recession – even more so in parts of the developing world. For several countries there was substantial help from OPEC to offset the oil price increase; but many others were seriously affected.

The world economy has failed to return to its earlier buoyancy. The western industrialized countries had grown at more than 4 per cent a year from 1950 to 1960, and more than 5 per cent from 1960 to 1973, but from 1973 to 1979 they grew at an average rate of only 2.5 per cent a year. The East European economies also grew more slowly, from over 9.5 per cent a year in the 1950s, and over 6.5 per cent during 1960–73, to less than 5.5 per cent during 1973–7 –

although figures for the East European countries are not strictly comparable with those for the West. Although some developing countries managed to maintain their growth momentum and their import demand – which helped to prevent an even worse recession in the industrialized countries – there was a marked slow-down after 1974 in Latin America and, most seriously, in the least developed countries, many of them in Africa. Their exports stagnated and their *per capita* incomes – little more than $100 – increased by just over one per cent, i.e. by $1–$2 per year.

Where growth has slowed down in developing countries it has, of course, aggravated an already grave unemployment situation; in the Third World unemployment and underemployment are measured in hundreds of millions. And unemployment has been rising also in the industrialized world. By 1979 there were over 18 million unemployed in the OECD countries. Many sectors of their economies – especially older industries like steel, shipbuilding or clothing – were in danger. Slow growth, inflation, the fluctuations of exchange rates, the rising costs of environmental protection and the problematic future of energy all added to the uncertainty of businessmen who held back from new investment.

The oil price was not responsible for all these ills, but oil has obviously become critical to the world economy. And in the North–South context the OPEC action has been of profound significance. For the first time a group of countries outside the circle of the industrialized world was able to exert its own powerful economic pressure. It belonged to the South and identified itself with the South's aspirations for fundamental reform of international economic relations. This gave the whole North–South dialogue a new impetus, though it still did not produce great progress in the 1970s.

As the decade drew to a close, the world economy was in serious difficulties, and the institutional framework which had served it since the war was inadequate to resolve them. Protectionism was on the increase, with no machinery strong enough to arrest it. In the monetary sphere arrangements for balance of payments adjustment or for an orderly pattern of exchange rates were not in sight. That there was a need for fundamental reform could hardly have been clearer.

Changing the World Economy

The governments and people of the South have the primary responsibility for solving many of their own problems; they will have to continue to generate most of their resources by their own efforts, and to plan and manage their own economies. Only they can ensure that the fruits of development are fairly distributed inside their countries, and that greater justice and equity in the world are matched by appropriate reforms at home.

The South needs and wants to be more self-reliant, to complete the process of political independence with economic independence. But that does not imply separation from the world economy. It means rather the ability to bargain on more equal terms with the richer countries, to obtain a fair return for what it produces, and to participate fairly in the control and running of international institutions. Many leaders in the South have complained that while the North may be prepared to spend money on alleviating southern poverty or distress, it is reluctant to surrender control over economic decisions. But this issue of sharing of power cannot be evaded.

Later chapters of the Report will discuss the major North–South issues. Commodity producers want to add more value to their products before they sell them: to export sawn planks or furniture instead of timber logs, instant coffee instead of coffee beans, refined metals instead of ores. But here the countries of the South run into tariff and other barriers in the major markets. An equally pressing need is for financial support to stabilize commodity prices and earnings. Most of the middle-income countries, and nearly all the poorer ones, depend very heavily on agricultural and mineral exports. Even Brazil or Malaysia, both middle-income countries which have moved into manufacturing, still rely heavily on coffee, rubber or tin. All these producers depend on prices which fluctuate widely, and which can force them to sell on a falling market at less than the cost of production. Price stabilization would be helpful to the purchasing countries as well.

Obstacles to Third World Industrialization

This in turn is part of the broader issue of access to markets. Exports of manufactures are important for developing countries' industrialization, but the North is raising obstacles against these too: including more 'non-tariff' barriers, such as formal or informal quotas, government subsidies or purchases restricted to their own domestic companies. Within the internal trading system of the transnational corporations the prices of manufactures, commodities or services can often be adjusted to the disadvantage of the developing countries. Further, a number of developing countries now count on the earnings of migrant workers as a critical source of foreign exchange. Pakistan for example receives almost as much from its workers abroad as from its total exports. But the migrants are often insecure and subject to discrimination; a recession can rapidly end their contracts, sending unemployment back to their home country. This labour market, like the market in commodities or manufactures, has weak sellers and powerful buyers.

In the international market for technology, the South faces other difficulties. Developing countries need to build up their own industry and research, and they are often in a weak position to bargain with the transnational corporations which control much of modern technology. They may benefit from direct investment, but the gains have not always been fully shared, which has caused political tension. They can buy technology through licences, but only on terms set by foreign corporations. They do not wish to lose control over their economies, they want to be able to treat on fair terms and with equal expertise with the transnational corporations.

The South needs, above all, finance. Most rich countries have accepted the target of giving 0.7 per cent of their GNP in the form of official development assistance, but few have lived up to it. Most aid goes to finance the foreign exchange costs of projects, but many of the poorer countries also need support for local expenditures and for imports of non-capital goods. Some of the more prosperous countries in the South have recently borrowed extensively from commercial banks, causing heavy problems in rolling over their loans, which by the end of the 1970s were causing anxiety to borrowers and lenders alike. And many developing countries will need much more finance over the next twenty years to produce any real improvement in health and nutrition, in mineral and industrial development, or in sustaining satisfactory growth

Among monetary issues, there are a number of particular concern to the South, as well as many in which North and South alike have an interest. The mechanisms for creating and distributing international means of payment are strongly influenced by the national policies of a small number of major countries, and the South is calling for a greater influence in decision-making.

Limited Progress in Negotiations

On these and other issues the South has been negotiating with the North for many years. UNCTAD set an extensive agenda for reform at its meeting in Geneva in 1964, which was further elaborated in New Delhi in 1968, in Santiago in 1972, in Nairobi in 1976 and in Manila in 1979. The North has moved on some issues. They agreed to a Generalized System of Preferences in 1968 by which individual developed countries allow duty-free imports of some manufactures from developing countries, though this has been subject to many restrictions. The European Community has negotiated trade preferences with a large group of developing countries, most of which had earlier colonial connections, culminating in the second Lomé Convention of 1979; but their impact on development has so far been modest. Multilateral trade negotiations have taken place in GATT. North and South have had talks within other international institutions; thus monetary reform was studied in the Committee of Twenty within the IMF which by 1974 had reached some agreement on the objectives, although not the means, of reform.

There was a spate of intense activity in the first half of the 1970s. In 1973 a summit conference of the Non-Aligned countries in Algiers adopted an Action Programme calling for 'a new international economic order'. This strategy of structural reforms was refined and adopted at the Sixth and Seventh Special Sessions of the UN General Assembly in 1974 and 1975. The 1974 General Assembly adopted the Charter of Economic Rights and Duties of States. The new importance of OPEC brought renewed world attention to the North–South dialogue, and led to the Conference on International Economic Cooperation (CIEC) which opened in Paris in December 1975. These talks continued intermittently until mid-1977, but they ended without any substantial agreement, except one in principle on assisting the poorest countries.

There was some movement in other areas. UNCTAD had introduced in Nairobi an Integrated Programme for Commodities whose centrepiece was the Common Fund which would help to stabilize commodity prices. This proposal achieved partial agreement in 1979, which some regarded as a negotiating gain, others as a false start; but negotiations on the Common Fund continue. On the Law of the Sea there was complex and laborious work involving both North and South, resulting in 1979 in an agreement in principle to set up a Sea-bed Authority. There were also negotiations about new codes for the transfer of technology and for the conduct of transnational corporations. There were discussions about the burden of debt, and after the CIEC talks the debts of some of the poorest countries were cancelled. But the main proposals for change have made little headway.

The most recent worldwide assembly was the fifth session of UNCTAD in Manila in 1979. While there was some concrete progress on a few secondary items, on the major questions of structural change which divide North and South there was virtually no movement towards any agreed measures which could be rapidly implemented. Did the delegations of the South perhaps not concentrate enough on the vital issues of mutual interests? Or were countries of the North simply lacking the political will to make major concessions?

East European Involvement

Attitudes in the Third World towards the East European countries were also changing. They had long argued that they were not responsible for the colonial heritage of other powers. Developing countries appreciated that the Soviet Union had moved from great backwardness to a modern industrial power in a short time. Eastern Europe can often offer long-term trading agreements, and their support has sometimes provided an escape from exclusive dependence, both military and industrial, on western countries.

In recent years Third World countries have expressed the wish for an increase in volumes of aid from and trade with eastern countries and for their greater involvement in international economic discussions. The international links of the eastern countries are growing; developing countries increasingly insist that their achievements and manifest influence in international affairs and the fact that many of them buy the Third World's commodities and sell manufactures to them on much the same terms – with significant exceptions as everyone else, confer a responsibility to participate more fully in international aid and trade with developing countries. At their Arusha meeting in 1979 the Group of 77 called for 'an increasingly more active role' to be played by the East European countries in bringing about the early establishment of a new international order.

The East European countries have expressed their willingness to cooperate further and they have also shared in international initiatives to solve global problems. Members of this Commission have had contacts with East European leaders. The Secretariat had a dialogue with Soviet experts of the Institute for World Economy in Moscow, who assured them that they were observing the problems of the Third World closely. They pointed out that they had undertaken great efforts for the development of the people within their own boundaries, and also in a number of developing countries. They stressed the quality of Soviet aid and argued that necessary military expenditures limit their capacity to provide greater foreign assistance. They emphasized the need for improvement in East–West relations and progress towards disarmament. The Soviet experts were fully aware of the great needs of developing countries. They strongly favoured changes in the international economic and financial system and institutions.

Many developing countries regard the Soviet Union as ranking in living standards among the industrialized countries. It is therefore hoped and expected that the Soviet Union and other eastern industrialized countries will increase their participation in world trade and in economic, scientific and technical cooperation, particularly with developing countries. Bolder political decisions in eastern, as well as in western and Third World countries, are needed to achieve a true international cooperation in the interest of development.

Participation of China

China is the largest developing country, with nearly a quarter of the world's population, and its experience has many lessons for others. While setting itself the long-term goal of industrialization, it gives the highest priority to agricultural production. It is strongly committed to population control. Even though China's annual income per head is less than $400, it has provided significant aid and technical assistance to other countries, both in quantity and quality.

The Commission sent a small team to China as guests of the Chinese People's Institute for Foreign Affairs, who discussed policies and attitudes to international economic relations, and were also informed of China's own progress in modernization. China is interested in closer exchange with the international economy in trade, finance and investment, and is now considering membership of the Bretton Woods institutions and GATT. It is already receiving offers of large credits from many sources. We welcome this trend for the closer participation of China in the international economy, which will benefit China and the rest of the world.

Unity to Avert Catastrophe

Current trends point to a sombre future for the world economy and international relations. A painful outlook for the poorer countries with no end to poverty and hunger; continuing world stagnation combined with inflation; international monetary disorder; mounting debts and deficits; protectionism; major tensions between countries competing for energy, food and raw materials; growing world population and more unemployment in North and South; increasing threats to the environment and the international commons through deforestation and desertification, overfishing and overgrazing, the pollution of air and water. And overshadowing everything the menacing arms race.

For these trends to continue is dangerous enough, but they can easily worsen. A number of poor countries are threatened with the irreversible destruction of their ecological systems; many more face growing food deficits and possibly mass starvation. In the international economy there is the possibility of competitive trade restrictions or devaluations; a collapse of credit with defaults by major debtors, or bank failures; a deepening recession under possible energy shortages or further failures of international cooperation; an intensified struggle for spheres of interest and influence, or for control over resources, leading to military conflicts. The 1980s could witness even greater catastrophes than the 1930s.

Such developments are not improbable; but we do not believe them to be inevitable. Current trends do not have to continue, let alone worsen. We believe that nations, even on grounds of self-interest, can join in the common task of ensuring survival, to make the world more peaceful and less uncertain. A fundamental change in relations between North and South as well as between East and West is crucial to this task. The world is a unity, and we must begin to act as members of it who depend on each other. It is not enough, as one of our Commissioners put it, to sit around tables talking like characters in Chekhov plays about insoluble problems. We have to lift ourselves above the immediate constrictions, and offer the world a plan and a vision of hope, without which nothing substantial can be achieved.

2   Dimensions of Development

Development never will be, and never can be, defined to universal satisfaction. It refers, broadly speaking, to desirable social and economic progress, and people will always have different views about what is desirable. Certainly development must mean improvement in living conditions, for which economic growth and industrialization are essential. But if there is no attention to the quality of growth and to social change one cannot speak of development.

It is now widely recognized that development involves a profound transformation of the entire economic and social structure. This embraces changes in production and demand as well as improvements in income distribution and employment. It means creating a more diversified economy, whose main sectors become more interdependent for supplying inputs and for expanding markets for output.

The actual patterns of structural transformation will tend to vary from one country to another depending on a number of factors – including resources, geography, and the skills of the population. There are therefore no golden rules capable of universal application for economic development. Each country has to exploit the opportunities open to it for strengthening its economy. Structural transformation need not imply autarky. Some countries might find it feasible to pursue inward-looking strategies that rely, at least in the early stages, on using their domestic markets. Others may diversify and expand their exports. Exports can become more fully integrated with the rest of the economy, as the domestic market comes to provide a larger base, or as export industries secure more of their inputs from local sources. Yet others will concentrate initially on distributing income more evenly in order to widen the domestic market for locally produced goods and to lay the foundations for a better balance between the rural and urban sectors. But all countries need an international environment that will be responsive to their development efforts. Herein lies part of the rationale for a new international economic order.

Statistical measurements of growth exclude the crucial elements of social welfare, of individual rights, of values not measurable by money. Development is more than the passage from poor to rich, from a traditional rural economy to a sophisticated urban one. It carries with it not only the idea of economic betterment, but also of greater human dignity, security, justice and equity.

The Nature of Poverty

Few people in the North have any detailed conception of the extent of poverty in the Third World or of the forms that it takes. Many hundreds of millions of people in the poorer countries are preoccupied solely with survival and elementary needs. For them work is frequently not available or, when it is, pay is very low and conditions often barely tolerable. Homes are constructed of impermanent materials and have neither piped water nor sanitation. Electricity is a luxury. Health services are thinly spread and in rural areas only rarely within walking distance. Primary schools, where they exist, may be free and not too far away, but children are needed for work and cannot easily be spared for schooling. Permanent insecurity is the condition of the poor. There are no public systems of social security in the event of unemployment, sickness or death of a wage-earner in the family. Flood, drought or disease affecting people or livestock can destroy livelihoods without hope of compensation. In the North, ordinary men and women face genuine economic problems – uncertainty, inflation, the fear if not the reality of unemployment. But they rarely face anything resembling the total deprivation found in the South. Ordinary people in the South would not find it credible that the societies of the North regard themselves as anything other than wealthy.

The poorest people in the world will remain for some time to come outside the reach of normal trade and communications. The combination of malnutrition, illiteracy, disease, high birth rates, underemployment and low income closes off the avenues of escape; and while other groups are increasingly vocal, the poor and illiterate are usually and conveniently silent. It is a condition of life so limited as to be, in the words of the President of the World Bank, 'below any rational definition of human decency'. No concept of development can be accepted which continues to condemn hundreds of millions of people to starvation and despair.

Eight Hundred Million Destitute

Precisely how many people in the Third World live in such conditions of poverty, no one can say. The International Labour Office estimated the number of destitute at 700 million in the early 1970s. World Bank estimates today put them at 800 million. This suggests that almost 40 per cent of the people in the South are surviving – but only barely surviving – in the kind of poverty we have been describing, with incomes judged insufficient to secure the basic necessities of life.

Mass poverty remains overwhelmingly a rural affliction, and it is rural poverty that seems so harshly intractable. The mass urban poverty of Kinshasa, Mexico City or Cairo is a relatively modern phenomenon. For all its squalor, it is one step up from rural deprivation. To some extent, that is why these cities have grown. But the poor in India, Bangladesh, Pakistan, Indonesia and nearly all of Africa, are still, to the extent of 70 per cent or more of the total population, in the rural villages.

Differing Conditions of Poverty

People are poor in two kinds of circumstances: in countries which have reached relatively high average levels of income, where this income is not well distributed; and in countries which have low levels of income where there is little to distribute. Poverty in the North is entirely of the first kind. There are pockets of poverty, and deficiencies in housing and other services, all the less defensible for existing in the midst of what several commentators have called 'overdevelopment'. In the South, the great majority of the 800 million poor live in the low-income countries of sub-Saharan Africa and South Asia, though many better-off countries have large layers of acute poverty which show that the benefits of growth have not trickled down to the poorest. This does not necessarily mean that these governments are indifferent to their poor or lack the political will to improve their lot. But some of the richer ones, especially in Latin America, could do much more: the growth performance of Latin America in the 1970s (of about 7 per cent per annum), if sustained, could enable them to solve their problems of extreme poverty. In Latin America as a whole, the absolute poor number about 100 million; in twelve out of twenty-three countries where reliable estimates exist, over one-half of the population has incomes insufficient to buy a basket of goods and services deemed essential for a minimum level of welfare.

The experience of some countries confirms that, where assets are distributed more fairly in the first place, sustained economic growth can provide jobs and better conditions for the poor. The better-off countries have sufficient resources to mitigate extreme forms of poverty; if they can maintain high growth rates, they can eliminate it. But for the elimination of poverty in the world as a whole the outlook is bleak. Recent World Bank projections (which contain fairly optimistic assumptions about economic growth, but do not incorporate any major changes in international or national development efforts) suggest that there will still be 600 million absolute poor in the countries of the South by the year 2000.

Low-Income Countries

For most developing countries of Africa and Asia, the seeming failure to distribute wealth is a symptom of a deeper distress which many of them do not have the resources to tackle. Their rate of growth in the past two decades – less than 3 per cent per year – has not been enough to make much difference to the poor. Their total resources, even if they were equally divided, are insufficient to support their populations. These countries, with a GNP per head of less than $250, had a combined population of 1215 million in 1976. More than half this number live in absolute poverty. Four large countries of Asia – Bangladesh, India, Indonesia and Pakistan – contain about two thirds of the world's poor. Another third is made up of countries that have been defined by the United Nations as 'least developed' (including Bangladesh). These countries have very different resources and economic structures. India, Indonesia and Pakistan, for example, are major producers of manufactures, including textiles, shoes and electronics; they have a developed infrastructure, with sophisticated commercial and financial services, scientists, engineers and managers; and they will be better able to help the poor if they can sell more exports, with access to the markets of the industrial countries. But virtually all these countries have two-thirds or more of their workers in agriculture, and all of them rely heavily on exporting raw materials. These are among the chief economic causes of their slow growth.

Half or more of the total product of these countries comes from agriculture; and this is part of their problem, since a higher rate of growth in agriculture depends both on mastering the vagaries of nature and on adapting social institutions. In many African countries food output has grown more slowly than population, which has worsened the conditions for the ever-growing number who earn their living by farming. In Asia also there has been a disappointing record, though there are some more promising experiences. In a number of countries, including India and the Philippines, the new crop varieties of the 'Green Revolution' produced substantial agricultural growth, at least from the mid-1960s to the mid-1970s. The expansion of food production and agricultural employment in the low-income countries is crucial. Historical evidence shows that the absolute number of people dependent on rural employment declines only in the later stages of development, when manufacturing has taken over as the leading sector in growth. Even in the early stages agricultural progress is linked to overall development as it needs markets both in and outside agriculture.

The international environment has not been particularly favourable to the poor countries. Prices of the commodities on which they depend heavily for export earnings have fluctuated erratically and have over long periods deteriorated in relation to the prices of their imports, especially capital goods and oil. In the long run the only effective solutions to these difficulties are diversification, greater flexibility and overall development. But the possibilities of diversification are circumscribed by limited access to the markets of industrial countries which are in numerous cases highly protected against processed products. Moreover, stabilized and remunerative prices of their commodities which can promote greater flexibility for their economies can only result from a better framework for commodity trade as a whole. International agreements on relevant commodities (in particular cotton, hard fibres, tea, oil-seeds and coffee), finance for national stocks and diversification measures are of particular importance to many of the poorest countries.

With a more favourable international economic environment some of the low-income countries would gradually become able to reduce their dependence on concessional assistance. But for the poorest countries, aid for promoting necessary structural transformation will continue to be essential well into the next century.

Newly Industrializing Countries

It would be highly misleading to present the Third World as an unchanging picture of widespread poverty. Even among the low-income countries progress is occurring, the beginnings – and in some cases much more than beginnings – of structural transformation. In a number of developing countries, moreover, there have been truly remarkable advances. In terms of sheer economic growth rates, the most striking cases have been the 'newly industrializing countries', which have been thrusting ahead with manufacturing growth. The Latin American ones – Argentina, Brazil, Mexico – have a quite old-established industrial base, which has increased rapidly in the postwar decades. A spectacular example is Brazil, whose economy at current growth rates will by the year 2000 rival in size that of the Federal Republic of Germany. It is also an important trading partner and thus a stimulus to growth for other countries in the South. Several of what used to be called 'peripheral' countries are now becoming significant nerve centres of industrial production.

Other smaller industrializing countries illustrate how fast the economic map of the world is shifting. They have been able to take advantage of the international division of labour in highly competitive world markets. Many of them are in South East Asia – Republic of Korea, Hong Kong, Malaysia, Singapore, Taiwan – but they also include Yugoslavia, with its different social system. Their economies as a whole have been sustaining an average growth from 5 to 9 per cent over a decade and a half. There are other countries which have begun relatively recently to penetrate export markets with their manufactures. Colombia, the Philippines, Thailand.

Already the names of these 'NICs' have become more familiar to consumers in the North, since they first noticed a few years ago that their sports shoes were made in Korea, their camera in Singapore, or their television set in Taiwan. The future progress of these countries depends considerably on the trade and financial policies of the North. They may suffer new setbacks with the development of micro-processors, which could reduce some of their advantages. While they owe much of their expansion and technology to the multinational corporations, they remain very vulnerable to the corporations' trading practices. And their debts pose serious problems, which we discuss elsewhere. Can the dynamism of these countries be integrated in an era of world economic expansion in the 1980s? Or will it be repressed through protectionism and the failure of global economic management? On this question depends not only their own future, but the hopes of many other countries looking towards industrialization.

Oil Exporters

Another group, the oil-exporting developing countries, has become rapidly richer in the last few years. The three with the highest *per capita* incomes – Kuwait, Qatar and the United Arab Emirates – are all special cases with very small populations. Indonesia and Nigeria, on the other hand, are far from wealthy; between them they have over 200 million people, and huge development problems for which oil revenues provide only a partial solution.

.But whether rich or poor, almost all oil producers still have serious economic difficulties. The better-off (Gabon, Iran, Iraq, Libya, Saudi Arabia, Trinidad and Tobago and Venezuela) depend heavily on oil and most of them lack the infrastructure and amenities of countries which have been prosperous for longer. With the proceeds of today's oil they need to create a balanced productive economy to sustain their populations in the future when there will be little oil left.

Elementary Needs: Health

The overall features of development take on their human character when we consider the satisfaction of elementary needs. We look first at the three major areas: health, housing and education. In health, there is some cause for hope as well as concern. Most people in the Third World are living much longer today than they were only two decades ago. In sub-Saharan Africa, it is true, life expectancy is still very low: the average is only about 45 years. But in large parts of South and East Asia, in North Africa and the Middle East, people can expect to live 10 to 15 years longer. Much of this has been achieved by controlling communicable diseases, including cholera and malaria. (The latter has unfortunately recently increased, though causing fewer deaths, after being almost under control in the 1960s.) The elimination of smallpox – achieved by the World Health Organization and collaborating countries – was one of the triumphs of the 1970s.

But poor health is still the likely fate of much of the Third World. The population censuses of 1970–71 showed that death rates were not declining as fast as expected. Health authorities were running into the more intractable conditions of poverty and malnutrition, poor hygiene and sanitation, all in turn contributing to high infant and child mortality. There are still countries in Africa where one child in four does not survive until its first birthday. Blindness afflicts 30 to 40 million people in the Third World and threatens many tens of millions more – whether from river-blindness, vitamin A deficiency or water-borne infections. No one knows how many people are undernourished and hungry, but much evidence suggests that the number could be more than one-fifth of the whole Third World, or 500–600 million people; some estimates put it at one billion.

Lack of safe water is a major cause of ill-health; in virtually half the world water supplies are uncertain. Four out of five people living in the rural areas of developing countries do not have reasonable access to even relatively unpolluted water. Even in towns with a public water supply one out of four do not have access to it and, of those that do, more than half receive intermittent and unsafe supplies. In the countryside women often have to cross long distances to secure their minimum requirements of water for the family. Sanitation is an even worse problem causing numerous water-borne diseases, to which children are particularly susceptible. Between 20 and 25 million children below the age of five die every year in developing countries, and a third of these deaths are from diarrhoea caught from polluted water. All these deaths cannot be eliminated just by providing safe water and sanitation; but there can be no lasting improvement of public health without them. In 1977 the UN Water Conference of Mar-del-Plata in Argentina set an ambitious goal: safe drinking water and hygienic conditions for all by 1990. So far over 100 countries have undertaken (with the help of WHO) self-critical surveys to determine the extent of outstanding needs, and of required external support. To attain the Mar-del-Plata goals, it is estimated that the current rate of investment must be almost doubled in towns and cities, and increased fourfold in rural areas.

Improving health requires efforts far beyond medical care; it is closely linked with food and nutrition, with employment and income distribution and with the international economy. But there are a number of priorities within the health sector itself. In 1978 the WHO held a conference in Alma-Ata, in the Soviet Union, on Primary Health Care. This set a target for governments and the world community, to attain for all people by the year 2000 'a level of health that will permit them to lead a socially and economically productive life'. Primary health care was the key to attaining the target; the conference also asked the governments to link health care to other sectors. The WHO has, in addition, backed an important Action Programme to give developing countries greater opportunities to obtain and produce medical drugs, and to make special provisions for the poorest countries to obtain essential drugs. And the WHO among its health activities has initiated a major programme to control and prevent blindness.

The costs of raising health services to an acceptable level are in themselves relatively small. The WHO estimates that $3 per child would be sufficient to immunize every newborn child in the developing world against the six most common childhood diseases. With present birth rates this amounts to $0.12 per person per year spread over the total population of those countries. To provide primary health care for all might, on the basis of pilot studies, be estimated to cost some $2.50–$4 per person annually. Clean water and sanitation, on the other hand, do require considerable investments, especially in urban areas. Typical costs for simple standpipes or wells can be roughly estimated at $10 per person for water in rural areas; the costs for house connections rise to $75 in rural areas and twice that in urban areas. For sanitation, typical costs are $5 per person in rural areas and $15 to $200 in towns, depending on whether sewerage is included.

Not only more resources, but greater political determination is needed to reform orthodox medical systems and to encourage cooperative community activities for the improvement of primary health care. But clean water and sanitation will remain an unattainable objective in poor countries without development aid. The 1980s have been designated as a Decade for Drinking Water and Sanitation; in order to remedy an intolerable situation, we call for its aims to be fully supported.

Elementary Needs: Housing

The need for housing is fundamental. But most developing countries have not been able to give it priority, and the individual is commonly left to fend for himself. The results may not be known statistically, but they are familiar to anyone travelling through the Third World. One recent study showed that one-third to two-thirds of all families in Ahmedabad, Bogotá, Hong Kong, Madras, Mexico City and Nairobi could not afford the cheapest new housing currently being built. The rush to the towns has created the same kind of misery as existed in the nineteenth-century cities of Europe and America. But industrialization in those days was labour-intensive, so that the cities grew as the jobs expanded; the migration in today's developing world is often due to the lack of opportunity in the countryside – it is 'rural push' as much as 'urban pull'. The consequences of high birth rates and rapid migration are all too visible in many cities of the Third World, with abysmal living conditions and very high unemployment or underemployment. The strains on families, whose members are often separated, are very heavy. In São Paulo in Brazil, the population was growing at around 6–7 per cent annually in the late sixties and early seventies, in such appalling conditions that infant mortality was actually increasing. The fact that people still migrate to these cities only underlines the desperate situation which they have left behind.

Many lessons are to be learnt from rehousing schemes undertaken in recent years in different parts of the world. The kind of housing required obviously depends on the climate and environment and no one pattern can be offered as a global model. It is relevant that most of the developing countries where the needs are greatest lie in warm climatic zones. Experience shows that, apart from the need to keep down costs and rents, the key factors are the supply of minimal essential services by public authorities, security of tenure in relation to local land laws, and proximity to work places and other social facilities. But it will be many years before even these essentials are universally available.

Elementary Needs: Education

In education, which is the key to much achievement in other fields, there has been comparatively consistent progress. Spending on schools and teachers has gone up faster than the growth of population nearly everywhere, with many more enrolments to primary and secondary schools in the 1960s, and this progress has continued in the early 1970s: primary enrolment went up by over ten percent a year between 1970 and 1973 in a fifth of African and a third of Asian countries. But there has been much less success in bringing more girls into the schools: they formed less than forty per cent of primary school enrollees in 27 out of 34 African countries in 1970, and in 9 out of 37 other developing countries for which information is available. Only in 17 was the proportion forty-eight per cent or higher. Secondary enrolment has grown much more rapidly than primary, but from lower levels: only in one-third of Asian countries, and in two-fifths of the countries of Latin America and the Caribbean, have more than forty per cent of the relevant age groups been enrolled in secondary schools. In many countries children are needed to work on farms or otherwise earn some income, as was the case in the North not too long ago. In poor families there is often a conflict between the need of the young for education and the need of the family as a whole to enlist children as supplementary producers or earners of income. A report on child labour in the Third World, produced by the ILO in 1979, gave shocking evidence of the numbers of children working long hours for negligible wages – conditions which show once again to what lengths families are driven by painful necessity.

Literacy in general has made varied progress. About one-third of adults in developing countries were literate in 1950; only a little over one half were literate in 1975. Literacy in Latin America rose from 65 per cent in 1960 to 75 per cent in 1970; in Asia, from 45 to 53 per cent; and in Africa from 20 to 26 per cent. But there are still 34 countries, according to the UN, where over 80 per cent of the population are illiterate. In contrast, higher education has often expanded too fast in relation to many countries' ability to employ graduates, and has sometimes taken a disproportionate share of educational budgets. Almost every country has begun to worry about the problem of 'educated unemployment', and to ask the question: are schools and universities teaching the right subjects to the right people?

Neither illiteracy nor other deficiencies in education will be easily overcome. UNESCO and other international agencies have embarked on extensive programmes, which deserve full support, to reduce illiteracy and to provide education for all. But, as with health, education ramifies into the economy, politics and society, reflecting inequalities and entrenched interests as well as the absence of skilled people and materials.

Needs Cannot Be Separated

These different needs, for health, housing or education, as well as the most fundamental need for food, all provide a clear and practical challenge both to the countries themselves, and to the industrialized nations without whose help the poorer countries can hardly succeed. But the idea that these problems are quite separate, and can be solved by specific initiatives, can no longer be believed. Whatever may be accomplished by medical aid, housing drives or school grants, the only way to achieve major improvements in these areas is to help the economies of these countries to grow and industrialize so that they will increasingly be in a position to help themselves; and this can only be brought about through a change in the international economic environment; through more purposeful collaboration between North and South, and much more systematic assistance from the North.

Women in Society

Any definition of development is incomplete if it fails to comprehend the contribution of women to development and the consequences of development for the lives of women. Every development policy, plan or project has an impact on women and cannot succeed without the work of women. And development with justice calls urgently for measures that will give women access to better jobs; that will diminish the arduous tasks that hundreds of millions of women face in their domestic and agricultural occupations; and that will distribute more fairly between the sexes opportunities for creative work and economic advancement.

Yet economic development is often still talked about as if it was mainly a subject for men. Plans and projects are designed by men to be implemented by men on the assumption that if men, as the heads of households, benefit from these projects, the women and the children in those households will benefit too. Women's problems still tend to be regarded as separate, rather than as facets of the culture and structure of all societies. Women's progress needs to be treated as a conscious element in every programme directed towards development.

Experience shows that some projects will not succeed at all unless they give positive incentives to women employed in them; some, such as the introduction of new crops, are quite likely to have adverse effects upon women's welfare; some industrial developments which recruit women as a source of cheap labour may harmfully affect both the distribution of work within the household and the quality of family life. Even welfare projects designed specifically for women and children have been found to have negligible impact unless arrangements are built in to make certain that the benefits reach them.

Women participate in development everywhere. But they are not equal participants because very frequently their status prevents them from having equal access to education, training, jobs, land ownership, credit, business opportunities, and even (as mortality statistics show in some countries) to nutritious food and other necessities for survival. The development of production-oriented societies and the use of capital (whether socially or privately owned) have mostly widened the gap between the different evaluations which society accords to men's and women's work. As the majority of inventions and technical improvements have been applied to what have been traditionally regarded as men's jobs, the effect has been to increase men's dominant role. If economic modernization is not balanced by deliberate social and institutional reform, it may work to the comparative detriment of women. As long as women have unequal access to education, technology and other assets affecting their productivity, the 'unequal exchange' which many commentators see as characteristic of North–South relations will in a not wholly dissimilar way obtain between men and women. For this to be overcome women in developing and industrialized countries must achieve equal status, equal opportunity and equal pay for equal work.

Development Depends on Women

The sexual division of labour goes far back into history and reflects wide cultural differences. Today everywhere traditional jobs are undergoing change, and this process will often require altering conventional attitudes, to overcome inequality. It is now increasingly recognized that change in family values and relationships is a precondition for the success of wider attempts at economic and social transformation; but it has also been revealed how resistant to change men can be.

Many development objectives have added benefits if they take into account the effects on women. Two of women's arduous tasks in most poor rural areas are gathering firewood, for which they must walk further and further afield as forests are cut down, and carrying water over long distances. The providing of alternative fuels would not only help to check deforestation; it would also give women more time for education, income-generating activities and social and political participation. Clean and more convenient water supplies would provide similar benefits for women, as well as being vital for health. Multiple benefits can also come from setting up day centres: children get better nutrition while mothers can be mobile and older girls stay at school. We have already referred to women's role in providing food. As the Economic Commission for Africa has said: 'While the global community cries out against the possible starvation of millions unless food production and distribution are improved, Africa's food producers – the women – continue largely to be ignored.' We also commend to governments and international agencies the FAO and World Bank guidelines on how to include women in their programmes. Women in fact need to be involved in all stages and at all levels of projects and programmes.

Women: 'Statistically Invisible'

No political system today automatically assures the equal status of women, and production-oriented societies generally tend to undervalue their contribution. Statistical methods still largely ignore the contribution of women when it takes place within the household rather than in the labour market, and they also tend to ignore the economic contributions of women because their employment is often concentrated in the so-called 'informal sector' or is seasonal and thus difficult to measure. UN statistics also underestimate the number of households in which the woman is the *de facto* economic head because they use biased definitions of head-of-household instead of a criterion reflecting actual economic contributions. Thus women remain statistically invisible. Yet their contributions are indispensable and basic. And many of them play an unquantifiable but important role – which they wish to share more equally with men – in safeguarding the health and capacities of coming generations.

Development inevitably alters the division of labour between the sexes; and some new jobs – in clothing factories or electronics – may provide opportunities for women. But when traditional societies are replaced by the modern money-system, women are often excluded and their status undermined. They lose their traditional jobs, but their household tasks remain outside the expanding money economy which determines status and the value of labour. Mechanization and automation can also handicap women if their lack of education, training or unionization keeps them out of new technical jobs. The ILO expects the proportion of women working in developing countries to diminish as traditional occupations disappear more rapidly than new ones are created. Men tend to see women as threatening their jobs, particularly when they receive less pay for similar work. But women as well as men need job opportunities, which provide recognition as well as income.

Special Hardships of Women

Women also suffer special hardships when men migrate from the countryside to the towns, or from one country to another: they are left behind as the head of the household, and often have to find jobs under difficult conditions, especially when legal barriers inhibit their right to make economic decisions. The suddenness of change is often accompanied by deeper poverty, at least in the short term. And where women migrate without their families (as often happens in Latin America), great social strains can ensue. More effective trade union representation for women is needed in such circumstances; and consideration could be given to promoting measures whereby business enterprises would devote funds to industrial training programmes for women.

Women bear many other hardships in the poorest countries. The greatest health hazards occur among children and pregnant women; but the design and distribution of health facilities rarely reflect this fact. This contributes to the situation observed in many low-income countries, that women's life expectancy is lower than men's (the opposite of the position in rich countries); that more than half of them suffer from anaemia; and that in some large poor countries their health appears to be worsening. But women cannot do much to improve their lot while authority and information remain in the hands of men. Even family planning can be affected by this inequality. Studies have shown a desire on the part of women in some countries to limit their families, while their husbands are against it. Sometimes this results from the husband's thinking more of the economic capacity of additional children, while the wife pays more attention to the burdens of child-bearing and child-rearing. But sometimes it is the expression of traditional attitudes to fatherhood, which mothers do not necessarily share. As long as women remain primarily responsible for child care, they should have a greater say in influencing the size of the family.

In all these areas governments, educators and opinion-makers have an important responsibility for fostering change. International programmes already exist. But the UN institutions, like most governments, and the multilateral institutions responsible for the programmes remain largely male preserves, with few women in their agencies at senior levels; this sets a poor example and makes it harder for them to reach women elsewhere. The UN conference held in Mexico for International Women's Year – 1975 – tried to draw attention to all these problems, but it needs to be more effectively followed up. We are now halfway through the UN Decade for Women (1976–85), which stresses equality, development and peace; and the world conference on women to be held in 1980 will review progress, specifically in the areas of employment, health and education. We call on governments to give these endeavours their full support.

The Need for a New Outlook

We argued at the outset that in the long run countries have to strengthen their capability to sustain development, through structural transformation. There is an analogy for individuals and families. Meeting essential human needs will require substantial public expenditures and welfare, but ultimately only the provision of remunerative employment will ensure development and be consistent with human dignity. The most basic of all needs is the right to participate in change and to share in the outcome.

This chapter reflects the importance of connecting economic development with human values and cultures as they are expressed in each individual country. No matter how enlightened the plans for the economic and social betterment of people's conditions, they will achieve little unless in parallel the battle is fought at the same time in both North and South, to liberate people from outworn ideas, from the grip of narrowly conceived national interests and from the passions and prejudices inherited from the past. A new international economic order will need men and women with a new mentality and wider outlook to make it work, and a process of development in which their full capacities flourish.

3   Mutual Interests

We discuss in the next chapters of our Report a series of measures which together would offer new horizons for international relations, the world economy and for the developing countries. In formulating our proposals we have been conscious of the arguments for and against them, and have tried to show where we believe them to have a positive balance of advantage for all sides. Taken together, they gain additionally through what they contribute to each other. We are convinced that the mutual interest of North and South will be served, that the world will be a more secure and prosperous place, if these proposals are adopted. This principle of mutuality of interest has been at the centre of our discussions. But it is a mark of the uneasy relationships between North and South that even to speak of mutual interests can cause suspicion. If international reform goes no further than reflecting what is in the mutual interest of all parties, will it go far enough? Will it not excessively reflect the dominant interests of the powerful?

We do not believe that mutual interests alone provide an adequate basis for all the changes that are needed. Especially as far as the poorest people and the poorest countries are concerned, the principal motives for our proposals are human solidarity and a commitment to international social justice. There must be an end to deprivation and suffering. It cannot be accepted that in one part of the world most people live relatively comfortably, while in another they struggle for sheer survival. As we shall argue, there are material reasons for trying to end this state of affairs – international political stability, expanding export markets, the preservation of the biological environment, the limitation of population growth. But we speak of solidarity as something that goes beyond mutual interests.

Mutual interests also do not provide a sufficient basis for change in the uses of economic power in the world, which we believe to be essential. The 'haves' are rarely willing to relinquish their control and their resources and share them with the 'have-nots'. Naturally there are conflicts between North and South; the most fundamental being questions of power and the numerous ways in which economic and even military strength confers on countries, organizations and corporations in the North the ability to manage the world economy to a considerable degree in its own favour. Some key elements of such power have recently materialized in the hands of a few countries in the South, especially the OPEC members – but not in a way which removes the predominance of the North.

An Opportunity for Partnership

The extent to which the international system will be made more equitable is essentially a matter for political decision. We are looking for a world based less on power and status, more on justice and contract; less discretionary, more governed by fair and open rules. A start must be made in that direction, and the obvious places to start are those where positive mutual interests in change can be identified. We believe there are numerous such interests. But greater efforts are required to place them at the centre of debate. The North–South dialogue has suffered from the atmosphere which prevailed in the past of southern 'demands' and northern 'concessions'; it is only in more recent years that prominent leaders of opinion have begun to call for the dialogue to be regarded as an opportunity for partnership, one in which all sides can work for their mutual benefit.

Conflict should not be ignored. There are some actual and potential economic conflicts: over the prices of the South's commodities and the North's manufactures and technology; over financial and monetary systems and institutions; over the relocation of industries; over the control and the sharing of scarce mineral and especially energy resources. But a number of perceived conflicts are not truly conflicts between the North and the South as homogeneous opposing groups. Some of the conflicts are between or within individual countries; they are often conflicts between a country's short- and long-term interests. There are also a variety of issues where a large part of the population in a northern country would benefit from a particular policy change which helps the South, while another would lose. It is when the interests of those who fear to lose dominate northern policy that the conflict expresses itself as one between North and South.

Understanding Interdependence

A sceptic might ask: if these mutual interests exist, why have the measures that embody them not been implemented long ago? Are people and governments not aware of the mutuality of interests? Or are there other considerations which weigh more heavily? A number of answers can be given. First, in some cases there really is insufficient public knowledge of the facts. For example, the media in the North often refer to the 'flood' of cheap manufactures imported from the South, the 'threat' from their growing industries; but how much attention is paid to the North's markets in the South? How well known is it that a large share of jobs in the North depend on selling to the South, that many goods would be far more expensive to northern consumers without these imports? Second, the interest for a given country may on balance be positive overall, but within the country there may be immediate versus long-term interests or other conflicts. Which of these interests has the upper hand in making government policy is a matter of politics and of political leadership.

Further, in a particular negotiation, even where both sides stand to gain, either may feel unwilling to give in, because they are not gaining enough, or because the other gains too much. This is especially true in negotiations between unequals, where if inequity is to be redressed the gains cannot be equal, and where all too often the uneven bargaining strength determines the outcome – or, as has frequently happened in the past, prevents any agreement. Finally, there are sometimes considerations which overshadow mutual interests. This is nowhere clearer than in disarmament where, as we observe elsewhere, the great common interest of mankind in reducing the cost and the growing risk of armaments is thwarted by mutual suspicion between states or groups of states.

Our proposals are not revolutionary; some are perhaps a little ahead of current thinking, others have been on the table for many years. We envisage them as part of a process of negotiated reform and restructuring. And we hope that the understanding of their interrelationships will strengthen the will for change.

The Transmission of Growth

We have noted in our first chapter the importance of growth in the

North to economic development in the South. It helps to provide expanding markets for the South's products and, politically, to enhance the climate for more generous policies, and in particular to ease the strains of adjustment to the South's industrialization. Only recently has attention begun to be paid to the other aspect of the matter. That the South needs the North is evident. But what of the North's need for the South? In what sense can the South be said to be an 'engine of growth' for the North?

It is now acknowledged that in the post-1974 period when the capital surplus oil exporters placed large funds in the commercial banks, borrowing by the better-off developing countries played a large part in 'recycling' these funds and ensuring that they were turned into export orders for northern manufactures. Without this, the recession of that period would have been much worse; the effect has been estimated in one study to have been comparable in magnitude to a significant reflation of the West German economy; another study, by OECD, suggests it was equivalent to 900,000 jobs in the industrialized countries every year during 1973–7.

The Potential Effects of 'Massive Transfers'

The dynamic developing countries have the capacity for high rates of growth; many of them, less concerned about inflation, were willing to borrow for domestic expansion in the early 1970s when northern capital markets experienced slack demand. With major prospects for resource development and industrial investment, they constitute in a sense a new economic frontier, with fewer of the special economic difficulties and social and political constraints operating in the North. But they need a high level of borrowing to cope with their indebtedness. The capacity and willingness of the major actors in this cycle of activity to continue lending and expanding their markets will be critical factors in averting a crisis in the early 1980s, and in promoting the longer-term growth of the world economy. The prospects will be far better for all if the dynamism of the newly industrializing countries can be accommodated in a more expansionary phase of the world economy.

Advocates of various schemes of 'massive transfers' of funds from North to South have argued that such action would amount to a pump-priming of the world economy, which would help it out of recession in the short term, and contribute to higher growth in the longer run. Critics have questioned the validity of this argument. Why should northern governments, hesitant to stimulate their own economies in a period of stagflation, find more virtue in a process of stimulation which operates via the developing countries?

One answer to the critics might be that export orders from developing countries would not be as inflationary for the North as demand generated domestically by public expenditure, if these orders went to sectors of industry which have excess capacity. However, this may not be a very significant factor. But the criticism seems to assume that only exports from the North are stimulated, whereas the exports would of course be matched by imports that have a counter-inflationary impact. The process of transfer of funds has a twofold effect. In the first place, part of the case for these transfers is to prevent an unnecessary addition to recessionary forces. As we argue in Chapter 15, there are several reasons for thinking that the recycling process of recent years will not repeat itself through the unassisted operations of the financial market; evidence is presented there to suggest that strong positive measures are needed to ensure that recycling continues to take place in a constructive manner.

Expanding World Trade and Markets

Secondly there is the broader view. We are talking of a stimulation of world trade as a whole, with its attendant opportunities for specialization and increasing productivity. There is ample historical evidence that expansion of trade is and has always been one of the mainsprings of the world economy. For most countries, balanced trade expansion is a less inflationary form of raising the level of economic activity than stimulation through increases in domestic public expenditure. The large-scale transfers we will propose are seen therefore as measures both to support growth in developing countries directly, and to permit a significant expansion of world trade. It is in this sense that we view them as contributing to growth and employment creation in the North as well as the South.

As we shall see, the transfers also have other functions in specific sectors such as minerals, energy and food, or in commodity price stabilization and investment. And they are important to the stability of financial markets and the international credit system. We also discuss economic cooperation among developing countries as an additional basis for enhancing their economic prospects. All these are important features of the growing interdependence of the world economy. They relate to measures for overcoming specific obstacles to growth and for curbing inflation. If progress can be made on these fronts, a further effect will be a considerable enlargement of markets in the South. Further, a part both of short-term recession and long-term stagnation has been the failure of productivity to rise in the North; a combination of continuous investment in the South and adjustment of northern industries will over time greatly strengthen the world economy – productivity is not helped by expensive prolongation of the life of uncompetitive industries.

The interdependence between North and South in the world economy which we can now discern more clearly highlights not only the ways in which they are complementary in growth and trade, but also the possible incompatibilities implicit in unbalanced growth. Apart from the adjustment problem in manufacturing production, one of the biggest difficulties ahead could be the competition for scarce exhaustible resources, especially in the field of energy, if economic growth among the rich countries were to continue at the intensity of use (and rate of expansion of use) of these resources exhibited in the past. Both the patterns of growth and the technological choices of North and South will bear on this issue. It is clearly an area where international cooperation is not just desirable but essential if conflict is to be avoided. Our Report makes proposals for such cooperation which we see as being of crucial importance for the world and its economy.

Access to Markets

A key problem which has to be solved if long-term world growth is to reach and stay at higher levels is that of access to northern markets for the South's manufactures. This issue demonstrates the complexity of arguments about 'interests'. If there are direct sufferers from competitive imports from the South, they are the industries and workers making the same product in the North. If their lobby is powerful and a protective barrier is erected, their employment is safeguarded. But the consumer loses, being deprived of the less expensive imported product – keeping out these imports contributes to inflation. Our discussion of industrialization and world trade shows that the loss of jobs in the North due to imports from the South has been very small in relation to total unemployment; this is also a mere fraction of the loss of employment that takes place due to technical change. But the loss of jobs occurs often in depressed regions of the North, and among poorer people or those without skills who may have difficulty in getting reemployed. The political pressures created by threats to employment are all the more difficult to resist in times of recession and high unemployment, and when industrialized societies are having to adjust to revolutionary changes in technology. It must be noted also that quite a number of the pressures for protection in the North today result from competition between producers in northern countries.

Protectionism Hurts

Yet the very protectionism that the recession encourages could itself be one of the greatest enemies of recovery. In the concern with jobs, it is often forgotten that North–South trade is a two-way street. Unless the South exports to the North, it cannot in turn pay for the North's exports to the South. Today the industrialized countries have a large positive balance of trade in manufactures with developing countries. The dependence of the industrialized countries on the markets of the South is substantial and is becoming larger still. In 1977, Japan, the US and the EEC sent more than one-third of their exports to the Third World, with the proportion reaching 46 per cent in the case of Japan. US exports to the developing countries were more than four times those to Japan and nearly twice those to the EEC, and the EEC's exports to the Third World were three times those to the US and twenty times those to Japan. From 1976 to 1977, the EEC's exports to the Third World increased by 20 per cent, and in 1975 when its exports actually declined to the US and other developed countries they increased by 25 per cent to the Third World. The importance of this trade to employment is illustrated by the fact that one job in twenty in the United States is in production for export to the Third World. Protectionism therefore endangers jobs of workers producing export goods for sale to developing countries, a fact often missed in discussions of the 'threat' which imports pose to jobs at home in industrialized countries; and inflation, which those imports reduce, also endangers jobs when it leads to contractionist policies.

The great challenge for the North therefore is to cope with the difficulties of adjustment so that world trade can expand; to see its trade with the South not as a threat but as an opportunity; to see it not only as part of the problem but as part of the solution. In the end, failure of the mature industrial economies to adjust to the realities of international competitiveness may deprive them of their prosperity and impose far costlier and more disruptive adjustments than those which their current measures of protection attempt to postpone. The industrialized countries cannot expect their valuable exports to developing countries to continue (and the large loans by commercial banks to several of them to be repaid) if they do not permit them to earn their way by selling their manufactures in return. The challenge to the South is to develop the necessary expertise and trained manpower to ensure their own industrial development and to respond positively to the trade opportunities created by improved access to the markets of the North. Considerable mutual interests of North and South lie in the changes in the world economy implied by the South's industrialization.

Earning More from Commodities

Our proposals on commodities are of two main kinds: those which relate to the development of processing and marketing in the producing countries, and those which relate to price and earnings stabilization. In the case of the former, the benefits to the North lie in more stable supplies, and wider markets in the South from their growing incomes. As with manufactures, the processing industries of the North will face intensified competition; but the extent of employment losses likely to be caused by such competition will be even smaller.

In the case of commodity price stabilization, international action can clearly convey benefits to both North and South. For the producing countries, stabilization offers an end to damaging fluctuations in foreign exchange earnings which can make a mockery of domestic economic management. Price fluctuations have often led to wasteful investment cycles and distress sales on falling markets, aggravating debt problems. For the importing countries, stabilization both eases the decisions of individual economic units which can rely on more predictable prices for long periods, and conveys macro economic benefits. In particular, stabilization would avoid the lasting inflationary effects of commodity price cycles: in their upward phase they induce price increases for manufactured products, whose prices are often not reduced to the same extent when commodity prices fall.

An important current issue is the establishment of floors at reasonable levels below which export prices of developing countries' commodities will not be permitted to fall. There is no reason why this should be disadvantageous to consumers, who have an interest in secure supplies of raw materials and thus steady rates of investment in raw-material production. This in turn depends on remunerative prices for producers, as well as other factors.

The North, and especially Europe and Japan, depends on the developing countries for a very large share of primary products. For coffee, cocoa, tea, bananas, hard fibres, jute, rubber, and tropical hardwood, both the EEC and the US depend entirely on imports from the Third World. In several important minerals Japan and the EEC obtain over 90 per cent of their supplies from imports, in large part from the Third World; the US and Canada, themselves major mineral producers, also depend on imports from developing countries for a number of key minerals. Sixty per cent of world exports of the major agricultural and mineral commodities other than oil originate from the Third World.

Energy, Environment, Food

Our suggestions on energy also seek an expression of common interests. Managing the transition from exhaustible to renewable energy sources will require in particular a major effort to develop new sources of energy. This is something to which the North – including the eastern countries – can contribute with their technology, their research and their capital for investment. There are clearly major benefits to the North in making financial and other arrangements to encourage energy exploration, research and development in the South. These should include solar energy development, particularly to assist the poorest countries. Without strong efforts to develop new energy sources, there is a danger that the lead-time for decisions will be too short and increasingly risky energy technologies may be adopted.

In the short term, oil is the critical problem. The future of the world economy is critically dependent on successful international cooperation to curb wasteful consumption, to promote equitable distribution at predictable prices, accelerate exploration, and deal with the related financial issues. An accommodation must be sought between producers and consumers which will inevitably have to go beyond questions of oil alone. It is in the interests of all that uncertainty be reduced as far as possible over the shorter- and longer-term prospects for oil and for other forms and sources of energy.

The environment is another obvious area where there is the clearest common interest. Important harm to the environment and depletion of scarce natural resources is occurring in every region of the world, damaging soil, sea and air. The biosphere is our common heritage and must be preserved by cooperation – otherwise life itself could be threatened. We have paid particular attention to the problems of poorer countries, where the pressure of mounting necessity and the lack of alternative means of managing resources are causing damage – deforestation, desertification – whose consequences can spread well beyond the boundaries of the countries themselves, establishing an urgent case for international assistance.

In food, again, there are mutual interests. We are proposing major additions to aid for agriculture in the South, as well as stock-piling and financial measures for enhancing the stability of international food supplies and prices. This will represent a charge on the lending countries – but one from which they will benefit, since if food-deficit countries are not assisted to produce more, and a satisfactory food security system is not established, shortfalls in food production in one part of the world can lead to inflation of food prices. Revised priorities are also required in many developing countries, to pay more attention to increasing agricultural production. In the absence of these measures the 1980s and 1990s could witness even worse scenes of starvation than have occurred in the 1970s, and dramatic rises in cereal prices everywhere.

Transnational Corporations

One of the controversial issues we have examined is the role of transnational or multinational corporations. In recent years in fact the various parties in international negotiations have been getting somewhat closer together. A very substantial mutual interest lies in harnessing the economic strength and experience of the multinationals for development. For home countries, profitable and secure overseas investments are desirable; the industrial countries would benefit particularly from the development of energy and other mineral resources in Third World countries. The host countries also have much to gain, provided that the effects of the involvement of multinationals which bring costs and disadvantages can be regulated. Under such regulation the technology, skills and capital of the multinationals can assist the expansion of developing countries' industry and exports of manufactures, and their mineral development; commodity trade could also be rendered more profitable to the producing countries.

Many of the specific items of negotiation, such as disclosure of information and tax liability, are of as much interest to the North as to the South. Indeed the important role of these corporations in world production, processing and trade, as well as other developments such as their increasing technological cooperation with several eastern countries, makes the multinationals issue today one of global rather than solely North–South concern.

The Financial and Monetary Systems

Our proposals in the monetary field keep in mind the necessity of a more orderly monetary system for the world economy as a whole, as well as for meeting the needs of the developing countries. Greater stability in the exchange rate system encourages both trade and investment. Such stability increases the confidence of holders of assets, be they surplus oil producers or other potential investors. The adequacy of international liquidity is a factor in damping cyclical fluctuations in economic activity, in limiting the incentives for protectionism, and in assisting commodity producers to ride out periods of deterioration in their terms of trade. Improvements in the balance of payments adjustment process such as we propose can help to prevent increased contractionist pressures in the world economy.

In the financial field we have identified a number of unmet needs, and have suggested how they can be met in a new approach to development finance. The measures for greater universality and automaticity in raising revenues, and our proposals for institutional reform and innovation, would amount to a significant strengthening of cooperation among all countries to promote development. They would constitute a step towards co-management of the world economy.

We have already argued that the large-scale transfer of resources we propose later in the Report will contribute to the expansion of world trade, and therefore to growth and employment in North and South. But we do not rest all our case for increased and improved aid on this argument. We are well aware that in several aid-giving countries public support for foreign assistance is strongly motivated by humanitarian concern and moral principles – concern which we share. That part of aid which will consist increasingly of grant-like flows to the poorest countries and regions cannot for the most part be claimed to bring to the donors economic rewards of quite the same extent as hard lending to better-off countries. It must be justified mainly on humanitarian grounds. But there is a broader interest in the North in providing such aid. We do not believe the world can live in peace or even that the North can prosper indefinitely if large sections of the South – with hundreds of millions of people – are shut out from any real prospect of progress and left on the margin of survival.

Towards a Genuine Society of Nations

North–South relations in recent years have become an increasingly important part of international politics as well as economics. One ambition of this Report is to propose steps along the path to what could genuinely be called a society of nations, a new world order based on greater international justice and on rules which participating countries observe. This requires nation states to exercise mutual restraint among themselves, and in particular to be concerned about the less fortunate members of such a society.

Several of the topics we discuss bear on the question of peace within this world order. A halt to the arms race must be a key goal of international endeavour; negotiating disarmament measures would both make the world safer, and release resources with the help of which many other problems could be resolved. In this search for peace, North–South relations are themselves crucial, not least over energy and mineral supplies, which could be the cause of serious conflict if not brought within a framework of international agreement. Increased East–West cooperation both between themselves and in partnership together with the South must also be encouraged, for its own sake and as a contributing factor to peace. Such issues are among the most difficult and the most important objectives we have discussed.

Concern for the future of the planet is inextricably connected with concern about poverty. Continued rapid population growth in the next century could make the world unmanageable; but that growth can only be forestalled if action is taken to combat poverty in this century. Much the same is true for the biological environment, which is threatened with destruction in many countries as a direct result of poverty – though in others as a result of ill-considered technological decisions and patterns of industrial growth. These problems – nuclear weapons proliferation is another – can only be resolved by North and South acting in cooperation, and their mutual interests in doing so are only too obvious. The conquest of poverty and the promotion of sustainable growth are matters not just of the survival of the poor, but of everyone.

In much of our discussion, and in Chapter 8 specifically, we discuss the responsibilities of the South to complement measures of international social justice with domestic ones to achieve the same ends. Poverty cannot be overcome without determined efforts, both international and national. Here too there are mutual interests. It is to the North's advantage that the South manage its own economies effectively – and the North can assist it to do so. Such assistance would be the more effective if it overcame political inhibitions, showing equal willingness to cooperate with countries relying heavily on public sector enterprise and with those more orientated towards the free market economy. Stronger economic cooperation among developing countries can help to promote growth in the South in ways which do not depend on the North – this too is in the mutual interest.

Reforms Are Interconnected

The picture of a different world which we are trying to present rests to some extent on an attempt to go beyond a piecemeal treatment of North–South issues. The picture as a whole may be more inviting than some of its details. We are convinced that a world which carried out our recommendations would be more just, safer, and more prosperous than one in which countries continue in adversary postures sustained by the sterile negatives of the past. We say this not only because the recommendations have value in themselves, but because they contribute importantly to each other. Mineral problems, for example, cannot be fully resolved without action on the financial front, on the issues affecting the multinationals, and in the field of commodity agreements. The energy question requires action in these areas, and also a broader framework of international agreement. Debt, the international banking system, commodities, and access to markets for manufactures are closely interrelated. One can spell out numerous interconnections of this kind. There are interdependencies not only between countries but between issues.

We do not suggest that the measures we propose are without cost to the North. The North must share its resources and its control of institutions; it must be willing to work for some changes in the way markets operate, which is presently to its advantage. But we do suggest that the North as well as the South gets much in return, both in straightforward economic benefits and in a reduction of uncertainties and instability. And there is not only the capturing of mutual gain to be considered, but also the avoidance of mutual loss. It is not difficult to envisage a world in which the measures we propose are not carried out; and in which the path of the future leads to reciprocal impoverishment.

The Moral Imperatives

All the lessons of reform within national societies confirm the gains for all in a process of change that makes the world a less unequal and a more just and habitable place. The great moral imperatives that underpinned such reforms are as valid internationally as they were and are nationally; but experience confirms that there are other imperatives also, rooted in the hard-headed self-interest of all countries and people, that reinforce the claim of human solidarity. World society now recognizes more clearly than ever before its mutual needs; it must accept a shared responsibility for meeting them. After two years of consultation together, and with many of the world's most eminent people from the various fields of international development, we are convinced that there are gains for all in a new order of international economic relations and hope for humanity in achieving them. Both North and South have an interest in the preservation of hope.

4 The Poorest Countries

The Commission has been especially concerned with examining the problems of the poorest countries: a special working group was formed which heard expert evidence; and one of the full meetings of the Commission was held in Mali in West Africa, which gave an important opportunity to see the problem at first hand.

The United Nations has singled out the 'least developed countries' for special attention. They are defined as: 'countries with severe long-term constraints on development assessed on three basic criteria: viz – *per capita* GDP of $100 or less at 1970 prices, share of manufacturing of 10 per cent or less of GDP, and 20 per cent or less literate persons aged 15 or more'. They have a population of 258 million (1977 estimate) or 13 per cent of the population of all developing countries. Their average income per head in 1977 was about $150, equivalent to $80 in 1970 prices, and their growth rate of income per head for the last two decades has been less than one per cent.

Most of the least developed countries – the present UN list includes twenty-nine of them – are found contiguously in two areas which we call the 'poverty belts'. One extends across the middle of Africa, from the Sahara in the north to Lake Nyasa in the south. The other, beginning with the two Yemens and Afghanistan, stretches eastwards across South Asia and some East Asian countries. These belts extend into other regions and parts of countries, for example parts of Kenya in Africa and, in Asia, Burma, Cambodia, Vietnam and parts of India. The point has been raised whether parts of countries which have the same characteristics and handicaps as the least developed countries should not be treated on a par with them. The Commission hopes that the United Nations will continue to review its criteria and make consequential changes in the lists to ensure that they include all countries deserving special attention.

Some of the countries in the poverty belts, like Bangladesh, have large populations; others such as Gambia are small in area and population. They each have different approaches to development; their economies have different degrees of openness. But each of them has a slim margin between subsistence and disaster; and they are all circumscribed by their ecology and their dependence on international market forces beyond their control. They exist in a fragile tropical environment which has been upset by the growing pressure of people. Without irrigation and water management, they are afflicted by droughts, floods, soil erosion and creeping deserts, which reduce the long-term fertility of the land. Disasters such as drought intensify the malnutrition and ill-health of their people and they are all affected by endemic diseases which undermine their vitality. Their poverty, harsh climate and isolation all make it harder to explore their resources, especially minerals. The sun, which might be a valuable source of cheap energy is presently a curse, sapping their vigour, while they are forced to use relatively expensive conventional forms of energy. They have to cut down their forests, degrading the environment in order to survive.

This condition has worsened in the 1970s. Not only has the poorest countries' growth slowed down further; but even the increased assistance from the international community has been offset by a decline in the purchasing power of their exports. They also have had to face more starkly the grim possibility that their ecosystem may not enable them to feed their people – unless urgent measures are taken now.

A Programme for Structural and Ecological Change

This mounting destruction of the earth's capacity to support life is not, we believe, an inescapable destiny. The record of stagnation and decline can be reversed: these people can begin to master their environment and thus gain hope for the future. But there must be immediate intervention to attack the root causes of poverty, for the stress on the ecosystem which is caused by people's needs makes it harder in turn for the vegetation and land to withstand the extremes of the climate. What might elsewhere be an awkward period of low rainfall becomes in these regions a period of famine and reversion to desert; a flood can take away the topsoil for ever. These countries must avoid the disastrous consequences of the deteriorating ecosystem: but the task is immense.

To achieve this change requires new priorities, and a definite time-frame. We know that the international community has widely recognized the special needs of the poor. We are encouraged by the recent redistribution of aid in favour of the poor countries. But we believe that unless their productive systems are radically altered, these countries will remain on international welfare just to enable them to survive, needing ever increasing aid.

A framework is needed within which these people can feed themselves, provide their own values of reference and look after their own future. Measures should be adopted which can help them to escape from the poverty trap. Education is important, but the masses of educated unemployed in India or Sri Lanka show in bitter relief the danger of partial solutions. We believe that the attack on mass poverty must be many-sided; it must create the means to escape from the dead-end of poverty, through agricultural development, industrialization, migration and other agents of change. These countries need to build up an infrastructure, and a political and administrative structure, which can give their people hope of breaking the equilibrium of poverty.

This means that much greater effort must be directed towards water and soil management, improving health, reforestation, developing energy and minerals, building up transport and communications and finding employment for the landless. These measures share common characteristics. They are long-term; they need guaranteed resources over a long period before they can be undertaken; and they would only give a direct return on their investment after a relatively long gestation period. They need a time-frame of 15–20 years, and their planning should start now. Many of these programmes would be best organized on a regional basis, and to implement them will require a unique institutional framework for cooperation. We note that at its Manila meeting in 1979 UNCTAD unanimously adopted a Comprehensive New Programme of Action for the Least Developed Countries covering many of the same fields as our own proposals.

Water and Soil Management

Agriculture provides 44 per cent of the poorest countries' GDP and 83 per cent of their employment. Yet they are not growing enough to feed their people; and projections indicate that they will encounter a food gap of at least 20 million metric tons by 1990, which amounts to about a third of their consumption. Studies by such organizations as the Food and Agricultural Organization

(FAO), and the International Food Policy Research Institute (IFPRI) show that this gap has many causes, including weak infrastructures, institutions and delivery systems, and the lack of research into appropriate technology. But the most fundamental difficulty is control and management of water. Crops in the more humid tropics of South Asia are damaged by severe floods from the rainfall during the monsoon, while the yields in the wet season in all humid tropical areas are limited by high cloudiness, by disease, by root-zone saturation and by losses of soil nutrients through leaching. Most African countries, but especially the Sahel zone (as well as Sudan, Ethiopia, Somalia and Tanzania), have much of their farming within semi-arid tropics where evapotranspiration is exceedingly high and rainfall can vary by 40 per cent from year to year.

Unpredictable rainfall makes agricultural planning difficult even in the best of circumstances; but once water is available all the year round the farmers are protected from the vagaries of the climate, which is the most important single measure to encourage them to adopt improved farming techniques. Irrigation with proper drainage gives greater yields, a more flexible choice of crops and more intensive farming. It also contributes to hydropower. There have been promising studies of major irrigation schemes, for the river basins of Senegal, Niger, Volta, Lake Chad, Rufiji, Kagera, Brahmaputra-Ganges, for example, and the Himalayan watershed and the Mekong. To exploit these basins would cost (it is estimated) at least $50 billion over the next 15–20 years. There is also scope for small irrigation projects undertaken by local communities. We recommend that bilateral and multilateral agencies should assist in studies and surveys to assess the costs and benefits of these water projects and in their finance and execution where viable.

Growing more food will also depend heavily on research, which can improve inputs of fertilizers and seeds, and result in more efficient methods of production and a better balance between production systems and the environment. The 'Green Revolution', which was a product of such research, has spectacularly increased grain production, but mainly in areas where irrigation was available or could be developed readily through tubewells; it has been less successful in areas with unpredictable rainfall or in semi-arid regions (including most of sub-Saharan Africa). Research is needed into new seed varieties of crops which can flourish in the soil and climate of these areas, for example millet, sorghum, tubers; into measures to maintain soil fertility, to control weeds, diseases and pests, and to prevent soil erosion. Above all, research is needed into particular, often small, areas, where the crops are related to the local climate and soil-type: the 'agro-economic specific zones'. By studying the actual environment in which the farmers work, researchers will then be in a position to give relevant advice to contiguous communities. This should be done in such a way as to exert considerable pressure on local governments to deal with the institutional issues that otherwise frustrate agricultural development, including agrarian reform. Governments should find ways to transfer workers in the slack season to improving the land with such activities as building, fencing, drainage or small irrigation construction. But such conversion needs a system of tenure and organization which can give people a secure stake in the land and can thus create incentives for this type of saving and investment.

Health

Human energy and innovation depends on good health. Yet most people in the poverty belts suffer from a combination of long-standing malnutrition and parasitic diseases; and some of these diseases, like sleeping sickness and river-blindness, prevent the farming of rich agricultural lands, hold back the breeding of domestic animals and reduce the productivity of the workers. About one billion people are at risk from malaria. River-blindness – which drives people out of the fertile areas of the Volta, Niger, Gambia and Upper Nile rivers – is estimated to affect 20 million people in Africa. Sleeping sickness, which also limits livestock grazing, currently afflicts 35 million victims; bilharzia is estimated to affect between 180 and 200 million people. The eradication of these diseases requires international support: the scale and complexity and the costs of the technology to cure them are beyond the economic means of these poor countries. The tropical and sub-tropical areas are particularly prone to these diseases. But once a disease such as malaria is brought under control, as was done in the Terai Hills of India, in the rice-growing areas of Sri Lanka and in the canal zone of Panama, major advances can be made in agriculture and other activities.

Health is a unique challenge, because it is a collective public function where improvement is soon noticeable. Reducing parasitic diseases demonstrates that there is no inevitability about people's lot; that human beings *can alter* their own environment and their prospects for the future. As the poor begin to realize their own capacities for directing their lives, they become more open to innovation and change. Reduced morbidity from malaria and river-blindness has already in the past encouraged farmers who have previously been debilitated to accept new farming techniques. Improving the health of infants also builds a promising start to human development. Health must therefore be tackled at two levels: disease vectors must be controlled and the socio-economic environment, including the provision of clean drinking water and a better living environment, must be improved. The most expensive items in disease control are the chemical compounds which are used to attack the disease vectors and the drugs used for treatment. Local efforts are made to defray expenses but it is hard to sustain a disease eradication expenditure of $40 per head when the average income is only $135, and international aid is essential. We also recommend that the efforts of the WHO and the World Bank in eradicating river-blindness should be extended to sleeping sickness, bilharzia and malaria; and the WHO should also intensify its research efforts into cheaper and more effective ways of controlling these diseases. These research needs are estimated at $560 million, but control costs will be in the range of $2.5 billion over the next twenty years.

Afforestation and Energy

In most of the countries in the poverty belts, nine-tenths of the people depend on firewood as their chief source of fuel, and in colder mountain regions for home heating. Unrestrained commercial exploitation and increased population have led to soaring wood prices: more and more physical energy is expended to satisfy the basic fuel needs, animal manures are diverted from food production to cooking and the treeless landscape extends further, with disastrous effects on the ecology.

The firewood crisis is intimately linked to the food problem in at least two ways. The destruction of the forests accelerates the erosion of the soil, increasing severe flooding and creeping deserts and reducing soil fertility. And the diversion of manure for use as fuel leads to a loss of agricultural nutrients, damaging the soil structure by failing to return manure to the fields. The result is a circular trap. As wood scarcity forces farmers to burn more dung for fuel and to apply less to their fields, the falling food supply will necessitate the clearing of ever larger, ever steeper tracts of forests which then intensifies erosion, which in turn further reduces soil fertility.

The energy crisis of the poor is in some respects less intractable than that of the rich. It cannot be solved through reduction in demand, for the needs are close to rock-bottom. But it can be solved. Unlike oil, forests are renewable when they are properly managed. The logical immediate response to the firewood shortage – and one which provides many incidental ecological benefits – is to plant more trees; many regions can raise fast-growing tree varieties which can be culled for firewood inside a decade. Reforestation is not an easy undertaking but with major international assistance it can be done. Experience in China has shown that the combination of a strong political commitment at the top with broad public participation and shared benefits at the bottom can provide a basis for rapid reforestation. Of course, it can only succeed if it is complemented with measures which assure the local inhabitants their essential needs; otherwise their efforts would be rightly directed towards conserving their own lives.

The energy needs of these countries go beyond wood fuel. Indeed, to carry out the ambitious agricultural programme proposed and to cater for the reduction of rural isolation, for mineral exploitation and for transportation, requires increased energy inputs in the form of oil and electricity – the type of energy that will drive motors. It is important to step up resources and assistance to encourage accelerated oil and gas exploration in these countries. There will also be a need to augment their capacity to import oil. Research into other energy sources should be intensified. Solar energy is particularly suitable for use in sunny rural areas (sun belts) where there is considerable dispersion of population and where the cost of distribution of electricity by transmission is high. The introduction of commercial solar energy into these areas would be a major catalyst for structural change. In some areas, use of solar energy can be considered immediately and in many more areas only a slight advance in solar technology is needed to make it economical in the near future. We support the provision of greater funds for the research and use of solar energy in the poverty belts.

Transport and Communications

Many countries in the poverty belts are not only landlocked but divided by mountains and hills which isolate their regions from each other. Effective development must call for extending transport and communications into the more isolated areas, which is essential for both internal and external trade, to link farming and other activities to the markets. The costs will be heavy, including substantial maintenance because of the difficult terrain and weather.

At the Conference on International Economic Cooperation (CIEC) during 1975–7 the participants recognized that the African continent suffers special disadvantages in problems of infrastructure, whether in transport and communications or in social and economic organization. They agreed that these were a serious obstacle to such critical goals as expanding food and agricultural production, as well as providing social services. They therefore supported the resolution of the Ministerial Meeting of the Economic Commission for Africa (ECA) which called for the launching of the African Transport and Communications Decade, 1978–88. In this decade, which was also supported by the UN itself, it is intended to harmonize, coordinate, modernize and develop communications of all kinds, including road, rail, water transport, telecommunications, radio, television and postal services. The ECA has since prepared programmes for the first phase from 1980 to 1983, whose estimated cost will be $8 billion. This would include $4 billion for roads and road transport (including the building of a transnational highway covering 31,500 km, with 43,000 km of feeder road links), $1.5 billion for railways and rail transport, and $1.4 billion for maritime transport and ports. We believe these proposals need substantial support from the international community, particularly from the European Community and some of the surplus OPEC countries ; and since these needs coincide with under-used capacity for transport equipment production in many industrial countries, there could be an opportunity to provide some assistance in the form of equipment as well as in funds.

Mineral Exploration

The isolation of the poorest countries, together with their lack of funds and political problems, have also made it especially difficult for them to survey their mineral resources systematically. The necessary financial resources and technical knowhow are in the hands of the transnational corporations and government agencies in the industrial countries; but the poorer countries with their weak bargaining power and lack of information about their own resources, are often reluctant to enter into contracts with transnationals. In our discussion of minerals we suggest how greater trust could be established in the negotiation of mineral contracts; and we propose increased finance for exploration which could be of particular value to these poorer countries. The control of their own exploration, together with the establishment and strengthening of regional mineral centres and national laboratories, could provide a new impetus to development.

The Landless in the Asian Poverty Belt

In Asia, with the rapid rise of population, many millions of people cannot now be accommodated on cultivable land, which is already over-extended, and they cannot easily be absorbed into other activities. In Bangladesh, it has been estimated that one-third of the people are marginal peasants with less than one hectare of land, poor tenant farmers and sharecroppers who are dependent on the larger landholders for work. Another third of the population is estimated to be landless. Land reform can only provide small relief for these people, since large holdings account for only 0.2 per cent of the total land. Investment in irrigation and flood control can provide the conditions for multiple crops which not only give increased yields, but generate a much higher demand for labour. The expansion of industry can help to give work to those who have no opportunities on the land.

Regional Cooperation and Regional Projects

These measures will not only help the poorest countries to generate and sustain their own development. They are essential to avoid catastrophe. We have limited them to those policy areas which can attract and use concessional finance without touching on internal national policies; thus they do not emphasize to the same extent many important ingredients of development, including education, administration and industrialization. They have an implicit bias towards regional projects, because many of the economies are too small to be viable on their own. Regional cooperation cannot be imposed; it must grow from within, on the basis of need. But it can be strengthened by external resources, and when countries make serious attempts to cooperate they deserve major financial support: particularly for the Sahel programme (covering Senegal, Mauritania, Mali, Niger, Upper Volta, Chad and Cape Verde), the Kagera River basin (covering Rwanda, Burundi, Tanzania and Uganda), the Brahmaputra-Ganges programme (covering Nepal, Bhutan, Bangladesh and parts of India) and the Mekong Committee's project (covering Cambodia, Laos, Vietnam and Thailand).

Financing and 'Absorptive Capacity'

The total financing needs of these least developed countries alone have been estimated by UNCTAD at $11 billion per annum for the 1980s and $21 billion per annum for the 1990s (in 1980 prices). This is based on the target of an annual growth rate of GDP of 6.5 per cent, and a rate of growth of domestic savings of 6.8 per cent. The funds required to meet the above regional projects are estimated in 1978 prices at a minimum of $4 billion per annum, additional to present aid, for the two decades 1980–2000. Most of this finance should be provided on grant or near grant terms and must be assured over long periods of time. This raises the question of the appropriate institutional framework for mobilizing resources which will be discussed below.

These countries do not have enough qualified people to organize the large volumes of investment that they need; they are thus said to lack the 'absorptive capacity' which is so crucial to development. But some of the problems of absorption have been created by the terms and conditions of present aid management, for example reliance on foreign exchange components of projects; far greater sums could be transformed into productive investment if they came in more freely usable forms. Greater technical assistance (especially if it is planned jointly with the recipients) could identify, prepare and implement projects in a way that would augment absorptive capacity; stable commitments to aid would ensure that many projects which are now shelved could be implemented. We therefore support the longer-term replenishment of IDA and UNDP funds, as well as other sources of finance that may become available. Financing of local costs can also enable these countries to use external funds far more effectively, as they are often short of local as well as foreign finance.

Institutional Framework for Planning and Financing

Regional programmes call for new forms of organization for planning and financing. The experience of the 'Club du Sahel', which is a very flexible association between the member countries and donor agencies, could be extended into a wider conception of regional cooperation. In this Club all the partners, Sahelian and non-Sahelian, informally meet on an equal footing to share ideas, to air differences and to search for new ways of achieving the objectives of the member governments. Such joint formulation of a programme enhances mutual trust, increases absorptive capacity and makes it more likely that the agreed projects will be carried out. We believe such a role can be played by regional economic commissions, like the Economic Commission for Africa and the Economic and Social Commission for Asia and the Pacific (ESCAP), which could establish units to prepare specific regional plans. Such units could also help the regional project institutions to articulate their policies and priorities for long-term development: they could encourage cooperation between donors and make it easier to mobilize resources.

Receiving governments often get money from different agencies, each with different lending criteria; and these must be properly coordinated. The assistance should be as far as possible channelled and earmarked through a single body for each poverty belt, which can be organized by the Regional Development Banks or Funds of Africa and Asia. The overwhelming needs of the poverty belts call for much greater flexibility especially in the means for investing in their infrastructure. This could be helped by forming a group such as a consortium or Task Force led by a major financial institution in which the donors and the recipients and the relevant Regional Commission's unit all participate to ensure the appropriate financing for the programme. Coordination by the recipients of regional aid of this kind would also be useful. It could be effectively undertaken by them through the establishment of a body responsible for these activities or through existing organizations. Such a body could help to encourage fuller participation by the countries themselves in the management of these aid programmes.

Helping People to Help Themselves

We believe that the richer nations must continue to give special attention to the poorest countries to help them to help themselves. They should step up their aid, directing it with effective planning into the critical areas of the ecology. They should provide emergency assistance as an addition to the longer-term programmes, not (as at present) as a large share of their total regular aid. Greater assistance, together with support for commodity prices, can augment the purchasing power of these countries and, with the new machinery for cooperation and coordination, a comprehensive programme could move the poverty belts towards self-sustained growth before the end of this century.

Recommendations

An action programme must be launched comprising emergency and longer-term measures, to assist the poverty belts of Africa and Asia and particularly the least developed countries. Measures would include large regional projects of water and soil management; the provision of health care and the eradication of such diseases as river-blindness, malaria, sleeping sickness and bilharzia; afforestation projects; solar energy development; mineral and petroleum exploration; and support for industrialization, transport and other infrastructural investment.

Such a programme would require additional financial assistance of at least $4 billion per year for the next two decades, at grant or special concessional terms, assured over long periods and available in flexibly usable forms. New machinery is required on a regional basis to coordinate funding and to prepare plans in cooperation with lending and borrowing countries. Greater technical assistance should be provided to assist such countries with the preparation of programmes and projects.

5 Hunger and Food

An End to Hunger

Poverty goes hand in hand with hunger. 'A truly major effort to eradicate hunger, with its human degradation and despair,' said the Executive Director of the UN World Food Council in January 1979, 'is a political imperative for building world cooperation and solidarity among all peoples and all nations.' As these words were spoken, a meeting was beginning in Geneva which was hoping to complete the negotiation of the International Grains Arrangement, a key part of a new international food order; but the meeting broke up without agreement. Compassion, solidarity, and self-interest all call for the urgent abolition of hunger. Yet progress has been stumbling and slow.

Eight hundred millions are estimated to be 'destitute' in the Third World today, as this Report has already noted: most of them by definition cannot afford an adequate diet. In some low-income countries studies have shown as many as 40 per cent of pre-school children exhibiting clinical signs of malnutrition. No one can state the exact numbers in the world who experience hunger and malnutrition, but all estimates count them in hundreds of millions: millions who will either die from lack of food or have their physical development impaired. It is an intolerable situation. The idea of a community of nations has little meaning if that situation is allowed to continue, if hunger is regarded as a marginal problem which humanity can live with.

An International Responsibility

Putting an end to hunger is a challenge to the world's economic system, requiring complementary national and international measures. Only major efforts of investment, planning and research can make enough food available for the six billion people the world will probably hold by the year 2000. But not only must the food be there; people who need it must be able to buy it. The reduction of poverty itself is equally essential for abolishing hunger. We concentrate here on specific needs in the spheres of food, agriculture and rural development, but all the Commission's recommendations on trade and finance are relevant to the issue. To conquer hunger, every family must have a reliable livelihood, which means much greater gainful employment in both agriculture and manufacturing.

Food production in all the developing countries rose by over two and a half per cent annually between 1950 and 1975; but demand for food has grown by well over three per cent a year as populations and incomes have gone up. As a result the developing countries have rapidly increased their imports of cereals, from relatively low levels in the 1950s to 20 million tons in 1960 and 1961, to over 50 million tons in the early 1970s, and nearly 80 million by 1978-9. On current trends the Third World could be importing 145 million tons of food by 1990, 80 million of which would be needed by the poorer countries of Africa and Asia. It is unlikely within the prevailing economic climate that these countries' own exports, or even additional aid, can finance such massive food imports. And even if the financing problems can be solved, there are doubts whether major grain producers could supply the amounts needed. The suffering, unless something is done, will be appalling.

If world food production does not grow adequately, there is also bound to be a repetition of the inflationary surge in world food prices that occurred in the early 1970s. We refer below to the problem of fluctuations in global supplies and measures to reduce them. But growth in food output is essential if persistent inflation in food prices is to be avoided. While some farming and commercial interests in the major grain-surplus countries would not object to higher prices, for most people and governments the avoidance of food price increases is a major objective. There are strong incentives, therefore, for both North and South to support the proposals we make in this chapter, and all countries, including those of Eastern Europe, have great responsibilities for their part in world food production.

Increasing Domestic Food Production

The first priority of food policy in developing countries, particularly in those of sub-Saharan Africa and South Asia which face the most serious deficits, is greater domestic production. Self-sufficiency is not necessarily sensible for all countries; for those with limited agricultural capacity, or for whom it is more efficient to develop exports to pay for food imports, it does not make economic sense. But if a country has two-thirds of its labour force engaged in agriculture and still cannot provide its own food, and if it has ceased to be self-sufficient in the last two decades without any corresponding increase in cash crops or other exports to pay for imports, there is obvious cause for concern. Thus Zaire twenty years ago was a net food exporter; now it spends about $300 million a year, a third of its export earnings, on food imports – which is a major factor in its debt and economic problems. Nigeria has increased its food production in recent years by only 0.5 per cent annually, while its population grew at 3 per cent and incomes were rising, so that far bigger food imports were required. In fourteen African countries agricultural growth has been slower than that of population in the whole period since 1960.

In Asia agricultural fortunes have been more varied. India has managed on average to keep food output growing faster than its population over the past thirty years; while Bangladesh has recently experienced both famine and glut. In both countries, as in most of the Third World, even in years when overall food supplies have been adequate, this has not put an end to hunger and malnutrition. Both food and incomes have not been evenly enough distributed, and ensuring that they are is a major task, in many developing countries, on top of the generation of adequate supplies. China has given food production the highest priority, and has managed – not without difficulties – to maintain adequate growth in food supplies and improve their distribution.

Food Must Be a Priority

In the fifties and sixties agriculture often suffered from relative neglect; many developing countries in their drive for industrial advance did not at first recognize the complementary functions of rural development. They were also pessimistic about changing agricultural technology and persuading cultivators to innovate – a pessimism which today would be unjustified. This perspective began to change in the early 1970s, when a large range of countries announced plans to concentrate more heavily on agricultural production, rural employment and improved nutrition. Progress remains difficult, against intractable soil and weather conditions, and – in numerous countries – conservative social organization and uneven distribution of landholdings. According to FAO data, food production grew more slowly than population in 58 out of 106 developing countries during the period 1970–78. But intensified efforts and revised priorities in many developing countries together with outside assistance can go a long way towards overcoming the precariousness of the present food situation.

Domestic Efforts Need World Support

In a broader perspective, self-sufficiency in food must be the aim of the world's major regions. This self-sufficiency does not exclude trade; nor should it confine some countries to agricultural production only while others industrialize. Some specialization should take place, to minimize costs. But a reliance on trade must not allow the world market in food to be a dominant factor. The market should have a regulatory and corrective role; but within an overall system governed by international measures for security of food volumes and prices, assistance for increased domestic production, and reliable food aid.

The poorer countries will need much additional help to increase their food output. Aid to agriculture in low-income countries was approximately $3 billion in 1977. Estimates by the International Food Policy Research Institute (IFPRI), the FAO and the World Bank indicate needs for additional assistance to agriculture up to 1990 from $4 billion to over $8 billion a year, matched by very considerable additional investment and recurrent expenditures by the countries themselves. The IFPRI estimate, from a study specially made for this Commission, calculated the full costs of overcoming the projected food deficits; on the assumption that the countries concerned would meet half the capital costs and 80 per cent of the recurrent costs of this agricultural programme, the amount to be covered by aid would be some $12 billion (1975 dollars) annually in the 1980s, calling for additional foreign aid of $8.5 billion (or $13 billion in 1980 dollars). This will have to be in the form of programme as well as project assistance.

Reaching the Rural Poor

There has been much change in recent years in attitudes in the international agencies towards agricultural assistance – but also on efforts to ensure that agricultural projects reach the rural poor. The Commission has been particularly interested in the International Fund for Agricultural Development (IFAD) which was constituted with about $1 billion at the end of 1977. The Fund was mandated to commit this money in three years, principally on projects to raise food production and consumption by the poorest people in the poorest countries. At first the Fund experienced some difficulties and had to rely on other agencies to identify projects, but by its second year it proved able to mount successful missions and locate appropriate projects, giving every promise of fulfilling its mandate over the three-year period. IFAD represents an important innovation in development finance since it combines funds both from OPEC countries and from the industrialized countries. Further, with 124 member countries, its management structure enjoys full participation of developed and developing countries, and has taken all its decisions by consensus. This Commission supports the work of IFAD and expresses the hope that its funding will be replenished.

Investment Is Better than Food Relief

We have already referred to the potential inflationary consequences of world food deficits in the international food market. If additional assistance is not forthcoming, there will also be far more calls for emergency food supplies, which are in the long view an expensive and irrational way of coping with food problems. Food relief programmes often cost more in one year than would the five-year local investment programmes which might have made them unnecessary.

The biggest single amount of investment required is for irrigation and water management. There are also very great needs in infrastructure, particularly roads, and transport and rural electrification, for greater use of fertilizers and pesticides, and for draught power. In many countries rural administration is weak and needs far greater attention. The continuing development and adaptation of new plant varieties depends on a sustained effort of research at international, regional and national centres. Plant development has made great progress, but there have been signs recently of flagging international support. Much more effort should be put into both development and research, where relatively modest sums can have a large and well-demonstrated impact on production.

Appropriate Farming Systems

It is important to appreciate that new models are needed for agricultural development in the Third World. The western agricultural model with its high degree of mechanization and use of chemicals cannot be simply transferred to developing countries. There are many examples of mechanization increasing output and employment, and chemical fertilizers and pesticides have contributed importantly to raising yields, especially with new plant varieties. But there have also been examples of unthinking transfers of inappropriate techniques, mechanization leading to significant job destruction at the local level and ill-advised application of agricultural chemicals. The need to develop farming systems appropriate to local circumstances, attentive in particular to employment creation in rural areas which may help stem the drift to the cities, and to ecological balance, is part of the case for increasing local research capacity.

Agrarian Reform

But the conquest of hunger calls for much broader international and domestic efforts to ensure that the additional food reaches those who need it, and that it is bought, either by individual families or by governments for subsidized distribution. But governments cannot sustain subsidized schemes for long, and an end to hunger can only be foreseen if there are more wage earners, and a more equitable distribution of income – a challenge for many developing countries where growth has bypassed the poor. Agrarian reform is a critical means to benefit the poor – though naturally the measures needed differ from country to country. In some areas the key issue is reform of tenancy to give greater security of tenure. In others it is to divide large parcels of land among those who can farm it more intensively. Yet others require consolidation measures to overcome the effects of excessive fragmentation of holdings which has already occurred. All these can increase the incentive for farmers' investment. Free and viable organizations of agricultural labour have an important role in raising rural incomes and involving the poor in rural reform and development. But poor farmers who are provided with land will require substantial credit and other forms of assistance, and land reform often temporarily disrupts production, imposing additional costs. Multilateral lending agencies could usefully give help for adjustment and institutional reforms associated with programmes for agrarian change.

Many aspects of rural development policy were given a possible new stimulus by the 1979 World Conference on Agrarian Reform and Rural Development. Developing countries expressed their determination to give priority to rural development, for which, the

Conference declaration emphasized, 'agrarian reform is a critical component'. They also emphasized that the present state of commercial, economic and financial relations between North and South – including current aid practices – were themselves an obstacle to accelerated rural development. Transnational corporations, in particular, were often developing cash crops for export at the expense of local food availability, and were contributing to the problems of global food supplies. Perhaps most significant of all was the Programme of Action adopted, under which countries would set up targets for themselves, and authorize the FAO and other UN organizations to help them monitor their progress; an important aim of the Programme of Action was to help countries integrate agricultural development and agrarian reform with overall development. The Programme of Action also called on governments to ratify and enforce the ILO's Conventions on freedom of association, and on rural workers' organizations and their role in economic and social development.

There are several other much-needed domestic improvements. Grain storage together with improved transport and communications are crucial for distributing food. In many countries with poor communications these require substantial investments. In drought-prone areas in particular where irrigation is not practicable they are essential for ensuring that food is available locally.

The Importance of Fish

Increased consumption of fish could also help to reduce hunger and malnutrition. This requires increased supplies and often promotion of new food habits. Most developing countries remain considerably below the average world intake of fish protein *per capita*. However, many smaller developing countries have technical and managerial difficulties which prevent the adequate exploitation of this resource. A new FAO programme has just been launched to help Third World countries develop and manage their Exclusive Economic Zones (EEZs – the 200 mile zones defined in the draft Law of the Sea) within which over 90 per cent of the world commercial fish catch is taken. International cooperation to ensure conservation of ocean fish stocks is essential. In addition, the development of freshwater fish-farming has considerable potential in many countries. It could provide an attractive opportunity especially for landlocked countries to improve the diets of their people.

Technical and managerial problems affect not only the actual fishing operations; they are also a major obstacle in bringing the fish to consumers: cooling chains and refrigerated transport are not sufficiently developed in many countries. Furthermore, modern technology is only beginning to develop means of processing large quantities of small fish for direct human consumption, and of exploiting resources not utilized so far, for example the krill of the Antarctic. At present, ocean fishing is largely in the hands of developed countries. To obtain a fair share in ocean fishing, developing countries would have to organize cooperation among themselves, especially among the smaller island states which are potential managers of some of the largest EEZs but which individually are not capable of developing an efficient fishing industry. Such efforts deserve the support of multilateral institutions and of advanced countries.

Food Alone Is Not Enough

Hunger and malnutrition are not removed by food supplies alone; health, education and other services are needed, with planning to ensure that nutritionally appropriate foodstuffs are available locally at prices which can be afforded. And in the whole question of conquering hunger women play a key part which requires greater recognition, help and rewards. They feed and care for the children, who are the most vulnerable to ill-health – a fact that programmes take too little into account; also, as we have stressed earlier, they play a major role as agricultural producers, often working with unsuitable technology, for low pay and in poor working conditions.

The joint tasks of satisfying the need for food and promoting rural development and agricultural advance include a considerable array of activities – even more numerous than those already mentioned. Soil management; the safeguard – or re-establishment – of ecological balance; the development of technologies adapted to local soils, climate, social and economic conditions; national planning *and* decentralization, designed to facilitate active participation by rural workers and their organizations; extension services; education and training at all levels; these are only some of the domestic priorities which have not been reviewed here, but which are also essential for attaining an end to hunger, and to make the world's food system function on a sustainable basis.

Hunger Cannot Be Isolated

The problem of hunger has to be faced both as a part of domestic economic development and in its links with the international economy. Agriculture cannot be treated separately from the essential complementary role of growth in the industrial and service sectors. First, the increased effective demand for food, necessary to continued production incentives in agriculture, must come in substantial part from growth in employment in the non-agricultural – though not necessarily urban – sectors. The rural landless and even those with small landholdings cannot be fully employed in basic food production and hence cannot derive adequate income and effective demand for food from agriculture alone.

Second, inputs for agricultural growth such as fertilizers or farm equipment – which have to be at appropriate prices – must either come from domestic production or from imports; in the latter case they have to be paid for largely by more exports, including manufactured exports. Third, the price farmers receive is not the only incentive they need for growing more crops; there must be attractive consumer goods from other sectors of the economy which they will want to buy. Fourth, investments in the infrastructure for agriculture are so expensive that part of the costs must in many cases be carried by other productive activities. Finally, manufacturing and service sectors have potential growth rates of 10 to 15 per cent compared to about 4 per cent in agriculture. Thus, giving due emphasis to agriculture is not a substitute for industrial development; it is a question both of the balance between industry and agriculture and of effective encouragement of the components of industrial growth which can assist agricultural development.

So the problem of hunger connects clearly with the rest of this Report. The expansion of trade and finance, including cooperation among developing countries, which can permit incomes to rise, is as important as producing more food or distributing incomes. The low-income countries need assistance both for rural development and for raising the entire productive capacity of their economies which alone can create adequate incomes and jobs. There are no shortcuts to eliminating hunger.

The Need for Secure Supplies

In the late 1960s and early 1970s, as a result of policy changes, grain stocks in the United States (which with Canada supplies 80 per cent of the world's traded wheat) were allowed to run down. Unfortunately in 1972–3 there were disastrous droughts in Africa south of the Sahara, and massive foreign buying by the Soviet Union as a result of poor domestic harvests. The result was a sharp rise in the price of wheat. Between 1972 and 1974 it had more than doubled, and did not settle back to earlier levels until the promise of a large world crop in 1976. In the meantime the World Food Conference in 1974, which was summoned in response to the crisis, placed renewed emphasis on the need for international agreements, and in particular for 'international food security'.

There are in fact major swings in grain production every few years. To cope with them negotiations for a new International Grains Arrangement opened early in 1978, and continued until February 1979, when they were adjourned *sine die*. Significant elements in the negotiations were provisions on reserve stocks, price triggers, and special measures in favour of developing countries. Within the arrangement, there was also to be a consultative Coarse Grains Convention without economic provisions, on which substantial agreement was reached. The operational principles of the Wheat Trade Convention were also agreed upon, but there were disagreements on a number of detailed matters, those dealing principally with the levels of trigger prices, and the special provisions for developing countries, including the size of stocks and assistance to build up reserves. Developing countries, because of their limited ability to hold reserves, insisted on the creation of a fund, to be managed within the Arrangement, to finance the construction of storage facilities, the purchase of grain and the costs of running the reserves. The developed countries were unable to accede to this, and limited themselves to suggesting a Committee to evaluate the storage needs in each developing country and to recommend appropriate action to donor countries and international organizations. It is estimated that developing countries would need to hold 5–7 million tonnes of a 20–30 million tonnes reserve; the acquisition and storage construction costs involved have been put at roughly $1.75 billion.

Freer Food Trade

World food markets are made more unstable by the array of controls on trade which are put up by the surplus producers – most of them the richer countries of North America and the European Community. They restrict the imports of most food products and periodically restrict exports through controls and taxes. The purposes are to maintain high internal production for maximum self-sufficiency; to provide high incomes for farmers; and to protect domestic markets from international fluctuations. But their policies have often produced expensive surpluses, which are frequently sold abroad with the help of subsidies – thus helping some developing countries but competing with exports from others.

These policies have accentuated world grain price fluctuations. In the wheat trade the price and stock policies in North America and Western Europe generated too much wheat in the surplus period before 1970, but created insufficient supplies during the shortage which followed. Since these countries do not consume much less when the price of wheat rises, the effects of a poor harvest can only be absorbed by reduction of stocks, by animals eating less, or by people in the poorer countries eating less. When world stocks are low, as they were in 1972, it is the poor who bear the brunt, as a result of high food prices: which is why greater food reserves are essential. But studies suggest that this need would be reduced if there were freer trade in foodstuffs both within and between North and South. There should be movement in both directions: adequate reserves and fewer trade restrictions.

Making Fertilizers Available

What will happen to agricultural production as supplies of oil become scarcer and so rise in price? The question is increasingly asked since 'modern' farming is heavily dependent on oil-based nitrogenous fertilizers. A higher price of oil inevitably puts up the price of fertilizers, and this will cause problems on which there cannot be complacency. At the moment there should be no clear danger of a worldwide shortage of fertilizers, nor is there yet an urgent need to introduce plant varieties less dependent on chemicals. Modern high-yielding plants are efficient converters of nitrogen into food, with the minimum non-food content, and making efficient use of sunlight. Fertilizers take only about 2–3 per cent of current oil production, and there should be no serious volume deficiency over the next 15–20 years, especially if conservation of energy allows more oil to go into petrochemical production.

In the longer run, when supplies of oil for fertilizers begin to diminish – which should not happen before the next century – there could be alternative sources of nitrogen from coal, or from the biological fixation of nitrogen in the soil. And where hydropower or other non-oil electricity is economic, it should be feasible to get nitrogenous fertilizer from the air through electrolytic derivation.

In the nearer future, it is worth noting that by increasing food production in developing countries, which rely more heavily on human labour and animal power, we consume less of the world's exhaustible resources than by producing more food in the richer nations. To produce food in the same region where it is eaten also cuts down the cost of transport, which itself uses up energy. And the yield of a given additional dose of fertilizer is higher today in the South than in the North where fertilizers are already intensively used. As input prices rise, the relative cost of food production will shift in the South's favour. But in the South as in the North care has to be taken to avoid ecological damage by excessive use of agricultural chemicals.

The rich of the world could also help to increase food supplies if they used less fertilizer for non-food purposes, and also if they ate less meat: to produce one unit of meat protein uses up eight units of vegetable protein, which could be consumed directly. While grass-fed cattle do not remove cereals, poultry and cattle which are raised on cereals consume a very large volume of them – from 3 to 9 kg for each kilogram of edible poultry or meat – sufficient to supply a large proportion of the world's hungry people with cereal products.

Such changes of habits may be distant. But in the meantime the fertilizer price problem, as distinct from the overall supply problem, raises serious issues. It is particularly important to guarantee fertilizer supplies at reasonable prices to low-income countries, and to this end the FAO in 1974 established, in cooperation with fertilizer-producing countries and the international fertilizer industry, the International Fertilizer Supply Scheme, by which fertilizer is made available for low-income countries, to be drawn on as needed at set prices.

Food Aid

Food aid will continue to be essential. It has been criticized in the past, whether for its political exploitation or for the disruption of agricultural incentives in the recipient countries. But the economic criticisms are now less often heard; food aid need not be a disincentive to agricultural production provided that effective demand for food is raised to clear the market at a price which rewards domestic producers. Many countries will take one or more decades before they can satisfy their internal food requirements, and enough food must be made available to them while they are building up their domestic capacity.

Requirements for food aid have usually been calculated

according to expected deficits. But they could be looked at differently if they were also related to programmes for increasing investment in agriculture such as we have envisaged here. Some two-thirds of that investment is for developing water resources, which requires large numbers of workers who themselves need much additional food. In India, for example, it has been calculated that as much as 60 per cent of the funds needed for irrigation projects may actually be spent in the end on construction workers' food. Food aid for such a purpose could eventually be phased out, but during construction it could provide a direct input.

Continuity of food aid, as with any other type of aid, is critical: countries must be able to rely on the amounts and their timely delivery, with sufficient advance notice to allow them to plan demand management and the physical organization of supplies. A government takes a political risk in making a public commitment to abolish hunger; those which do so should be assured of continuing support from the international community, though this need not imply food aid. There must be a reliable assessment of how much food aid is needed. The World Food Conference in 1975 set a target of 10 million tons a year, which has not yet been reached. Indeed, more may be needed if all targets are to be met in the near future, and especially if food aid is extended to support investment in agriculture and labour-intensive public works programmes. Food aid other than cereals is also needed; additional use of some EEC dairy surpluses, for example, could be made for this purpose. Food aid should of course be seen as a complement to other kinds of aid, and given without political strings; and food issues must always be considered in the context of national agricultural programmes. A new Food Aid Convention has been under negotiation to try to achieve these aims for some time; its renewal is a matter of urgency.

Even if all these measures are set in motion, emergencies arising from climatic and other causes will still call for urgent assistance. The Seventh Special Session of the UN General Assembly in 1975 recommended that an international emergency food reserve be set up for this purpose, with a stock of 500,000 tons of cereals. By late 1979 there was still no reliable mechanism for maintaining the reserve by annual replenishment; and contributions had only been of the order of 350,000 tons. Some experts suggest that 500,000 tons may be inadequate and that 750,000 tons will be needed by 1981; and the FAO has estimated that the emergency needs due to crop failures alone amount to some 2 to 3 million tons a year.

Some experts have expressed the view that the international food reserves and the emergency reserve referred to above will not by themselves solve all the problems of countries with fluctuating food import needs, and have proposed a financial food facility, to be located in the IMF or elsewhere. This would be available to low-income countries in times of domestic production shortfalls or unexpectedly abrupt increases of the price of food imports. Studies suggest that an average of $200 million per year would have kept cereal availability in the most seriously affected countries (excluding India, whose needs in a bad harvest year are much greater) within 95 per cent of trend since the 1960s. The Commission favours the creation of such a facility. The lower the levels of food reserves, the greater the need for it; and it is probably more efficient for some emergency needs to be covered by a permanent financial facility or by a mechanism which would quickly come into play when larger assistance is needed than can be accommodated by present arrangements.

An Imperative Goal

This Commission sees no more important task before the world community than the elimination of hunger and malnutrition in all countries. Conclusions similar to those we have reached are shared by many other bodies, including most recently the US Presidential Commission on World Hunger. We are well aware that this is not a limited task – it involves nearly all aspects of the world economy and the development process, to create and distribute both the required food and the employment and incomes which will enable the food to be bought by those who need it. But the world has the capacity to achieve such a goal; it is imperative that it does so.

Recommendations

There must be an end to mass hunger and malnutrition. The capacity of food-importing developing countries, particularly the low-income countries, to meet their food requirements should be expanded and their mounting food import bill reduced through their own efforts and through expanded financial flows for agricultural development. Special attention should be given to irrigation, agricultural research, storage and increased use of fertilizer and other inputs, and to fisheries development.

Agrarian reform is of great importance in many countries both to increase agricultural productivity and to put higher incomes into the hands of the poor.

International food security should be assured through the early establishment of an International Grains Arrangement, larger international emergency reserves, and the establishment of a food financing facility.

Food aid should be increased and linked to employment promotion and agricultural programmes and projects without weakening incentives to food production.

Liberalization of trade in food and other agricultural products within and betweeen North and South would contribute to the stabilization of food supplies.

Support for international agricultural research institutions should be expanded with greater emphasis given to regional cooperation.

6 Population: Growth, Movement and the Environment

The present staggering growth of world population will continue for some considerable time. It will be one of the strongest forces shaping the future of human society. Over one million people are added to the population of the world every five days, and it will increase in the 1980s and 1990s by close to 2 billion, which is more than the total number of people in the world during the first decade of this century. Nine-tenths of the increase will take place in the Third World. In the industrial countries the prospects are more uncertain – there might be very small increases but in some of them the population may even decline somewhat.

It is true that the population explosion seems to be abating. Fertility is going down in many countries in the Third World and their rate of population growth is no longer increasing. In some countries, including the People's Republic of China, birth rates have been reduced so much faster than death rates that growth rates have been cut in half. By the year 2000 world population is nonetheless likely to have grown from its present level of 4.3 billion to 6 or 6.5 billion. Rapid growth over a long time has produced a very young age structure in developing countries; the number of new families will grow so fast that even if each couple starting from today had only two children their population would increase by almost one-third.

Doubling Populations

The decline in fertility during the 1980s and 1990s is therefore not likely to make a great difference to the total numbers in the year 2000, but it is decisive to what happens after that. Depending on whether the decline in fertility accelerates or slows down, world population could, as projections show, stabilize – or possibly turn down – at levels anywhere between 8 and 15 billion in the course of the next century. Even on the assumption of continued fertility decline, the populations of most countries in the developing world are likely to reach at least twice their present size. Nigeria and Bangladesh are projected to have as many people as the United States and the USSR today, and India will have at least 1.2 billion inhabitants. The cities of the Third World are growing even faster than the total populations, and the biggest of them are likely to exceed 30 million by the end of this century.

It is easy to feel a sense of helplessness at these prospects. The growth of population at rates between 2 and 3 per cent per annum will produce a doubling of population in 25 to 35 years. This compounds the task of providing food, jobs, shelter, education and health services, of mitigating absolute poverty, and of meeting the colossal financial and administrative needs of rapid urbanization. It is also difficult to avoid the conclusion that a world of 15 billion people would be racked by a host of potentially devastating economic, social and political conflicts. Whether the nightmarish vision of a hopelessly overcrowded planet in the next century can be averted depends gravely on what is done now to hasten the stabilization of population.

Development Reduces Birth Rates

Many countries have shown both that economic and social development itself helps to limit population growth and that public policies can contribute directly to the decline of birth rates. The countries where birth rates have recently most declined have usually been those which have managed to spread the benefits of development widely. Even very poor areas, such as Kerala in India, have been able to give people new hope for a better life by involving them in the workings of development, improving their health, raising the status and educational levels of women as well as men, and ensuring adequate food supplies for the poor. Where this has been done, birth rates have tended to fall, while they have remained high in many richer developing countries which have paid less attention to the needs of the many.

There is a risk that the widespread trends of fertility decline may create the impression that the situation is taking care of itself. This could be unfortunate. International support for population policies is flagging at precisely the time when the commitment to, and political acceptance of, family planning policies is spreading in the

Third World. Over sixty countries, with 95 per cent of the population of the Third World, have adopted family planning programmes, although the degree of commitment varies. The needs for population assistance are great – for example, the United Nations Fund for Population Activities (UNFPA) can only meet two-thirds of the requests it receives.

Success in Family Planning

Those who have pursued such programmes vigorously have registered considerable success. China, which already has one billion people, has in the course of the 1970s reduced its rate of growth from 2.3 per cent to little more than one per cent; it aims at zero growth by 2000. Chile, Colombia and Costa Rica, the first countries in Latin America to adopt systematic family planning policies, have reduced their birth rates by close to one-third in the last twenty years, and the same is true of such East Asian countries as Hong Kong, Singapore and the Republic of Korea. The world Fertility Survey has recently analysed extensive data from fourteen developing countries and found fertility in most of them going down at a dramatic pace. The age of marriage of women is rising, which tends to limit family size, and the knowledge of family planning methods is becoming widespread – over three-quarters of the women in these countries, and in many others over 90 per cent, know of at least one such method. Other surveys have shown that striking changes are occurring not only in urbanized and educated populations but even in poor and rural ones. In Thailand marital fertility dropped by 20 per cent in the first half of the 1970s, and fertility in Java and Bali dropped by 15 per cent in the same period. In summary, except in Africa and in some of the poorest Asian countries like Bangladesh and Pakistan, birth rates are now falling significantly in most of the Third World. There are still countries which limit rather than promote access to family planning and where population growth is believed to be a source of national or ethnic strength, but their number is steadily shrinking.

Expanded and more effective family planning services are needed. But experience has shown that these are rarely effective unless they go hand in hand with community development, education, better chances for survival of infants and children, higher status for women, and other advances which require general economic and social progress. What is done to meet the challenges of poverty, ill-health and hunger is a primary contribution to checking excessive population growth. In the final analysis, it is development itself that will provide the most propitious environment for stabilizing the world's population at tolerable levels. In the creation of that environment, all countries have a mutual interest. The prospect of an overcrowded planet in the next century has little meaning to people who live on the margin of existence today.

Need for Population Programmes

We believe that development policies should include a national population programme aiming at an appropriate balance between population and resources, making family planning services freely available and integrated with other measures to promote welfare and social change. International support for population projects and programmes and for social and biomedical research needs to be greatly enlarged.

The pressures from rapid population growth are in the first place of concern to the countries where it occurs and where more than half of all investment and development efforts may be needed merely to keep levels of living from slipping even lower, and where unemployment and underemployment are accentuated by the steady growth of the labour force. But an increase in world population of such historic dimensions is also bound to have numerous consequences for the whole international community. The international movement of people is likely to increase, and the global pressure on the resources and the natural environment of the earth will become severe.

International Migration of Labour

The movement of labour across national boundaries has assumed very large proportions in the last decade. The large-scale migration of unskilled and semi-skilled labour, and of professional manpower, which has taken place in the last two decades has been a reflection of imbalances in income and employment opportunities and, to some extent, of constraints on the international flow of capital and trade.

The rich countries which have imported workers have controlled the number and character of the manpower and the duration of its stay; most of the movement has been temporary. Much of the demand has been structural, coming from industries which cannot keep or attract national workers. And although there has been a demand for more permanent workers, migrant labour in many countries is treated as a temporary workforce. This has created friction and hardship. The movement of migrant workers involves human beings, and its social aspects have understandably made it a sensitive and visible issue.

At present there are about 20 million migrant workers in the world, about 12 million of them from developing countries. An estimated 6 million are in the United States, most of them coming from Mexico – many illegally. Western Europe's share went up from about 2 million in the early 1960s to 6 million in the early 1970s but fell by one million with the post-1973 recession. More than 2 million of the migrant workers in Europe come from developing countries, mainly Algeria, Morocco, Tunisia, Turkey and Yugoslavia. Since the early 1970s, large numbers of workers have also gone to the oil-exporting countries of the Middle East: about 3 million at present, two-thirds of them from the region itself and the rest from South and South East Asia. South Africa has for many years attracted mine labour – around 400,000 at present – from the neighbouring countries of Botswana, Mozambique, Swaziland and Lesotho. Migrant labour is also of importance within East European countries, and there are labour flows among developing countries in parts of Latin America and in West Africa.

In all parts of the world the presence of migrant workers has raised sensitive political issues. In the United States, the regularization of non-legal migration has become an important question. In Western Europe, the situation of migrant workers and their families and their housing, schooling, and political status have attracted much public attention and caused lively debate. Uncertainties surround the future pattern and permanence of migration in the Middle East. The apartheid system in South Africa, which is a source of outrage in itself, is inflicted on workers who migrate there from neighbouring countries.

The Contributions of Migrants

A second and very different stream of migration is the 'brain drain'. In the early 1960s and 1970s well over 400,000 physicians and surgeons, engineers, scientists and other skilled people have moved from developing countries to more developed ones. The principal sending countries have been India, Pakistan, the Philippines and Sri Lanka. Most of the migrants have gone to the United States, Canada and Britain, others to the rest of Western Europe, Australia and the Middle East. Like migration in general, this kind of movement has had a long history – dating back at least as far as the drain of Greek brains to Alexandria around 300 BC. But never before has it been so extensive, nor based so largely on economic incentives. The brain drain has occurred in part because many students and professionals trained in developed countries have chosen not to return home.

Migration has given benefits to all parties. The sending countries have gained from the jobs provided to their nationals and often from the training and skills acquired by workers who later return. They have also benefited from the money sent back by migrants, currently about $7 billion annually from Western Europe and about $5 billion from the Middle East. These remittances have become a big foreign exchange earner for many developing countries where they sometimes match or surpass export earnings from commodities and manufactures.

Receiving countries have also derived many benefits from migrant labour which has contributed to their domestic product, made their manufacturing industries more competitive and held down costs in construction industries and service sectors. Skilled migrants have been particularly valuable as they have saved their host countries substantial costs in education and training.

On the other hand, the status of migrant workers is often unsatisfactory and precarious. And while countries of immigration have been able to control migrant flows to suit their needs, countries of emigration have been buffeted by fluctuations in the demand for migrant labour and in remittances, and they have lost skilled and semi-skilled manpower which they badly need.

Migrants and their Rights

National and international migration policies should protect and promote the interests of the migrant workers themselves, as well as those of their home and host countries.

Receiving countries differ widely in their treatment of migrants. Some admit them to citizenship in due course and allow them in the meantime some of the rights that go with it. Many others treat them as temporary workers, ineligible for many social security benefits and economic and political rights. Within the European Community, workers from other member countries enjoy the same rights as domestic workers. Some sending countries, for their part, only allow their citizens to migrate on condition that they maintain their citizenship and plan to return. The International Labour Organization (ILO) has formulated norms which provide for the respect of the basic rights of all migrant workers and ensure that migrants and their families get fair treatment in living and working conditions, in social security, health and safety; that they are allowed to reunite their families, to preserve their ethnic identity, and to join trade unions. We regret that these conventions have not been ratified except by a very small number of countries. All governments should adopt them and implement them both in spirit and letter.

Much migration takes place under illegal and abusive conditions. Traffickers in sending and receiving countries organize this trade for their own gain, and migrant workers are illegally employed in host country enterprises without health insurance, social security or proper housing. It is certainly in the mutual interest of all countries to take concerted measures to eliminate this trade in human beings, as the above-mentioned ILO norms prescribe.

More generally, governments should reach agreements, both bilateral and multilateral, to regulate international migration. With better planned and more orderly policies, fluctuations could be evened out, remittances be made more predictable, and return migration assisted when it occurs. Steps in this direction have been taken within the OECD in Europe; similar measures are needed elsewhere. The World Employment Conference in 1976 has made valuable recommendations in this direction.

When industrial countries suffer from economic recessions they frequently shift part of the burden on to developing countries by insisting on 'return migration' which in effect means exporting their unemployment back to the home countries where unemployment led to migration in the first place. This has recently happened on a large scale to countries like Turkey and Yugoslavia, causing simultaneously a sudden increase in unemployment and a sharp decrease in remittances. Such events are outside the control of the sending countries, and they should be helped to adjust to them. The IMF Compensatory Financing Facility has recently been extended to cover fluctuations in remittances as well as ordinary export earnings, which is an important step in the right direction. There is also room for more bilateral cooperation for meeting the adjustment problem.

Migration can provide new opportunities for developing countries to cooperate among themselves, particularly in the Middle East where receiving countries are rich in resources and sending countries have a surplus of skilled workers. The two groups have complementary interests, but this kind of continuing interdependence has to be managed in the long-run interests of both sides and of the migrant workers themselves.

The migration of people in search of better opportunities to make a living is an essential aspect of development and change and has been so throughout history. We are still far from a shared understanding of the principles that should guide international migration. In the meantime, the objective must be to build, on the basis of the interests of the countries concerned, a framework that is more just and equitable than the present one.

Refugees and Displaced Persons

A different flow of international migration that has become a distressingly regular feature of the modern world is that of political and religious refugees and of people who have been displaced by wars and political upheavals. It is estimated that in this century some 250 million people have fled their countries.

In recent years the problems have assumed an added dimension because refugees often have no intention of staying in the countries of first asylum nor do these in many cases see fit to keep and employ them. In the last three years there has been an average of 2000–3000 new refugees a day in the world. Situations giving rise to large and sudden movements of refugees have arisen on all continents. Some 4 million refugees and displaced persons for whom permanent solutions have not been found are in Africa alone, and even greater numbers exist in various parts of Asia. Altogether the number of refugees is of the order of 10 million.

The Universal Declaration of Human Rights states that 'everyone has the right to leave any country, including his own', also 'the right to seek and to enjoy other countries' asylum from persecution'. The attempt to translate these rights into practical realities is the concern of the United Nations High Commissioner for Refugees, a range of other international organizations, and many governmental and voluntary agencies devoted to humanitarian relief work. Increasingly, the attempt to improve the lot of refugees has come to focus on three objectives: first, to establish the principle of asylum to ensure that refugees are not repelled and sent back to the countries from which they have fled; second, to arrange for the care and protection of refugees in temporary asylum; and third, to search for permanent solutions such as voluntary repatriation or resettlement.

Asylum for Refugees

Refugee problems are not caused by population pressure. Their roots lie in intolerance, political instability and war. But the difficulties of assuring asylum and arranging for resettlement of refugees are greatly increased when receiving countries already feel overpopulated. Resettling rural refugees is difficult when land is scarce and rural under-employment extensive. The resettlement of urban refugees is also hampered by unemployment. Refugees sometimes have valuable skills, and countries are then more inclined to offer them admission; but countries of first asylum should not be left with the sick and the aged whom other countries do not want. In resettlement planning, consideration should also be given to arrangements which might help to maintain social links and identities among refugees.

Although one must hope that governments will in the future refrain from creating conditions which their citizens find oppressive enough to flee from, and that wars and other man-made disasters will be less frequent, it is necessary to be prepared for new emergencies. The demographic prospects for the coming decades suggest that it will only get harder to resolve such situations unless and until the principle of international burden sharing is accepted globally and the granting of asylum and the humane treatment of refugees become matters of genuine concern to the international community as a whole.

Pressure on Resources and Environment

A question we cannot overlook is whether the resources and the ecological system of the earth will suffice to meet the needs of a greatly increased world population at the economic standard that is hoped for. So far the bulk of the depletion of non-renewable resources and the pressure on the oceans and the atmosphere have been caused by the spectacular industrial growth of the developed countries where only one-fifth of the world's people live. But population growth in some parts of the Third World is already a source of alarming ecological changes, and its industrialization is bound to lead to greater pressure on resources and environment.

As we have noted elsewhere in this Report, the exhaustion of the world's oil supplies will force far-reaching change on the world economy in a foreseeable future, but most other mineral resources seem to be in relatively ample supply. The problems arising from their depletion stem largely from the character of their distribution and from the difficulties that may occur in their production and trade.

Renewable resources, however, may set narrower limits. The biological systems of the world are showing signs of strain. Thus the catch from ocean fishing has levelled off in spite of great improvements in modern fishing fleets. Depletion problems in relation to farming, water supplies and forestry are discussed in other parts of our Report. When the environment is overtaxed it does not harm only the countries directly faced with deterioration of the resource base but affects all countries through the ecosystem of the earth, as in the case of deforestation. The forests now covering about one-fifth of the earth's land surface are crucial to the stability of soil systems and to the survival of innumerable animal species and millions of human beings. They also help to absorb the excessive amounts of carbon dioxide emitted by the burning of fossil fuels, a process which threatens to warm up the atmosphere and could produce climatic change with potentially catastrophic consequences. The combined demand for firewood, farm land, and increased exports of forest products to industrial countries is causing a deforestation of 11 million hectares each year in the Third World. That is half the area of the United Kingdom. Deforestation also leads to impoverishment and erosion of the soil and increased flooding and silting up of rivers, reservoirs and harbours, as is happening in Panama, Bangladesh, Nigeria and many other countries.

Protecting the Environment

It is gratifying that there has been an awakening to the need to protect the environment from over-exploitation, pollution and contamination. The United Nations Conference on the Human Environment in 1972 was an important milestone, and much progress in awareness has been made in the years since then. It can no longer be argued that the protection of the environment is an obstacle to development. On the contrary, the care of the natural environment is an essential aspect of development.

Yet there is still much resistance. The costs of containing pollution are easier to calculate than the benefits of unpolluted air and water. There is also a temptation for a country to set lower standards than another in order to attract industry and create jobs. There is an obvious need to harmonize standards, to prevent a competitive debasement of them. Developing countries too are already experiencing industrial pollution and have an interest in establishing and enforcing standards for environmental protection. The same norms will not be appropriate for all countries, and they must make their own judgement of the trade-offs involved. But to seek to attract industry at the expense of environment might cause damage that is more costly to undo than to prevent, and it would also be likely to contribute to protectionist pressures in industrial countries.

Environmental impact assessment should be undertaken wherever investments or other development activities may have adverse environmental consequences whether within the national territory concerned, for the environment of neighbouring countries or for the global commons. There should be guidelines for such assessments, and when the impact falls on other countries there should be an obligation to consult with them. Development banks should be mindful of such factors in the development of their own projects, and be ready to assist environmental impact studies to ensure that an ecological perspective is incorporated in development planning.

Need for International Regimes

Maintenance of the global commons – especially the oceans, the atmosphere and outer space – and control of the accelerating utilization of them requires the establishment of international regimes. In the absence of such authority, over-exploitation and abuse could cause irreversible damage, especially to the interests of weaker nations.

The difficulty of making progress at the global level and securing agreement in these matters between countries of vastly different resources and interests has been starkly evident in the ongoing United Nations Law of the Sea Conference. The creation of an international Sea-bed Authority will represent a breakthrough, but there is a real risk that only the least valuable and most remote portions of the seas will be under its jurisdiction, and that responsibility for research and pollution control in the 'exclusive economic zones' of 200 miles or more will not be subject to internationally agreed codes of practice. Yet halting the destruction of the oceans is of vital concern to all mankind.

It is clear to us that the growth and development of the world economy must in the future be less destructive to natural resources and the environment so that the rights of future generations are protected. Few threats to peace and the survival of the human community are greater than those posed by the prospects of

115

cumulative and irreversible degradation of the biosphere on which human life depends.

Recommendations

In view of the vicious circle between poverty and high birth rates, the rapid population growth in developing countries gives added urgency to the need to fight hunger, disease, malnutrition and illiteracy.

We also believe that development policies should include national population programmes aiming at a satisfactory balance between population and resources and making family planning freely available. International assistance and support of population programmes must be increased to meet the unmet needs for such aid.

The many migrant workers in the world should be assured fair treatment, and the interests of their home countries and the countries of immigration must be better reconciled. Governments should seek bilateral and multilateral cooperation to harmonize their policies of emigration and immigration, to protect the rights of migrant workers, to make remittances more stable and to mitigate the hardships of unanticipated return migration.

The rights of refugees to asylum and legal protection should be strengthened. We also believe that commitments to international cooperation in the resettlement of refugees in the future will be necessary to protect countries of first asylum from unfair burdens.

The strain on the global environment derives mainly from the growth of the industrial economies, but also from that of the world's population. It threatens the survival and development opportunities of future generations. All nations have to cooperate more urgently in international management of the atmosphere and other global commons, and in the prevention of irreversible ecological damage.

Ocean resources outside the 'exclusive economic zones' of 200 miles should be developed under international rules in the balanced interests of the whole world community.

7 Disarmament and Development

Arms or Peace?

Recent developments have made the world more aware that the arms race has become a grave danger to the whole of mankind. The armaments of the superpowers and their alliances represent a precarious kind of balance which, given present political conditions, contributes to preserving world peace. At the same time they represent a continuing threat of nuclear annihilation and a huge waste of resources which should be deployed for peaceful development. The build-up of arms in large parts of the Third World itself causes growing instability and undermines development. A new understanding of defence and security policies is indispensable. Public opinion must be better informed – of the burden and waste of the arms race, of the damage it does to our economies, and of the greater importance of other measures which it deprives of resources. More arms do not make mankind safer, only poorer.

The world's military spending dwarfs any spending on development. Total military expenditures are approaching $450 billion a year, of which over half is spent by the Soviet Union and the United States, while annual spending on official development aid is only $20 billion. If only a fraction of the money, manpower and research presently devoted to military uses were diverted to development, the future prospects of the Third World would look entirely different.

In any case there is a moral link between the vast spending on arms and the disgracefully low spending on measures to remove hunger and ill-health in the Third World. The programme of the World Health Organization to abolish malaria is short of funds; it is estimated that it will eventually cost about $450 million – which represents only one-thousandth of the world's annual military spending. The cost of a ten-year programme to provide for essential food and health needs in developing countries is less than half of one year's military spending. Moreover, arms production is not just a matter of spending but of manpower and skills. It is profoundly disturbing to realize that in East and West a very large proportion of scientists and much of the scientific resources of universities and industry are devoted to armaments.

The obstacles to reversing these trends are formidable, but they should not be allowed to get in the way of serious discussion of the dangers of the arms race and the realization of the size of the economic burden that it involves. One of the chief enemies of disarmament is the sense of resignation and traditional acceptance that accompanies large defence spending, while the dangers are constantly mounting.

Disarmament and Arms Limitation

Mutual distrust between East and West stimulates the arms race, causing excessive and ever-increasing military expenditures. The biggest concentration of weapons, the crux of the arms race, is centred on the European theatre, and there is a danger of a further build-up of more destructive weapons in this area. But it would be wrong to ignore other areas of dangerous conflicts: the lack of a comprehensive peace-settlement for the Middle East; tension and violence in various parts of the African continent; strained relations between the Soviet Union and China, and the partially related crises in South East Asia.

In addition, the borders of developing countries left behind as part of the colonial heritage are the occasion of tension in certain cases and, like continuing racial conflicts, have sometimes been, and could again be, the source of military conflict. If major powers have the illusion that access to raw materials can be settled by military means as a last resort, North–South relations will become a major factor in international tensions.

The issues debated in the international disarmament talks – strategic arms limitation, balanced force reductions, the nuclear test ban treaty, measures against nuclear proliferation – move forward extremely slowly. Responsible leaders on both sides have so far shown a regrettable lack of courage. Some commentators have suggested that another reason for the slow progress is that these talks are cut off from the political and economic life to which they are so important. They continue as exchanges between armaments experts, attempting to reach binding and policeable agreements on highly technical issues, with the inherent danger that politics becomes the prisoner of technological developments. Another difficulty arises from the fact that negotiations only take place after new weapons systems have already been established and are starting to become outdated.

Competition in Destructive Weapons

SALT 2 could represent a major step forward, in terms of *détente*, in spite of well-known shortcomings. But even after SALT 2 is ratified and implemented, well over 10,000 US and USSR strategic nuclear warheads will remain aimed at military and civilian targets. There exists a much larger and as yet unrestricted number of so-called tactical nuclear weapons, including medium-range missiles. Their destructive force equals one million Hiroshima bombs. Therefore an agreement to control these weapons which particularly threaten Central Europe is a matter of great urgency, all the more so since new weapons are under discussion.

Competition in armaments between the largest military powers continues primarily in a qualitative rather than quantitative dimension; each new generation of weapons being more destructive than the system it replaces. Furthermore, the greater precision of nuclear weapons may lower the 'threshold' and thus increase the danger of war. Also, so-called conventional weapons now have devastating power. There is already a threat of the militarization of outer space with anti-ballistic weapons using lasers and particle beams.

In a parallel move to the future negotiations on SALT 3 the next important steps might be taken in Vienna where the talks on mutual balanced force reductions (MBFR) have been going on for several years. To counter the underlying lack of trust in East West relations calls for continuing the process of *détente*; for increasing the areas of peaceful exchange, of industrial and scientific cooperation to forge a beneficial interdependence between East and West. At the same time further agreements on confidence-building measures, as recognized in the Helsinki Declaration on Security and Cooperation in Europe of 1975, should be negotiated as soon as possible.

Arms Sales to the Third World

While the prevention of nuclear war remains the first ambition of disarmament, 'conventional' (non-nuclear) weapons account for 80 per cent of all arms spending. In fact all the wars since the Second World War have been fought with conventional weapons, and in the Third World, where they have killed more than ten million people. In some of these wars, such as in Korea and Indochina, the major powers were actively engaged; in others they have been in the background. Some of the most lethal wars have been fought with 'small' arms. The Lebanese civil war, for instance, has caused more deaths than all four Arab–Israel wars. The war in Cambodia is an even more tragic example.

The North's sales of conventional weapons to the South are increasing. These represent 70 per cent of all arms exports. But this trade is one between a few suppliers and a few receivers. According to the 1979 Yearbook of the Stockholm International Peace Research Institute (SIPRI), imports of the Third World in 1978 (in 1975 US dollars) were $14 billion, of which seven countries (Iraq, Iran, Republic of Korea, Saudi Arabia, India, Israel and Libya) account for $8.7 billion, the five Middle Eastern countries alone accounting for $6.6 billion. Some Third World countries, with Brazil in the lead, are now developing significant arms production capacity and are starting to export arms as well. But 70 per cent of the arms imports to the Third World came from the USA ($5.8 billion) and the USSR ($4 billion), with France ($2 billion), the United Kingdom ($660 million) and Italy ($620 million) the other leading suppliers. As the export of sophisticated arms is accompanied by an export of military-technical instructors, this can aggravate existing tensions.

The major powers sell weapons mainly to suit their own foreign policy or to maintain regional balances, rather than to benefit their economies. Smaller countries, for their part, use arms exports to subsidize their own military production, to provide employment in their own arms factories, and to assist their own economies. Arms exports from industrialized countries are now largely controlled by governments; such exports have nonetheless been increasingly subject to commercial pressures. The United States established its own government arms sales organization in 1961, which was followed by the other arms-producing powers. Where countries imposed export restrictions, these regulations were bypassed through the exports of factories or knowhow for military purposes.

Restraining Arms Exports

With the recession in the arms industry in the early 1970s –

following the end of the Vietnam war – and the emergence of new profitable markets, particularly in the Middle East, the drive to sell weapons to the Third World was intensified, often aimed at stimulating new demand irrespective of real defence needs. These military-industrial pressures in the North are often reinforced by and connected with contacts in the developing countries, many of which have military governments or strong military élites who want to be equipped with modern weaponry to enhance their prestige. Arms exports by Eastern Europe too have been influenced by the availability of surplus weapons and the need to earn foreign currency.

There should be restraints on the commercial pressures for arms purchases exerted by the North – both West and East. This is unlikely to be achieved without agreement between the arms-producing countries. The traditional justification of arms selling – 'if we don't sell them, someone else will' – cannot be accepted. In recent years the major powers have become more seriously concerned about the consequences of their arms transfers, and in December 1978 the United States and the Soviet Union held discussions in Mexico to try to limit transfers of conventional weapons to the Third World. There was some expectation that agreement could be reached over regions such as Latin America, where the issues seemed relatively simple. But the talks broke down over questions of supplying arms to other regions. This setback should not be allowed to discourage further attempts to limit conventional arms exports on a non-discriminatory basis. Some restraint might be achieved by the western powers alone, at least in relation to major arms importing countries, in the competition amongst themselves to sell weaponry to the Third World. But the whole international community should increase the effort to reach agreement to restrain delivery of arms or arms producing facilities to areas of conflict and tension; the major powers bear special responsibility in this.

We also believe there should be disclosure of all arms exports and of the export of arms-producing facilities. But this will not be an easy task, and would require global agreements.

The governments of developing countries like any others want weapons to strengthen their national security; but they must share the responsibility for restraint. Some of them have increased their military expenditure at a rate that bears little relationship to their security needs, at the expense of peaceful development. As massive arms imports require an adequate infrastructure, absorb scarce skilled labour and additional foreign exchange for maintenance imports, this all increases debt burdens. To reverse this trend will involve new priorities by developing countries and their leaders. But we recognize the difficulties of restraining arms procurement in areas of tension where large imbalances of military capacity exist, especially where this is combined with persistent oppression such as apartheid.

Nuclear Weapons Proliferation

Every effort must be made to secure international agreements preventing the proliferation of nuclear weapons. Many developing countries now regard nuclear energy programmes as essential to their economic future. Unfortunately, as is well known, these can in many cases be used later to provide nuclear weapons as a by-product. Already there is a prospect of thirty to forty nations being in a position to produce nuclear weapons in the next twenty years. However, it is one thing to produce a nuclear explosive device; it is another to produce one which can be efficiently used for military purposes. And a country which wanted nuclear weapons could produce them cheaper and faster directly than as a by-product of nuclear power development. Nevertheless, the possibility of proliferation is real and dangerous.

Developing countries cannot be denied the right to install nuclear power plants. In order to eliminate the misuse of nuclear power plants for military purposes, the inspection system of the International Atomic Energy Agency should be strengthened and accepted by all countries. This should be facilitated by meeting constructively the concerns of those countries which have not signed and ratified the Nuclear Non-Proliferation Treaty. The treaty under which Latin America was declared a zone free of nuclear arms could be an interesting model for consideration by other regions.

Measures to curb the global arms race have made only limited progress. They may have prevented some programmes from expanding and certainly the major powers have come closer together in appreciating the dangers and the costs of the escalation of arms production. But real disarmament, actual reduction of weapons and expenditure levels, remains elusive.

Taxing Military Spending

Various proposals have been made for taxes on military

expenditures, if they exceed some agreed level, and on arms trade. As we discuss in another section of this Report, a possible tax on international trade could include a tax on arms trade at a higher rate of tax than that on other trade. The likelihood of any international agreement on such measures is small at present. There are a number of objections to these proposals, including the fear that any tax on arms would in some sense 'legitimize' arms expenditures. Further, few countries make full disclosure of military expenditures, and in some countries such disclosure is quite deficient. Nonetheless, military expenditures and arms exports might be one element entering into a new principle of assessment for international taxation, and efforts to generate appropriate information for this purpose deserve encouragement.

Disarming for Peace and Development

The problem is to reduce the demand for weapons so that resources for development can be captured before they become armaments. But we make no simplistic assumption that what could be saved by limiting military expenditure could easily be diverted into development assistance. New economic and political priorities are also required.

An argument often heard (and as often overestimated) is that arms production and exports are essential to the North's economies and employment. This is a fallacy. While it is true that the arms industries have been a source of growth and jobs, they are certainly not irreplaceable. Conversion to civilian production could be achieved faster than is often assumed because the economic problems are easier to tackle than the political ones. Recent data from the United States and other studies, including one by the International Metalworkers Federation, confirm that investment in arms production creates fewer jobs than in other industries and public services. There is no reason to doubt that much of the capital and manpower presently employed in arms production or other military uses can be converted into producing peaceful equipment essential to development, including capital goods, as much research has shown. These and other questions relevant to disarmament are being reviewed by the UN Group of Governmental Experts on the Relationship between Disarmament and Development, which began its three-year period of work in 1978.

All over the world, and even in the North, there are large unmet needs in health and transport or urban renewal which could expand to reduce any demand gap caused by reductions in arms production. If people paid lower taxes – and on a world average one tax dollar out of six goes into military expenditure – they would not be at a loss for other goods on which to spend their money. There are also many areas of research and global cooperation more valuable to humanity, more likely to ensure its survival, than the improvements of the machinery of destruction to which so much of our resources are now devoted. But the fundamental need – from the world development standpoint – is for the industrialized countries to direct themselves towards peaceful high technology production, which could make use of the highly skilled manpower currently employed in arms industries.

The political problems of achieving a shift are not easy to resolve. Internal politics are interwoven with military-industrial connections which influence domestic and foreign policies, arms production and arms sales abroad.

A New Concept of Security

An important task of constructive international policy will have to consist in providing a new, more comprehensive understanding of 'security' which would be less restricted to the purely military aspects. In the global context true security cannot be achieved by a mounting build-up of weapons – defence in the narrow sense – but only by providing basic conditions for peaceful relations between nations, and solving not only the military but also the non-military problems which threaten them. The arms race, in which each participant acts in the name of national security – too limited a view of national security – has produced a situation in which the extinction of mankind is a real possibility. The goal of building up a globally respected peace-keeping mechanism, powerful enough to prevent conflicts turning into warfare, should be kept constantly in mind. A strengthened role for the United Nations in securing the integrity of states should result in the reduction of national military expenditures, thus freeing resources for more constructive purposes, including development assistance.

Our survival depends not only on military balance, but on global cooperation to ensure a sustainable biological environment, and sustainable prosperity based on equitably shared resources. Much of the insecurity in the world is connected with the divisions between rich and poor countries – grave injustice and mass starvation causing additional instability. Yet the research and the funds which could help to put an end to poverty and hunger are now pre-empted by military uses. The threatening arsenals grow, and spending on other purposes which could make them less necessary is neglected. If military expenditures can be controlled and some of the savings related to development, the world's security can be increased, and the mass of mankind currently excluded from a decent life can have a brighter future.

Recommendations

The public must be made more aware of the terrible danger to world stability caused by the arms race, of the burden it imposes on national economies, and of the resources it diverts from peaceful development.

The mutual distrust which stimulates the arms race between East and West calls for continuing the process of *détente* through agreements on confidence-building measures. All sides should be prepared for negotiations (including those on the regional level) to get the arms race under control at a time before new weapons systems have been established.

The world needs a more comprehensive understanding of security which would be less restricted to the purely military aspects.

Every effort must be made to secure international agreements preventing the proliferation of nuclear weapons.

A globally respected peace-keeping mechanism should be built up – strengthening the role of the United Nations. In securing the integrity of states such peace-keeping machinery might free resources for development through a sharing of military expenditure, a reduction in areas of conflict and of the arms race which they imply.

Military expenditure and arms exports might be one element entering into a new principle for international taxation for development purposes. A tax on arms trade should be at a higher rate than that on other trade.

Increased efforts should be made to reach agreements on the disclosure of arms exports and exports of arms-producing facilities. The international community should become more seriously concerned about the consequences of arms transfers or of exports of arms-producing facilities and reach agreement to restrain such deliveries to areas of conflict or tension.

More research is necessary on the means of converting arms production to civilian production which could make use of the highly skilled scientific and technical manpower currently employed in arms industries.

8 The Task of the South

In our Terms of Reference we agreed that we would 'pay attention to the responsibilities of the developing countries in their domestic policies, to match the efforts for international economic and social justice with efforts to promote the same ends among their own populations'. In this chapter we address this issue. We do so fully aware that domestic policies lie within the national domain, but mindful also that no examination of international development issues can be realistic without a full appreciation of the essential tasks which developing countries must themselves undertake in pursuit of real development.

And we do so without in any way wishing to suggest that changes in domestic policy must be a prior condition for reforms in the global system. The case for an international order conducive to development and both equitable and rational in terms of relations between countries is valid in its own right. It does not rest on the contingency of particular national policies whether social, economic or political. But the case for greater equity within nations is valid also; and it is directly relevant to the prospects for economic development and the improvement of the quality of people's lives which is its goal. It is in this context that we consider some of the special responsibilities that rest upon developing countries. We discuss national policies to alleviate poverty, and economic cooperation between developing countries; both are important and related to each other.

National Policies to Alleviate Poverty

In earlier chapters we have briefly reviewed the record of development in the postwar period and set out the dimensions of global poverty. The picture is a mixed one: in certain areas major strides have been made towards modernization but, except in a few countries, progress in attaining the social objectives of development has generally been disappointing. Economic growth has not always meant that living standards have improved for the broad masses of people. A few countries have succeeded in combining rapid economic growth with rising living standards for most of their population; but in the aggregate the number of people suffering from absolute poverty has continued to grow; unemployment and underemployment have worsened and in many cases inequalities in income and wealth have widened.

This outcome is a reflection for the most part of existing economic and social structures and past patterns of growth; these in turn have been influenced by international factors. Elsewhere in this Report we examine the operation of the international economy and show how it has contributed to frustrating the ambitions of the South for development. But there is an equally fundamental problem: those who benefit most from the present distribution of wealth and economic power, whether in the North or the South, commonly fail to give the highest priority to their shared responsibility for improving the lot of the poorest in the world. Present structures within developing countries are often reinforced both by domestic policies on investment allocation, public expenditure, pricing, trading patterns and exchange rates, and also by the ways in which northern concerns influence the organization of production in developing countries. In combination, these factors have frequently led to patterns of growth whose benefits accrue mainly to minorities who have been able to invest or work in the modern sectors of industry and agriculture or occupy the higher rungs of the public services and the professions.

Social and Economic Reforms

Rapid progress in reducing poverty will thus require changes in the international economic system as well as in national patterns of growth. The reforms we propose on international policies and institutions would provide additional resources and a favourable external environment for the global assault on poverty. But changes in the international system alone will not suffice. They must be complemented for most countries by social and economic reforms at the national level.

Developing countries differ widely in their levels of development, resources, structure and organization of production and patterns of income and wealth distribution. No single set of policies can suit them all. Nevertheless, the experience of the past two decades shows that many of them face similar problems and suggests a number of policy approaches relevant to a wide range of countries. In this section we attempt to highlight those development policies that, widely adopted, would signal to the international community a genuine commitment by developing countries to a more equitable sharing of the benefits of development as well as a determined effort to mobilize human and material resources for it.

The likelihood that these policies will be implemented depends largely upon internal political circumstances. There are political constraints to the adoption of our proposals, arising from vested interests and from the magnitude of poverty itself; but while we do not wish to prescribe for individual countries, it can still be argued that broad political participation and determined leadership are the best guarantors of policies such as we recommend. We believe that in the vast majority of developing countries much more could be done to achieve equitable development.

Elements of an Anti-Poverty Strategy

If the poor are to gain directly from growth and participate fully in the development process, new institutions and policies are needed to achieve redistribution of productive resources to the poor, generate rapid expansion in jobs and income-earning opportunities and provide social and economic services on a mass basis. A shift of development strategy to achieve these ends will depend on political will, efficient economic management and effective mobilization of resources. But domestic efforts to achieve development cannot be restricted exclusively to direct anti-poverty policies and programmes; they must be seen within the broader framework of policies for promoting rapid growth and structural transformation of the economy. Nor should anti-poverty policies imply that the flow of aid be restricted to financing only small-scale projects directly and immediately benefiting the rural and urban poor. Financially and economically viable projects in the modern productive sector, including sophisticated technology and large-scale economic infrastructural projects, are an important element of the development process requiring international support.

Although institutional changes and policy thrusts will need to vary from one country to another, it is useful to classify countries into two broad groups. The first comprises countries where some of the essential reforms have already taken place. Both middle- and low-income countries, including some of the least developed, fall within this group. Many of the middle-income countries among them have already gone far in meeting the essential needs of their people. For the low-income countries in the group, the overriding priority is rapid growth. Equal shares of poverty do not necessarily imply a progression to equal shares of wealth; for this both the mobilization of domestic resources and an increased inflow of external resources are crucial. They will need, as growth gathers momentum, continuously to adapt their institutions and policies to prevent the new economic power and wealth being concentrated in the hands of a small minority. In certain countries this may mean some sacrifice of quicker growth in favour of broader but surer development which minimizes social strains; in others, research suggests, redistributive strategies may accelerate growth.

The other category includes the majority of developing countries where better distribution of productive resources and incomes has still to be undertaken so that the essential needs of all the people can be met and initiative and productivity encouraged, particularly in rural areas. In some middle-income countries, where the poverty problem is of relatively modest dimensions and the state derives significant revenue from productive resources, the main need is for policies to redistribute income and assets and to expand employment opportunities rapidly. For the others, both middle- and low-income, where poverty exists on a considerable scale, a broader package of policies including agrarian reform, promotion of small-scale enterprises and significant changes in the organization and delivery of public services is essential.

The Priority of Agriculture

Seventy per cent or more of the poor in developing countries live in the rural areas. In the past, many countries have put disproportionate efforts into developing the urban and industrial sectors. But the neglect of agriculture has often caused *per capita* food production to stagnate or even fall, and food prices to rise. Rural poverty has thus increased and inequality has become wider. We believe that a necessary condition for faster overall growth is sustained increase in agricultural production, especially in food crops. This will call for a high proportion of development funds to be directed to rural areas for infrastructure, credit, storage, marketing, extension services, research, agricultural implements and production inputs such as fertilizers and improved seeds and pesticides.

We know from experience, however, that unless such action is accompanied by structural changes, the impact on rural poverty may be negligible or even negative. In many countries, there are sharp disparities in land ownership: a minority of landlords and large farmers, often 5 to 10 per cent of the rural households, may own 40 to 60 per cent of arable land. The rest of the rural population is crowded on small, often fragmented pieces of land; many own no land at all. In many cases, a high proportion of rural land is held on a tenant or sharecropping basis with the landlord appropriating large shares of the total crop. Such agrarian structures are both unjust and inefficient. In some countries the large holdings are underutilized and output per acre is lower than on small holdings. To reduce rural poverty and increase food production, agrarian reform and the promotion of farmers' and workers' organizations are priority issues. Such reforms are also necessary to enable large masses of people to participate more fully in society.

Assisting the 'Informal Sector'

Apart from those in the agricultural sector, people suffering from extreme poverty are found in the so-called 'informal sector' of the economy. Workers in this sector derive their often meagre incomes from a myriad of small-scale activities: repairs, manufacturing, construction, trade, catering and other services. With inadequate growth in job opportunities in the modern sector, the informal sector has grown rapidly. It is characterized by ease of entry, labour-intensive processes of production and distribution, traditional or easily acquired skills, low wages, and the use of local materials and simple tools and machinery. In many countries, official policies have tended to neglect, or even to discriminate against, this sector.

In order to utilize the potential of the informal sector in assisting development, there is need to assist it through easier access to credit, training to upgrade skills, technical advice on product improvement, and the provision of better tools and infrastructural facilities. Encouragement of sub-contracting by larger firms and of purchases by the public sector can provide new sources of demand. Joint purchases of inputs and assistance with marketing can enhance the bargaining strength of individual units and enable them to compete more effectively with larger domestic and foreign enterprises.

In some countries the magnitude of the poverty problem is such that all these measures will need to be supplemented by special programmes of employment creation through public works schemes. If well planned and executed, these schemes can, while augmenting the income of the poor, allow fuller utilization of labour, especially during slack periods, and result in the creation of useful infrastructure, enhancing social amenities and productive potential especially in the rural areas. Such programmes might cover soil conservation; reforestation; small irrigation dams, canals, and channels, land reclamation, drainage and flood control schemes and roads. Great care will need to be taken to ensure that the poor benefit from the employment, income-earning opportunities and assets created by these schemes. Agrarian reform and appropriate forms of workers' organizations may be a necessary condition for the success of large-scale public works programmes.

The choice of technology has an important bearing on employment and productivity in agriculture and non-farm small-scale enterprises. Most developing countries are characterized by technological dualism: while modern industry and agriculture use highly advanced technology, peasants and workers in the traditional sector often rely on centuries-old technologies. Perhaps the greatest technological problem facing developing countries is the essential need to upgrade technology in traditional agriculture and the informal sector.

Social Services

The satisfaction of the essential needs of the poor requires a combination of private and public goods and services. While sufficient employment opportunities and access to productive assets can help the poor to gain the income required to satisfy some of their needs, governments have to meet other needs through programmes in education, health, housing and water supplies.

In most countries, governments do not have enough resources to provide such services for the bulk of the population. The problem is often compounded, as a disproportionate share of available resources is used to provide services of a high standard to a small minority of the population, usually in urban areas. Several countries have been trying out alternative ways of organizing and delivering such services with particular emphasis on reaching the poor segments of the population. As was discussed in Chapter 2, simpler, cheaper yet effective programmes can be devised to reach deprived groups within a relatively short period of time. In health, housing, water supply and other services, what matters is the

131

determination to reach the maximum number of people with services appropriate to the country's means. This is even true in education, where a number of countries have shown that it is possible to make extremely rapid progress with relatively limited resources in this area. Their efforts involve the use of the maximum number of educated people as part-time teachers, better utilization of existing facilities, and the inclusion of some elements of basic literacy education in nutrition, health and family planning programmes.

There is greater recognition today of the importance of population planning to development. In an increasing number of countries, cultural and social attitudes at all levels of society are changing, and information and facilities for family planning are now provided. We stressed in Chapter 6 that they are more effective if they are provided as part of a development effort emphasizing the provision of work opportunities and of health and educational facilities for the mass of the people. In a number of countries, rates of population growth have begun to decline significantly with wider access to health, family planning and education services, more education and employment for women, and improvements in the living standards of the poor; we support the further limitation of population growth by such broadly based programmes.

The Importance of Planning

Success in altering the pattern and process of growth outlined earlier will depend critically on political factors, on efficiency in policy formulation and implementation, and on the mobilization of domestic resources. An increase in the volume and intensity of employment and in the use of local materials should augment resources for development. But to permit an expanded investment effort and improved social and economic services, the consumption of luxury goods and services may have to be restrained through import, consumption and excise taxes, and in many countries additional revenue can be raised through taxes on land and capital gains, and higher tax rates on individuals and companies. Control of tax evasion and improvements in tax collection can add to resources. Economic rates for use of public utilities – electricity, water, transport, etc. – are another means of enhancing revenue, and in many cases can themselves influence the distribution of the benefits of growth.

The importance of efficient planning and economic management can hardly be overemphasized. More people need to be trained for high as well as middle-level positions in planning, management, engineering and a variety of other professional, vocational and technical subjects, and training must be made more relevant to local circumstances. The application of cost benefit analysis in evaluating public sector programmes and projects can bring significant savings. It is possible to curb wasteful expenditure on bureaucracy, on prestige projects, and on military programmes which are not always undertaken in relation to external threats. Sound economic management may also call for the reform of the price system better to reflect the real costs of resources, including capital, foreign exchange and interest rates on savings.

Development Requires Participation

This will need to be accompanied by efforts to encourage people to organize themselves. Workers and peasants, women and youth organized in trade unions, cooperatives and other groups – will often be the guarantee of implementing reforms in many social and economic areas. Furthermore, such organizations can help in decentralizing development activities, in mobilizing resources, particularly through self-help and public works projects, and in providing social services, extension services, credit, training and inputs on a group basis. Decentralized government or administrative systems could help in this process. In achieving the main objectives of development, no system lacking in genuine and full participation of the people will be fully satisfactory or truly effective.

Ways in which the poor can be helped to participate in the development effort must be determined by each country in the light of its problems and possibilities. The suggestions made in this chapter may suit some, not others. But the case for a new international economic order will lose much of its moral force unless it is geared to a global effort to eradicate mass poverty. A determined effort must be made at national level, and the international community can and must extend its fullest support by helping to meet the manpower, material or financial shortages which may come in its way.

Economic Cooperation among Developing Countries

The actions which developing countries can take at home or pursue in cooperation with industrialized countries do not exhaust the paths open to them. At the Arusha Ministerial Meeting of the Group of 77 in 1979 a decision was taken to form a 'short-term action plan for global priorities in Economic Cooperation between Developing Countries' (ECDC). More and more the developing countries are giving attention to furthering their development through such cooperation. Efforts to set up regional integration schemes and regional development banks go back a long time. More recently, however, the search for increased self-reliance and economic independence has led to a stronger emphasis on mutual cooperation.

This thrust does not imply that the South wants to dissociate or 'delink' itself from the North. On the contrary, it has coincided with a marked shift towards export orientation and with expanding trade with the North. Moves by developing countries towards self-reliance on a national and collective basis should be seen as an attempt to reduce economic dependence on the North, to rely more on themselves and to promote their dignity and fuller independence. Self-reliance does not imply autarky. The developing countries seek to exploit the growing and as yet unrealized mutuality of interest among themselves arising from their increasing interdependence. Since existing disparities in development and power can give interdependence with the North an asymmetrical character, they aim not only to reinforce their own independence but also, through enlarged cooperation among themselves, to secure a better share in global economic management.

The failure of northern growth to have a significant impact on the South, the meagre results from years of intensive North–South dialogue and negotiations, the persistent recession in the industrialized countries and their limited prospects in the foreseeable future for a return to the growth rates of the 1960s – all these factors have strengthened the view that an increased contribution must come both from domestic economic processes and from policies of mutual cooperation among the developing nations themselves.

There have also been other positive factors. The emergence of new opportunities and the complementarities that exist among developing countries have increased awareness of the potential for promoting development through South–South cooperation. This potential can only be realized when each partner sees net benefits in such cooperation. But it also offers the chance for the countries of the South to make a commitment to bear their share of collective responsibility for the poor of the planet.

New opportunities have arisen with the emergence of some developing countries as capital-surplus countries or as exporters of capital goods; and with the newly industrializing countries displaying increasing technological sophistication. The scope for economic cooperation expands as Third World countries develop. The North should welcome the increased desire of developing countries to be more responsible for their economic and political destiny and to utilize unexploited opportunities for economic cooperation among themselves. Accelerated development of the South, however promoted, must ultimately bring benefits to the North as well – in terms of increased opportunities in an enlarged and more buoyant world economy. Given the dynamics of economic development, expanding trade among developing countries has not meant and will not mean fewer opportunities for trade with the North. The interest of the industrialized countries in enhancing South–South cooperation could be reflected more clearly in their policies towards ECDC.

Regional Cooperation

The trade of developing countries with one another is growing faster than their trade with the North. In 1976, 22 per cent of the South's total exports and 32 per cent of its exports of manufactured goods went to the South. The fulfilment of the Lima target, to which we refer in Chapter 11, requires further growth in trade between developing countries; if developed countries fail to roll back protectionism and continue to experience low growth, developing countries will need to expand their trade with each other even faster.

Regional and sub-regional economic integration remains an important means for the pursuit of ECDC. Some attempts at sub-regional integration have run into difficulties, and progress overall has been slow. This is hardly surprising since poor countries are even less able than rich ones to accept the short-run burdens of regionalism, however significant the long-run benefits might be. These difficulties have been aggravated in recent years by the greater need to insulate national economies from severely adverse external economic influences. Yet, in spite of difficulties, regional schemes such as the Andean Group and the Association of South East Asian Nations (ASEAN) have continued to make substantial advances. Now that the political, economic and institutional requirements are better understood, sub-regional integration and other forms of close cooperation offer a viable strategy for

Improving Technology

In speeding up industrialization and agricultural development, developing countries should not lose sight of the character and quality of their industry. In technology they can do much to upgrade their indigenous technological capabilities through collective efforts. They can share skills and establish where necessary regional and sub-regional centres to adapt and develop technology. In such initiatives the more industrially advanced developing countries like India, Brazil and Yugoslavia can take a lead.

Technical cooperation among developing countries (TCDC) is now recognized as an important aspect of ECDC and the work of UNDP in particular in assisting it deserves international support. Greater attention is now given to the use of the more relevant skills and technical knowledge available in developing countries for the solution of problems in other such countries; but much more progress in technical cooperation among developing countries can be made: for instance, since consultancy services from developing countries encourage adaptation and the use of equipment designed in those countries, wider use of such services would help South–South trade and technology development.

International Support for ECDC

An international environment and international organizations providing technical and economic assistance should give positive support to cooperation among developing countries. Ways in which international assistance can supplement the South's effort are: untying of aid to allow equipment and technology to be purchased from developing countries; the relaxation of 'rules of origin' in preferential tariff arrangements; the encouragement of multi-country industrial projects; the provision of support for regional integration schemes. Measures of support for economic cooperation among developing countries as agreed at UNCTAD V in 1979 could, if implemented effectively, be a substantial complement to the efforts of developing countries themselves.

Third World Organization

Increased support for ECDC from international organizations does not eliminate the need for the developing countries to set up their own technical support system. Some functions such as the organizing of their weak and fragmented bargaining power and the preparation of negotiating positions and strategies can best be undertaken by a Third World organization. These functions arise from the South's involvement in international negotiations. But the goals the South seeks to pursue through ECDC would also be served by such an organization. The great diversity of interests among developing countries strengthens rather than weakens the case for such a body. An organization of this kind could be particularly useful to the smaller countries facing complex and varied international issues. In relation to the above functions it would be additionally helpful if the existing UN Regional Economic Commissions could be strengthened, and supplemented, for example along the lines of the Sistema Economico Latinamericano (SELA).

A Third World organization is essentially a matter for decision within the South. It should not be seen as evidence of a posture of confrontation on the part of the developing countries but rather as a Third World counterpart of existing northern institutions for cooperation – an organization for economic cooperation among developing countries.

Recommendations

In any assault on international poverty, social and economic reforms within developing countries must complement the critical role to be played by the international environment for development, which itself needs to be made more favourable.

In countries where essential reforms have not yet taken place, redistribution of productive resources and incomes is necessary. A broader package of policy improvements would include expansion of social services to the poor, agrarian reform, increased development expenditures in rural areas, stimulation of small-scale enterprises, and better tax administration. Such measures are important both for satisfying elementary needs and for increasing productivity, particularly in rural areas.

The full potential of the informal sector to contribute to economic development requires the provision of increased resources in the form of easier access to credit, and expanded training and extension services.

The strengthening of indigenous technological capacity often requires a more scientific bias in education, the encouragement of a domestic engineering industry, increased emphasis on intermediate technology and the sharing of experience.

Improved economic management and the increased mobilization of domestic resources are essential to the promotion of development. In many countries there is scope for improvements in such fields as taxation policies, public administration and the operation of the pricing system.

Wider participation in the development process should be encouraged; measures to achieve this could include decentralized governmental administrative systems and support for relevant voluntary organizations.

Regional and sub-regional integration, or other forms of close cooperation, still offer a viable strategy for accelerated economic development and structural transformation among developing countries, especially the smaller ones. It supports industrialization and trade expansion and provides opportunities for multi-country ventures.

Developing countries should take steps to expand preferential trade schemes among themselves. This could be encouraged by such measures as the untying of aid.

Developing countries should give special attention to the establishment and extension of payments and credit arrangements among themselves to facilitate trade and to ease balance of payments problems.

The emergence of capital-surplus developing countries provides special scope for the establishment of projects on the basis of tripartite arrangements involving developing countries alone or in partnership with industrialized countries. Such arrangements should be supported by both developed and developing countries. Tripartite projects – including, when appropriate, industrialized countries – should be encouraged by nations with complementary resources such as capital and technology.

Developing countries should consider what forms of mutual assistance organization might help them to participate more effectively in negotiations and in the work of international organizations and to promote economic cooperation among themselves.

9 Commodity Trade and Development

Most of the Third World's export earnings come from primary commodities – 57 per cent in 1978, or 81 per cent if oil is included – and commodities contribute as much as 50 or 60 per cent to the gross national product of some countries. There is often a high dependence on a very limited number of commodities in the exports of many developing countries. While economic progress will depend increasingly on manufacturing, improved earnings from commodities under present circumstances could make a substantial contribution in assisting development. Many defects and imperfections have constrained the operation of commodity markets. The developing countries have had little opportunity to participate in the processing, transportation, marketing and distribution of their commodities. Many have also faced volatile prices; tariff and non-tariff barriers against exports, especially of processed products; declining prices in real terms for long periods; inadequate investment and uncertainties in mineral exploration and development; a tendency towards market concentration among importers and hence unequal bargaining power.

The Objectives of Commodity Policy

The developing countries need to find ways of strengthening their commodity sector so that it contributes much more to the development of the whole economy and becomes less vulnerable to unstable markets. There is now abundant empirical evidence to show that they can greatly increase their domestic value added, their employment and their foreign exchange earnings by expanding the processing of their raw materials. The UNCTAD Secretariat has recently estimated, on the basis of 1975 trade figures, that for ten commodities local semi-processing could provide the developing countries with gross additional export earnings of about $27 billion per year, more than one and a half times what these commodities now earn. This would, of course, involve substantial investment. Greater participation by developing countries in marketing, transport and distribution could yield further significant gains.

Until very recently international cooperation in fields such as processing, marketing and distribution did not hold much promise as an area that might be amenable to international negotiations. The focus of attention has therefore been on stabilization arrangements, made more urgent by the upsurge of price instability which occurred during the early 1970s. Stabilization of prices has also become identified as an area of mutual interest between North and South. The North is becoming increasingly concerned to ensure that periods of rising prices do not aggravate its own inflation and that volatile prices do not hinder investment and the long-term adequacy of supplies. The South has always been concerned about the harmful effects of unstable prices on innovation and productivity improvements in the sector itself, and more generally on its fiscal and economic planning. Commodities are the South's lifeblood, especially for the poorer countries, and to know what damage is done by the vagaries of the market is to understand why the South feels so passionately about them.

Commodity Development

The production and export of agricultural and mineral commodities create the base for the establishment and expansion of processing industries in developing countries. These could help to advance and diversify industrialization, a necessary development in the light of the quantitative restrictions on some of their labour-intensive light manufacturing industries. But the expansion of domestic processing is also severely hindered by the tariff and non-tariff barriers imposed by industrialized countries. Developing countries can export rice to the European Community free of duty; but they face a 13 per cent tariff, or variable import levies, on many forms of processed rice and rice products; the US puts a tariff of nearly 15 per cent on milled rice. Untreated wood goes in free to Australia, but the duty on sawn timber was recently raised from 7 to 14 per cent. Crude palm-oil faces a 4 per cent tariff in the EEC; when it is semi-refined the tariff is 12 per cent. There are also non-tariff barriers and technical regulations which hinder domestic processing.

Even where the tariffs on processed products may seem low, they are high in relation to the enhancement of the value of commodities added by processing. This 'effective protection' on processed products is a serious hindrance to developing countries' exports. When the tariff rate escalates with the degree of processing, as it normally does, the effective rate of protection is always higher than the nominal rate. The problem has been eased only to a minor extent by the various rounds of the multilateral trade negotiations and the Generalized System of Preferences. The removal of tariff escalation and other trade barriers and the consequent relocation of processing industries nearer the source of raw materials could be greatly facilitated if ways were found of implementing effective adjustment policies. Our proposals on industrial adjustment are discussed in Chapter 11.

A further hindrance to the development of processing is the tendency for freight rates to be higher on processed products. Since freight rates for some products are as high as tariffs, freight rate escalation could be as serious a problem for these products as tariff escalation. A recent study has shown that, for exports to the US market, freight rates as a percentage of f.o.b. values of processed products, as compared with their primary counterpart, were three times higher for rubber exported from Malaysia, and twice as high for leather from India and wood from Brazil. (To the extent that these differences reflect differences in the cost of handling they are not, of course, open to the same objections.) The expansion of domestic processing is also hindered by restrictive business practices. Factors such as scale economies, the large amount of capital required for some ventures, and the inadequacy of marketing arrangements are also relevant. A concentrated effort to identify and overcome unnecessary constraints on processing is urgently required.

Besides the expansion of processing, developing countries which depend heavily on a few commodities naturally want to produce them more efficiently, and to diversify into other sectors in order to be less exposed to the risks of the market. Inadequate research and development has led in many cases to only limited improvements, and to little progress in the search for new uses for natural products. Recent steep increases in the production cost of petroleum-based synthetics provide a breathing space for some natural products; the opportunity should be taken to put commodities on a better basis for securing productivity improvements.

Market promotion is another area in which great imbalance exists between natural and synthetic products or between commodities produced by developing countries and those or their substitutes produced by developed countries. Joint action by producers in developing countries to undertake generic market promotion could be an important means of obtaining a better balance.

A Bigger Share for Producers

Available data shows that returns to developing country producers tend normally to be less than 25 per cent of final consumer prices. The market power possessed by importers, processors or distributors is one cause of this low share. The small share in any case indicates the scope for increased earnings by developing countries from their commodities. While increased domestic processing would facilitate greater participation in marketing, efforts to secure improvements must not be concentrated on processing alone, and must include market promotion and the improvement of market structures. Thus the share of tea-producing countries in the price of tea at the supermarkets in the consuming countries can vary from as little as 20 per cent to as much as 40 per cent depending on marketing and taxation conditions. In the case of many commodities the immediate issue is not that of securing more competitive markets, but action to provide balanced bargaining power – the kind of action that farmers in developed countries have taken through cooperatives and farmers' associations to secure fair returns for their products.

In the Common Fund for commodities which is now in its final stages of negotiation in the UN, one 'window' – the Second – will be concerned with financing commodity development activities, and many developing countries regard these activities as the Fund's most important contribution. Existing development agencies, both bilateral and multilateral, help to finance projects in these sectors, but they have sometimes been at cross-purposes because they have focused on countries rather than on individual commodities, and have sometimes increased supplies when market prospects have been weak. Other projects have been turned down because of objections from producers in the North and for other reasons: for example, in the US, Congressional pressure was exerted to try to prevent the World Bank from lending for palm-oil development. Adequate financial resources should be made available to the Second Window in support of such long-run objectives as storage, processing, marketing, productivity improvements and diversification, in view of the importance of these activities for the development of the commodity sector. At UNCTAD V, agreement was reached to establish a framework for international cooperation to enlarge the participation of developing countries in the processing, marketing and distribution of their products. The development of a concerted programme to assist in remedying these problems deserves the fullest support. Our proposals in other chapters on improvement in market access, the regulation of transnational enterprises, the control of restrictive business practices and technology transfer arrangements also have a bearing on these problems.

Price Instability

It will take time before developing countries are in a position to process a large part of their materials. Thus it is important to them to secure prices which are stable and remunerative in order to support their development and avert persistent payments deficits.

The prices of many commodities are very unstable and this very often leads to unstable incomes for commodity producers. The problem worsens for the numerous countries with a high dependence on one or two commodities, since they are denied the greater income stability that goes with a more diversified pattern of production. Some examples of countries which in a recent year have obtained almost all their export earnings from one commodity apart from oil – are Zambia (94 per cent from copper), Mauritius (90 per cent from sugar), Cuba (84 per cent from sugar), and Gambia (85 per cent from ground-nuts and ground-nut oil). Between 1970 and 1972 over half the non-oil developing countries obtained more than 50 per cent of their export earnings from one or two crops or minerals.

The consequence for import capacity and economic growth of high dependence on one commodity is clearly shown by the example of Zambia in recent years. There was a boom in copper prices from 1972 with the price peaking in April 1974 at $3034 per ton; then it suddenly fell to $1290 before the end of that year. But the prices of imports continued to rise so that the volume of imports Zambia could buy fell by 45 per cent between 1974 and 1975 and the GDP fell by 15 per cent. The gravity of this situation for Zambia is put in perspective when it is contrasted with the 'oil shock' of 1974. This resulted in an increased oil bill for the industrialized countries equivalent to about 2.5 per cent of their GNP. In numerical terms

Zambia's shock was six times greater; in human terms for this poor country, it was severer still.

The volatility of prices is due to special supply and demand conditions in commodity markets. On the demand side the trade cycle and changes in stocking policy in relation to market expectations cause an unstable demand pattern to which supply may not be able to adjust readily; for example, crops may already have been planted, and changing mineral production capacity takes time. Also on the supply side rigidities arise from unplanned variations in harvests. A further factor which could aggravate the situation is a weak financial or foreign exchange position which forces some producing countries to sell at inappropriate times in relation to market circumstances. This was a factor for instance in the sale by cocoa-producing countries, before harvesting, of the whole of their short 1968-9 crop, at a price one-third below the average price which prevailed after the harvest. The effects of price instability are sometimes further exacerbated by fluctuations in the exchange rate of the currency in which the commodity price is quoted, especially in long-term contracts under commodity agreements.

In some situations the activities of middlemen tend to result in heightened price fluctuations at the producer level. The concentration of market power on the buying side, a situation that is not unusual in commodity trading, and inflexible marketing margins and freight rates have been factors tending to transmit instability back to the producers in aggravated form.

Many rich countries are substantial producers and exporters of commodities. Their commodities are also sometimes affected by unstable prices. However, the adverse effects on their economies or on producers are usually ameliorated by such factors as lower dependence on commodities, exportation of commodities in processed or semi-processed form, and the adoption of internal price or income stabilization schemes. Food producers are usually insulated, for instance, from price or income instabilities and unremunerative prices by extensive market intervention arrangements which are buttressed by protective trade barriers such as the Common Agricultural Policy of the EEC and the agricultural support systems of the United States, Canada and other countries.

Remunerative Prices

Besides the issue of fluctuations, an important concern of developing countries has been the level of prices. Producing countries contend that there is a tendency towards a long-term decline in commodity prices relative to the price of manufactured goods, and they point to the constant pressure, at times considerable, towards higher unit costs in manufacturing in developed countries, and the fierce competition which tends to operate on the producer side in some commodity markets. They cite, as evidence of unbalanced pricing, the inexorable upward rise in the prices of manufactured goods while commodity prices are oscillating.

There has been some debate as to whether over the long run the terms of trade have been unfavourable to commodity producers. Over a very long period, there are serious measurement problems which are well recognized. There have been periods in the past when the terms of trade have been favourable to commodity producers and in fact some economists are of the view that the world may be heading again for another such period. However, whatever the general situation concerning historical trends, there is no doubt that there have been long periods of declining relative prices for commodities. One such period has been from the mid-1950s to the early 1970s. In such periods, reduced export earnings have had severe inhibiting effects on the efforts of poor countries to secure economic advances. When such a decline is due to products becoming uncompetitive, attempts to increase prices could be counter-productive. The only justification for price or income support schemes in such circumstances would be to provide adjustment assistance to ameliorate the impact of the decline. And in such circumstances, export earnings stabilization and investment in diversification might be more appropriate than price support since any attempt to maintain artificially high prices could only lead to a faster decline of the industry concerned.

Where low prices for commodities are due not to long-run market factors but to the short- and medium-term vagaries of the market, their continuation for extended periods has harmful effects not only on producing countries but also on consuming countries since investment is discouraged and thus the security of long-term supplies is jeopardized. There is now great concern that investment in mineral exploration and production might not be adequate in relation to long-term needs. The case of copper is usually cited in this connection. We believe that while the price level is not the only factor, it has been significant in the investment problem, and the provision of remunerative prices should be given due attention in producer/consumer arrangements. It is in the interest of both parties.

Price Stabilization Arrangements

The issues of unstable commodity prices and remedial arrangements for them have been an important concern in international trade for a long time. It is generally acknowledged that more stable prices would be beneficial to exporting countries by helping to maintain foreign exchange earnings and to facilitate fiscal planning and economic management. However, views differ on the extent of such gains, not only because of variation in the assessment of the effects of instability, but also because of recognition of the difficulties of securing effective stabilization arrangements. In the postwar period, attempts have been made to establish international commodity agreements, but difficulties have been experienced in negotiating them and, even where they have been established, they do not appear to have realized their full objectives. Recently under UNCTAD a more concerted effort has been made and, in spite of the difficulties, there has been a growing awareness of a mutual interest for both producing and consuming countries in securing more stable and remunerative prices. So far, however, only four agreements are in existence – sugar, tin, coffee, cocoa; negotiations for one other – rubber – have been concluded recently.

The industrialized countries have two major interests: greater security of supply and more stable prices. Many industrialized countries are heavily dependent on commodity imports from the South; for example – apart from oil – coffee, tea, cocoa, natural rubber, jute and hard fibres, and a number of minerals such as nickel, copper, manganese and tin. This dependence is particularly marked in Europe and Japan. In future the industrialized countries both in the West and the East are likely to become more dependent on importing minerals and raw materials from developing countries; their supplies will depend on investment, which in turn will depend on the reduction of price and other uncertainties and the provision of more remunerative prices. Because of the greater interdependence between the industrialized countries themselves, any disruption of supplies to any one country affects the rest, and has far-reaching consequences for all of them.

The control of inflation has become a major concern of industrialized countries. The reduction of growth rates is closely connected with the adoption of anti-inflation measures. It is estimated that output loss from 'stagflation' in industrialized countries is now running at about $400 billion per year. At the time of writing this Report the prospects for both reduced inflation and improved growth rates are worsening. Views differ on the inflationary consequences in industrialized countries of unstabilized commodity prices. One study undertaken in 1977 for the Overseas Development Council in the US indicated a gain equivalent to $5 billion for the developing countries from a simulated stabilization programme covering eight major and five other commodities over the period 1963–73; the estimated gain to the US from avoiding GNP losses which would have occurred without the programme was equivalent to $15 billion over the same period. While there are considerable difficulties involved in such calculations, we believe that stabilized commodity prices could make a contribution to the reduction of inflation.

There are several reasons which explain the failure to establish effective International Commodity Agreements (ICAs). Consumers lose interest in stabilization when prices are declining, and producers lose interest when they are rising. Interest in price stabilization is unequally divided between consumers and producers since commodities are a much smaller proportion of the total trade of consuming countries than of the producing countries. Agreement between producing and consuming countries on the price range to be defended has always been difficult. Differences among producers, sometimes reflecting conflicts of interest between new and established producers, have stood in the way of a consolidated negotiating position. And finance to support buffer stocks and other stabilization measures have not been readily available.

The Common Fund and its 'Windows'

In the light of these difficulties, a more comprehensive and integrated approach to the commodity problem has been discussed in recent years. In consequence UNCTAD IV in Nairobi in 1976 adopted an Integrated Programme for Commodities and set up a timetable for the negotiation of the Programme, which was to comprise mainly a Common Fund and International Commodity Agreements for a substantial number of commodities of export interest to developing countries. The key role was assigned to a Common Fund – which according to the proposal was to command capital resources eventually of $6 billion – for the financing of buffer stocks and other price stabilization measures. The paid-in capital from member governments was to be $1 billion originally and $2 billion eventually. Borrowing would provide the remaining $4 billion.

Since then, there have been intensive negotiations, both on the proposed Common Fund and on individual commodity agreements. The proposal being considered is for a Common Fund with two Windows. The First would finance buffer stocks and the Second other investments which could help the production, processing and the marketing of commodities. In March 1979 agreement was reached on the principal elements of the Common Fund.

The principal difference between the March settlement and the original proposal for the Fund is that the initial paid-in capital for supporting stocking operations has been reduced to $400 million as compared with the $1 billion (to be increased by a further $1 billion at a later stage) proposed by the developing countries. However, unlike the original proposal, the Fund will also now receive cash deposits from International Commodity Agreements associated with it, equivalent to one-third of their maximum financial requirements. On the assumption that $6 billion of capital resources would eventually be required for the Common Fund, these cash deposits would provide a further $2 billion. Beyond this the two schemes show substantial similarities. Both schemes contemplate $4 billion of borrowing on the $6 billion model. However, while in the original proposal the necessary borrowing instruments would come from all members of the Fund, in the case of the March settlement they would also be subscribed directly to the Fund but only by those members of the Fund that are participating in the commodity agreements concerned.

Negotiations on the final arrangements for the establishment of the Fund are now taking place. We urge that every effort be made to conclude these negotiations and establish the Fund as early as possible especially since the main arrangements for financing the Fund have already been agreed. The main advantages of the Fund are the access it would provide to a specialized financing facility for support of International Commodity Agreements, the economies that could accrue from the joint financing of buffer stocks, and the encouragement it would provide to the coordinated financing of commodity development policies related to market stabilization. The Fund also envisages the financing of activities to assist producers of commodities where price stabilization agreements may not be possible.

Serious doubts have been expressed about the adequacy of the financing arrangements which have been agreed for the Fund. Experience would of course assist in the determination of the financing needs. Every effort should be made to ensure that this new venture in international cooperation is given the opportunity to succeed. In this connection, the financial arrangements would have to be observed carefully in connection with their viability, and their adequacy in ensuring the effective pursuit of the objectives of the Fund.

Mutual Interests in Commodity Trade

We mentioned above our belief that there is a substantial mutuality of interest in stable and remunerative prices for commodities. A number of imperfections and aberrations have been indicated in the operation of commodity markets. These have in many cases developed in the free market. We believe that stabilization schemes should be concerned with providing corrections for these imperfections. They should ensure that the market provides the appropriate signals for investment and consumption decisions, and prices which are remunerative to producers and fair to consumers. As such they should not be seen as unnecessarily interventionist but as having a positive role.

Despite these considerations, and sometimes because of doctrinaire concerns about intervention with the operation of market forces, some industrialized countries have approached the establishment of international commodity agreements negatively. This factor, together with difficulties in accommodating the diversity of interests between participants, has been at the heart of the problem of establishing and operating International Commodity Agreements. These difficulties have led to the suggestion that export earnings stabilization schemes, or compensatory financing, might be the best approach to the commodity problem. We see complementary roles for price and income stabilization agreements. Price stabilization has important functions especially in encouraging investment, stabilizing consumption, reducing inflationary pressures, and strengthening the purchasing power of commodity exporters.

International Commodity Agreements

The UNCTAD Integrated Programme involves some new approaches to the establishment of International Commodity Agreements. Given adequate resources the Common Fund could encourage the establishment of new agreements and assist the operation of existing ones. But we do not believe that it would provide answers to all the problems faced by exporting countries.

There is also need for additional forms of support in International Commodity Agreements, especially in relation to the stabilization mechanisms adopted within Agreements. Price ranges have proved difficult to negotiate, adjust and support. Serious consideration should be given to such issues as whether minimum prices alone or export taxes might not be more appropriate and easier to negotiate and administer in some circumstances; but action to establish reasonable price floors, where possible, is highly desirable.

International Commodity Agreements involve a cooperative arrangement between producers and consumers. This is a valuable institutional development which could be a means through which mutual interests in international commodity trade could be pursued. Of course, the benefits of a new regime for commodities must reach the real primary producers, namely the men and women working on the plantations and in the mines. Some commodity agreements contain provisions on labour standards. The observance of these provisions should be secured.

The role of ICAs should evolve and the emphasis should accordingly be on how to make them work more effectively. The alternative – improved compensatory financing schemes – would not be adequate to cope with such imperfections as volatile and unremunerative prices and market concentration on the buying side. The absence of International Commodity Agreements could in some cases encourage the search for solutions through confrontation and cartelization. This would not be a healthy development and would have adverse consequences for international economic cooperation. We believe that greater support should be given to International Commodity Agreements, and negotiations presently taking place on them should be concluded as rapidly as possible.

National Stocks

Where international agreements have not yet been established, or where they have proved difficult to establish, the availability of finance for national stocking could be beneficial to producing countries in discouraging selling at inappropriate times. Some countries have already undertaken such stocking on their own but poorer countries are unable to afford it. The provision of such finance in particular circumstances, especially to poorer countries, would give further encouragement to national stocking whether through internal or external financing, since greater benefits would accrue to all concerned from the greater price support that would result. The Common Fund should be given the capability to finance national stocking outside ICAs.

Stabilizing Export Earnings

Earnings stabilization schemes, also known as compensatory financing schemes, must be complementary to price stabilization schemes. Even where ICAs exist they may not succeed in removing all export income fluctuations. In the case of agricultural exports, fluctuations in earnings may be due to variations in output caused by the vagaries of nature. In situations of reduced output, if prices are prevented from rising because of a price stabilization scheme, this might lead to a reduction of export earnings below normal levels. A calamity like drought or flood may easily wipe out a whole country's crop. Then there are some commodities that are not easily storable, for example bananas. It is important to provide for situations like these, in addition to stock-piling and other price stabilization measures. This has been the main argument in favour of compensatory financing schemes.

We believe that compensatory financing could play even a larger role than this. There are commodities that are not easily amenable to price stabilization arrangements and UNCTAD may have been somewhat optimistic in the list of commodities it specified for the negotiation of ICAs. However, compensatory financing schemes normally provide finance after the shortfall has occurred; it is surely better wherever possible to prevent, by price stabilization measures, earnings fluctuations and other difficulties from arising rather than to compensate them after they have occurred.

Existing arrangements to stabilize the export earnings of the developing countries have been of value. The drawings on the IMF Compensatory Financing Facility between 1976 and mid-1979 were almost half of the total credit extended by the IMF to developing countries. In relation to commodities an important consideration for the future is whether the Facility could be adapted to accommodate adequately the needs that arise from the fluctuations in commodity export earnings. As it is at present, the Facility provides for general export earnings shortfalls but qualification for compensation requires also that there be a balance of payments problem. There are maximum limits to drawings which are related to quotas rather than the extent of shortfalls, and compensation is earned on the basis of nominal rather than real earnings. A proposal for a new complementary facility in relation to the needs of the commodity sector for compensatory financing deserves further study, as was called for by UNCTAD V.

In addition to the IMF Facility, there is an export earnings stabilization scheme – known as Stabex – under the Lomé Convention between the EEC and African, Caribbean and Pacific (ACP) countries. In the recent renegotiation of the Convention, the scheme – which stabilizes the earnings from individual commodities and which is concerned, with minor exceptions, with exports to the EEC – has been improved in terms of its product coverage. The size of the Fund for the five-year period 1980–85 is limited to 550 million European Units of Account (EUA) or about $750 million; the scheme will not cover minerals in spite of requests from ACP countries; and iron-ore, the only mineral included at present, will be phased out. However, a new facility – a mineral assistance scheme – with a fund of 280 million EUA or about $380 million will be introduced to assist ACP countries which depend significantly on six specified minerals to maintain their production and export capacity. Loans will be provided on a very soft basis – a forty-year repayment period with a ten-year grace period and interest at one per cent – for each mineral when there is a significant decline in production or export capacity.

The IMF Facility has recently been improved. Further improvements are recommended in a later chapter. Unlike the IMF Facility, Stabex provides compensation in the form of grants rather than loans to the least developed ACP countries. Further changes in the IMF Facility should move in this direction.

Mineral Supplies and Investment

The world is awakening to the fact that it is using up natural resources which are finite and cannot be renewed. The principal consumers are in the rich and industrialized countries, which themselves have the largest share of the deposits of most minerals which have been so far discovered, but which nevertheless draw much of their supplies from developing countries. The industrialized countries at present produce two and a half times as much minerals per head (including fuels) as developing countries, but they consume sixteen times as much, which is why they depend so largely on imports. About 70 per cent of the world's imports of fuel and non-fuel minerals come from developing countries, and the proportion shows a rising trend.

Economic growth with modern technology depends on these resources; and the realization that they are exhaustible is an intimation of mortality which raises disturbing questions. It is certain that the pace and pattern of economic expansion which has characterized the last century cannot be extended indefinitely.

Declining Mineral Exploration in the South

A general exhaustion of the world's resources is not expected this century, although petroleum resources will be greatly reduced. The UN study of the future of the world economy (the Leontief Report, published in 1977) suggested that lead and zinc, and possibly also nickel and copper, might become scarce by the end of the century. Some concern has been expressed about supplies of other minerals such as mercury, phosphorus, tin and tungsten; though for these and other minerals continued improvement of extraction technology, new discoveries and recycling may stave off scarcity. But the world will have to become much more concerned with locating the most economic sources of raw materials; that in turn requires an appropriate allocation of the exploration effort, which must precede actual mineral production by ten or more years. The recent pattern of such exploration has been very unbalanced. In the last few years as much as 80 to 90 per cent of the spending on exploration has been concentrated in a very few of the developed or newly industrializing countries, whereas it has almost entirely ceased over large areas of the Third World.

Traditionally mineral exploitation in developing countries has been dominated by international mining companies, which provided capital, technical knowledge and marketing facilities, and bore the exploration risk themselves. There has often been a lack of balance of costs and advantages to developing countries. This pattern of exploration and investment has now broken down. The mining companies place much of the blame for the situation on the instability of concession agreements in Third World countries, and on the erosion of what they regard as their contractual rights by nationalization or enforced renegotiation.

There are other fundamental causes. Developing country governments, having asserted sovereignty over their natural resources, are now reluctant to sign these resources away in far-reaching concession agreements negotiated at a time when they know little of the extent and richness of their own potential discoveries, and when their own negotiating position *vis-à-vis* an exploration company is certain to be weak. Mining companies, however, are unwilling to sink money in major exploration ventures in developing countries unless the full terms on which any discovery is to be exploited are fully negotiated in advance and, preferably, guaranteed by an international body.

This situation has been exacerbated by the slack demand and the low prices that have prevailed for many minerals through much of the 1970s. The consequence is a situation which redounds to the disadvantage of the industrialized mineral-importing countries and of the potential developing country exporters. The consequences of the current misallocation of today's mineral exploration effort will be delayed – for major mining projects take at least seven to eight years after the time of discovery (and often expenditures of up to $1 billion) to reach the stage of production. Such consequences, which will take the form of selective mineral shortages, price instability, severe inflationary influences and the failure of many developing countries to develop potential deposits, are nonetheless certain.

The Need for Secure Agreements

Here, therefore, is an area where new initiatives, involving imaginative new arrangements, can clearly be in the interests of North and South alike. Measures are needed to speed up exploration and exploitation of deposits in developing countries, while assuring a full share of the benefits of mining, processing and exportation to the host country governments.

The first step needs to be the provision of finance for increased exploration in the Third World. Exploration accounts, on average, for only about five per cent of the total costs of investment in non-fuel minerals (as compared to a rough average of 25 per cent for oil), but the risks involved are high. Developing countries cannot afford and in general would not be willing to finance such exploration expenditure themselves. Existing finance agencies, such as the World Bank Group and the Regional Development Banks, have been traditionally reluctant to undertake such risks, although they have recently become more willing to lend for exploration and development of fuel minerals.

And yet, until mineral development and exploitation agreements can be negotiated on the basis of assured and equally shared knowledge about the extent and potential value of deposits, concession agreements are bound to be unstable. It is a necessary feature of the traditional-style agreement that whenever a really rich deposit is discovered, a country's non-renewable resources will appear in retrospect to have been signed away too cheaply and the popular demand for renegotiation will be irresistible. The need is therefore for a multilateral financing facility to provide resources which can be converted into a loan and part of the initial financing of the project if a commercial deposit is discovered, developed and exploited. The existence of this multilateral facility would reflect international responsibility for and a common interest in mineral exploration.

Limitations of the UN Revolving Fund

The UN Revolving Fund for Natural Resource Exploration, which has been in operation since 1975, goes some way towards meeting this requirement. But under the Revolving Fund's arrangements, successful exploration is expected to cover the costs of unsuccessful ventures as well. Such an expectation is unrealistic for poor countries. The attempt at collective risk-sharing amongst Third World countries requires replenishment charges to be high (two per cent of the gross value of production over 15 years), and this has discouraged use of the Fund, which is still small, and based initially on voluntary contributions from some industrialized countries. The Fund in principle deserves wider support. But if it is to stimulate more exploration in the poorer countries its repayment terms will have to be relaxed, and it could reasonably spread the risks of financing over a far wider circle of countries interested in future mineral supplies. Much more finance is needed in exploration for energy, where the UN Revolving Fund is not active.

More Financial Channels for Exploration and Development

Once exploration has been completed and the extent of a deposit is known, it will become much simpler for host country governments to reach equitable and stable contracts with foreign companies and to attract long-term loans. The World Bank and the regional banks are now initiating or increasing their financing of energy and mineral development, and involvement of these bodies in financing agreements is often reassuring to both host governments and investors. But there are still some countries which do not attract private investment or which do not wish to become dependent upon such investment for developing their energy and minerals. In the whole field of energy and minerals financing there remain large gaps; these gaps are most pronounced with regard to the provision of finance for the equity contribution of host country governments towards joint ventures in mining, and towards the costs of facilities for further processing of mineral products within developing countries.

Lending for mineral exploration and development should be put on a systematic and expanded basis. While we recognize the limited activities of the UN Revolving Fund, the World Bank and other international agencies in this field, the sensitive issues already referred to make it crucial that the needs for increased mineral financing be met by an institution in which the developing countries have an equal share in decision-making and management. Our discussion in a later chapter of the role of transnational corporations also bears importantly on these issues.

Technical Assistance

In preparing their own mining laws and codes, in building up their new institutions, and when they are negotiating with international mining companies and lending bodies, developing country governments are also likely to need technical advice. When arrangements for further processing are being negotiated, advice may be needed on how to overcome the many artificial barriers to establishing such processing practices, which discriminate against them. It is crucial that no doubt should exist concerning the technical competence of such advice or the fact that it is rendered in the exclusive interest of the host government concerned. Such technical assistance might be provided by the financing facility proposed above.

Recommendations

The commodity sector of developing countries should contribute more to economic development through the greater participation of these countries in the processing, marketing and distribution of their commodities. Action for the stabilization of commodity prices at remunerative levels should be undertaken as a matter of urgency.

Measures to facilitate the participation of developing countries in processing and marketing should include the removal of tariff and other trade barriers against developing countries' processed products, the establishment of fair and equitable international transport rates, the abolition of restrictive business practices, and improved financial arrangements for facilitating processing and marketing.

Adequate resources should be provided to enable the Common Fund to encourage and finance effective International Commodity Agreements which would stabilize prices at remunerative levels; to finance national stocking outside ICAs; and to facilitate the carrying out of Second Window activities such as storage, processing, marketing, productivity improvement and diversification.

Greater efforts should be made to bring to a rapid and successful conclusion negotiations on individual commodity agreements wherever these are feasible.

Compensatory financing facilities should be expanded and improved to provide more adequately for shortfalls in real commodity export earnings.

The mutual interest of producing and consuming countries in the development of mineral resources requires the creation of new financial arrangements, leading to more equitable and stable mineral development agreements, greater assurance of world mineral supplies and increased developing-country participation in their resource development. A new financing facility, whose primary function will be to provide concessional finance for mineral exploration, should be established on the basis of a global responsibility for investment in mineral development.

10 Energy

In the course of the 1970s the cost and availability of energy, and particularly of oil, has become a worldwide concern. All countries have become dependent on petroleum products to maintain their transportation systems, industrial and agricultural production, national defence and other vital functions. Most of them depend on imports of oil and natural gas from other countries. The mere threat of a disruption in international supply lines sends shock waves through national societies and the world economy. At the same time, the depletion of the world's oil resources is proceeding so rapidly that the transition to other sources will be necessary in a foreseeable future.

Energy shortages take many forms. Sudden rises in petroleum prices affect all countries; but while pleasure motoring continues on a large scale, fishermen in poor island communities like the Maldives may not get oil at all to operate their boats, or farmers in India and Pakistan to work their irrigation pumps. The energy crisis in much of Africa and Asia means the shortage of firewood: poor families have to search further and further to find wood to cook their rice or wheat, while more and more of the land is denuded of trees. Many developing countries are experiencing balance of payments difficulties or economic stringency as higher expenditures on fuel force cuts elsewhere. The long-term solutions lie in the development of alternative and renewable energy sources; but the short-term difficulties are acute. Both require nothing less than a global strategy for energy.

Energy problems are closely linked to many of the issues we have discussed in previous chapters and will raise later. Oil is the leading commodity in world trade, making up as much as one-eighth of it. It has been subject in the past to control by a few multinational corporations. The scale of its use and of the monetary flows by which it is paid for are so great as to affect the prosperity of every country and the balance of the world's financial and monetary system, which is now seriously threatened by world economic conditions in general. The fair distribution of oil and the development of substitutes are likely to call for exceptional measures of international collaboration in the future.

Implications of the Energy Transition

The supply of energy, particularly of oil, has become a prominent North–South issue. Yet there are significant areas of agreement about oil. It is now widely accepted that during the 1960s when the industrial societies and a few developing countries were rapidly expanding their use of cheap oil, the price failed to reflect the depletion of resources. Oil was 25 per cent cheaper in 1970 in relation to the prices of other goods than in 1955. A higher price was essential to constrain consumption and to help ensure the consideration of long-term requirements and the development of alternative fuels to take the place of oil. Even at higher oil prices, there is much waste, especially in industrial societies, and frivolous use of a resource which is needed for world survival.

Ever since the first commercial strike of oil in Pennsylvania in 1857, its economics have been controversial. When oil supplies were controlled by cartels or groups of companies, prices reflected their market position at a particular time. There have since been significant changes in the control of supplies. In the 1960s a number of 'independent' companies began to challenge the monopoly power of the major oil companies; and in the 1970s producing countries increasingly took control, making long-term contracts with the 'oil majors'. In the 'spot market' where oil is sold outside long-term contracts, prices react sharply to sudden short-term surpluses or gluts. The spot market used to handle relatively marginal quantities, but in 1979 it acquired considerable importance. Experts are unsure whether this will continue to be the case, or whether it is a temporary phenomenon resulting from the new supply patterns.

Any assessment of world oil prices must take into account both the need for conservation and long-term supplies, and the critical need for oil, at least for the next two decades, both in industrialized nations and in the Third World. In the immediate future oil will remain the lifeblood of industrial society. While the long-term aim of energy policy must be to reduce the dependence on this diminishing resource, the fact must be faced that during the transition no country can escape serious disruption if its supplies of oil are drastically reduced. To navigate through these dangerous political narrows, achieving a fair distribution of oil while ensuring long-term alternatives, provides a major challenge to world statesmanship.

Disparities in Use

The use of energy in the world is grossly unbalanced. The consumption of energy per head in industrialized countries compared to middle-income and low-income countries is in the proportion of 100:10:1. One American uses as much commercial energy as two Germans or Australians, three Swiss or Japanese, six Yugoslavs, nine Mexicans or Cubans, 16 Chinese, 19 Malaysians, 53 Indians or Indonesians, 109 Sri Lankans, 438 Malians, or 1072 Nepalese. All the fuel used by the Third World for all purposes is only slightly more than the amount of gasoline the North burns to move its automobiles.

The oil-importing developing countries obtain about two-thirds of their commercial energy from oil, an even higher proportion than the OECD countries (half) or Eastern Europe (a third). The North has greater scope for conserving energy by relatively painless adjustments or by introducing less energy-intensive technologies. Most countries of the South have only a modest consumption of oil but, as they provide for their industries and rural communities and move away from traditional fuels, they will inevitably have to increase their use of oil and other commercial forms of energy very considerably. In recent years, however, a number of developing countries have had difficulty in obtaining even the relatively small quantities of oil they need currently.

While the North's consumption of commercial energy doubled between 1960 and 1976, that of the developing countries tripled: but it was still only one-fifteenth of the consumption in the West, or one-twelfth of that in Eastern Europe. The developing countries import only about 10 per cent of all traded oil. There is rightly a great interest now in alternative sources, such as solar energy, which may in the end be particularly suited to developing countries; but they should not be obliged to adopt expensive new technologies prematurely. They have a legitimate need for an expanding share of oil in the years to come.

Scope for Conservation

The industrial countries will have to alter lifestyles which they have based on abundant energy. This need not have severe economic consequences. The relationship between growth in GNP and the consumption of energy has been found not to be immutably fixed: indeed, figures for the OECD countries show a modest decline in energy use per unit of GNP in the last few years. Consumption grew rapidly in recent decades because people bought more cars, appliances, heaters or air conditioners, and because cheap oil stimulated energy-intensive technology. Over time, there is major scope for conservation and adjustment to higher energy costs. Recent studies of many industrial countries have shown that with only moderate changes in attitudes and practices the *per capita* consumption of energy can be substantially reduced without great sacrifice of economic growth.

At the Tokyo Summit of 1979 leaders of western industrialized countries made an undertaking to limit their oil imports up to 1985 to the levels prevailing in 1977–8. We believe it is time for the major oil consumers – today 85 per cent of the world's oil consumption takes place in the industrialized world – to set themselves ambitious targets for energy conservation. Developing countries also must make such efforts whenever possible. This can be done in various ways including overall consumption targets and standards for consumption in various uses such as vehicle mileage and building insulation. Ultimately such standards should themselves become the subject of international agreement and surveillance.

Oil Production and the Problems of the 1980s

About one-quarter of the world's commercial energy today is oil produced by OPEC members. As far as concerns any major increase in production in the near future from known and guaranteed oil reserves, the Middle East is the main source. In the short run, any expansion in world energy consumption has to be met chiefly by oil.

A number of factors bear on the planning of Middle East production. In the first place, the producers view the management of oil as something which affects all countries, and for which all countries have a responsibility. They are keenly aware of the depletability of oil, and that until very recently consumers acted as if supplies were unlimited. They express the view that future generations will hold them to blame for failure to manage this precious resource. There are also more technical reasons why higher output may be resisted. It is likely that the faster the off-take from a given oil-well, the smaller the volume of oil the well will ultimately yield. As the oil is pumped out, gas is released which may have to be flared off and wasted. And of course there are economic considerations. Burning oil in combustion engines is one of its lowest-value uses; conversion to petrochemicals is more important and more profitable and indeed is a growing tendency among Middle East producers.

For capital-surplus oil exporters, one of the biggest questions is what they receive in return for their oil; as long as oil is priced and paid for mainly in US dollars, the health of the dollar is a critical factor. And if the exporters exchange their dollars for long-term financial assets, the permanence of the value of those assets is equally critical. If a producing country does not need oil revenues for immediate payments for imports, there is a real question about the good sense of exchanging a depletable and increasingly valuable resource, which can easily be kept in the ground, for anything whose long-term value may be less certain.

New Sources of Oil

For all these reasons, significant increases in Middle East oil production are problematic. And further, any such increases will require major investments in billions of dollars. If new capacity is to become available in any near future, decisions on those investments must be taken relatively soon. But in the current world situation the decisions are very difficult to make. All these considerations underline the urgency of an accommodation between producers and consumers. They also underline the importance of conservation, which weighs heavily in the minds of producers.

There are other sources of oil supply in the industrialized countries and in the Third World. Recent major finds in Mexico show that there are still new reserves to be discovered, particularly in the Third World where, as with minerals, there is now far less exploration than in the industrialized countries which have already been intensively explored. The drilling density in prospective oil areas in industrialized countries is about forty times that in those of the oil-importing developing countries. Here the need for better North–South relations is fundamental. The mutual distrust between the major oil companies and many developing countries is a serious obstacle to exploration. The methods of finance and the safeguards and framework for fair negotiation and security which we propose in later chapters are specially urgent in the case of oil. The exploration and development of energy resources commonly involve the expertise and finance commanded by the big international companies, though there are increasing numbers of national oil companies and smaller private operators.

Need for Diverse Agencies

There is a need for a variety of agencies. The multinational companies are increasingly content to cooperate with multilateral agencies, but we do not believe that exploration should be confined to the major oil companies. In their new role in the overall supply structure the oil majors are making very considerable profits, which have attracted comment. Because of worldwide interest in these companies, special care must be taken to consider the reciprocal obligations of multinationals and host and home countries referred to in Chapter 12. At the very least these companies should increase their investment in oil development in the Third World. But the developing countries must obviously control the exploration of their own resources.

Production can be increased in some industrialized countries as well. Once again, it creates problems for surplus producers if industrial countries urge them to step up their production while they themselves go slowly and try to maintain their own resources.

An 'Emergency Programme'

In our final chapter we put forward an Emergency Programme for international negotiation, a crucial part of which covers the energy problem. It is no exaggeration to describe this as an emergency. Virtually all expert projections indicate a very tight oil situation in the 1980s, with increasing demand and great uncertainty about the state of supply. There is no need to dwell on the dangers that lie ahead: the vulnerability of supplies to political upheaval in any producing country; the threat of major hardships for developing countries; the dangers to the world economy – not to speak of the even greater dangers of possible recourse to military intervention by major powers who see their vital interests at stake in any serious disruption of supplies. The level of production is already a highly political matter, both in the national and international context, not least because the market incentives and supply patterns for current oil production do not create an orderly framework for equilibrating supply and demand. We therefore have no hesitation in putting forward a global energy strategy as a matter of the utmost urgency.

Alternative Energy Sources

The transition away from oil is made difficult by the fact that oil is an unusually versatile energy source which can be applied to many different uses and serve all the demands for highly concentrated energy which accompany urbanization and industrialization. And even if much new oil is discovered, the transition to other sources of energy will have to take place in an uncomfortably near future. Ultimately the human community must rely on inexhaustible sources of energy; solar in the broadest sense, which includes biomass, wind and tides; new forms of nuclear energy, supplementing hydro-electric and geothermal sources. But for the rest of this century oil, natural gas and other exhaustible sources of energy – particularly coal – have to meet most of the additional needs.

Most alternative energy sources are surrounded by problems – of technology, of risk to the environment and of costs. There are of course 'new' sources of oil such as tar sands and oil shales, from which synthetic oils can be produced. They present some of the same problems as coal, particularly in their large-volume mining methods, their needs for water, and requirements for cost-reducing research. Several industrial countries have enough coal to meet all their energy needs for decades or in some cases for centuries; but the human and environmental hazards of coal production and use were among the causes of the shift to other fuels. Accelerated research can and undoubtedly will diminish some of these hazards; it can also reduce the costs of converting coal to gas or liquid fuel. A greatly expanded role for coal seems inevitable in the next decades.

Nuclear Problems

Nuclear energy is another major alternative. For the immediate future it gives rise to legitimate concern. There is a risk both of accidents – as was underlined in the Three Mile Island incident in 1979 – and of long-term low level exposure, which make nuclear energy particularly alarming to the public. This option must be evaluated rationally and soberly. In view of the widespread apprehensions, safety precautions and regulations have to be more rigorous than for other energy sources. To rely on nuclear energy may ultimately require a resort to breeder reactors; but here the control of the fuel cycle is crucial. As we move further into the twenty-first century, nuclear fusion may also become available, promising virtually inexhaustible energy from a fairly benign process. But for the present stage of nuclear energy, the problems of radiation risk in power production and in the storage and transport of nuclear wastes are unsolved; the large demands on water and land made by nuclear installations are a matter of concern; in many countries public opposition to new nuclear stations is highly vocal. The nuclear alternative is thus problematic, and in most countries cannot be expected to make more than a partial contribution to overall energy use in this century.

Hydro and Solar Energy

Hydro-electric development is a well-known and feasible technology which must attract major new investment in the near future particularly in developing countries; high priority should be given to this at national and international levels. Solar energy, however, seems so far economical only in limited fields such as space heating, or generating electricity in remote locations. Great progress is reported in photovoltaic cells and thermal conversion, but a breakthrough in the storage of electricity is urgently needed. Given their solar exposure, it is possible that developing countries may at some point become relatively well off in energy terms, provided that really low cost technology is available. But research on a major scale is necessary to develop this technology. For some countries, especially poor landlocked countries with no indigenous fossil fuels, for whom even oil is made additionally expensive by heavy transport costs, solar technology is already competitive with other energy sources, and can become more so with further developments. We believe there is a strong case, in view of the mutual interest in assured world energy supplies, for the fruits of research on solar energy in the North to be made available on specially favourable terms to the poorer countries of the South. The oil-exporting countries themselves are anxious to use some of their funds for developing alternative sources of energy for the post-oil era.

Planning for the Future

During the rest of this century, most additional energy will almost certainly have to come from technologies which are already known. Some difficulties, like the higher costs and major investments in technologies, will be foreseeable; others will be less predictable, like nuclear accidents, oil spills or political upheavals in producer countries. But while the energy transition is inevitable, catastrophe is not; and it should be possible to mitigate the difficulties of the transition through proper planning and cooperation. The time lags will be long, and both the future supply of energy and the demand for it will depend on decisions taken by governments, investors and consumers today.

An International Energy Strategy

The greatest dangers facing the world in the short and medium term are supply disruptions, consequential price surges, and incompatible national policies.

The need to seek an international accommodation has been recognized since the oil crisis of 1973. Before the Conference on International Economic Cooperation (CIEC) in 1975–7, industrial countries wanted to concentrate first on oil and energy while the OPEC nations insisted on giving equal emphasis to the totality of the North–South dialogue, both because they saw themselves as part of the South, and because they had a special interest as oil producers in discussing other aspects of the world economy. They were naturally concerned about world inflation, which was diminishing the value of the currencies, particularly the dollar, for which they were exchanging their diminishing oil deposits; they were concerned about maintaining the value of their growing financial investments in the industrialized countries; they were anxious to have greater access to technology, to build industries which would survive after their oil ran out; they had a lively interest in the regulation of the multinational corporations, with which so much of their history had been interlocked; and the increasing importance of oil in world trade and payments gave them a growing concern in the functioning of the international monetary and financial systems. All this led them to insist that the problem of energy supplies was only part of the broader problem of restructuring the world economy; and at the same time, along with other nations of the South, they pressed for fairer terms for other commodities, and for a more equitable distribution of the world's resources. These problems are still on the agenda today.

The differences in perception should not conceal the important areas of common interest and potential agreement between producers and consumers, and the need for continuing dialogue. All parties have an interest in the creation of an international framework and a political climate which can provide a confident and trusting collaboration of all countries to ensure long-term exploration and development of energy, and an orderly transition from a world economy and industry based on oil, to one that can be sustained through renewable sources of energy. They have a shared interest in conservation and in avoiding abrupt price changes. And all must be aware of the special need to protect the poorer oil-importing countries. OPEC members find it difficult to meet the needs of these countries due to the lack of downstream facilities in their oil sector. It is suggested in some OPEC quarters, however, that special refinery facilities be established for groups of developing countries on a joint-venture basis between these countries and oil producers, which will guarantee the flow of crude from the producers to meet their needs and give them greater security.

A Global Research Centre

All countries must obviously formulate energy policies appropriate to their needs and resources. They must be able to make their plans on the basis of the most accurate available information, and coordinate their strategies as far as possible with other nations. Twenty of the West's oil-importing countries already belong to the International Energy Agency in Paris, in which recently there have been efforts to set targets for oil imports and make arrangements for monitoring them. We would recommend the setting-up of a global energy research centre under UN auspices which could in the first place provide a focus for information, research and projections. Such a centre could support in particular research in the field of renewable sources of energy. The UN conference in 1981 on New and Renewable Sources of Energy will offer an important opportunity to make progress in this field.

Protecting Poorer Oil Importers

Developing countries have found it difficult in times of serious shortages to obtain fuel required for their needs. The smaller ones in particular have tended to be left out of the system by the major oil corporations owing to their marginal importance as customers. In addition the oil-importing developing countries have been seriously affected by the sharp increases in the cost of their oil imports, which for many of them have in recent years absorbed a rapidly rising share of their foreign exchange earnings. There is an immediate need for arrangements to meet the financial requirements which such increases generate, over and above the general measures to strengthen their balance of payments through programme loans and other means. The financing of exploration for fossil fuels and the development of new energy supplies in the Third World, including natural gas, hydro-electric and geothermal energy, is also in the mutual interest and should receive international support.

Occasional disruptions in supplies will occur in the future as they have in the past, and contingency planning is essential. The oil-importing developing nations, which are in most need of protection, have so far been left out of international agreements. The Energy Commission of CIEC recommended that, in periods of reduced oil supplies, the most vulnerable developing countries should be given priority to allow them to meet essential requirements, and similar proposals have been raised elsewhere. There should be contingency plans to protect these countries in the event of acute scarcity.

Rejecting the Use of Force

The political dangers arising from the energy situation are underlined by fears expressed in the media and elsewhere that force might in some circumstances be used by powerful countries to ensure the security of future oil supplies. Such interventions would put world peace in jeopardy; even talk of them increases political tensions and makes solutions more difficult – we need hardly stress how essential it is that such notions be utterly rejected, and that the world's energy problems be solved by peaceful means.

Producer–Consumer Understanding

We believe it is both necessary and urgent to seek an understanding between producers and consumers on all internationally traded energy supplies. Such an understanding would comprehend the assurance of regular supplies of oil, more vigorous conservation, more predictable changes in oil prices, and the development of alternative energy sources. Several of these objectives require longer-term measures. But a start must be made with all of them. To this end we propose a major global agreement in our last chapter, which would include an international energy strategy, action on finance to accommodate developing countries' general borrowing needs and to ensure the recyling of surplus OPEC funds, and other measures of international economic reform, all of which taken together might begin to resolve North–South problems and lead the way to a more rational and equitable world order.

An arrangement between producers and consumers should include all countries. The Soviet Union produces more oil than any other country and is the second largest exporter after Saudi Arabia. It also earns half its hard currency from oil. It has the world's largest reserves of natural gas, of which it is the second largest producer (after the US) and the third largest exporter. Other countries of Eastern Europe have so far obtained 90 per cent of their oil imports from the Soviet Union, but they have in recent years begun to turn to Third World sources. And China is thought to have at least double the oil reserves of the US, with oil already accounting for 15 per cent of US imports from China. China is also the third largest coal producer in the world.

Energy must become the shared responsibility of the whole world community, and to reach an understanding will clearly require a serious attack on these and the other issues to which we address ourselves. All our futures could depend on the success which attends such global efforts.

Recommendations

An orderly transition is required from high dependence on increasingly scarce non-renewable energy sources.

Immediate steps towards an international strategy on energy should be taken as part of the Emergency Programme recommended in the final chapter of the Report.

Prices which reflect long-term scarcities will play an important role in this transition; orderly and predictable price changes are important to facilitate a smooth development of the world economy.

Special arrangements including financial assistance should be made to ensure supplies to the poorer developing countries.

International and regional financial agencies must increase substantially their financing of exploration and development of energy sources including the development of renewable energy resources.

A global energy research centre should be created under UN auspices to coordinate information and projections and to support research on new energy resources.

11 Industrialization and World Trade

The successive industrial revolutions of the past two hundred years in Europe and North America are now being followed by industrialization in Latin America, Asia and Africa, a natural and indeed inevitable development which is already beginning to change the pattern of comparative advantage in the world economy. Most countries in the Third World regard industrialization as a central objective of their economic policy. They see it, together with agricultural progress, as an integral part of development and structural change. The drive towards it reflects deeply felt needs for modernization and economic independence.

The developing countries have only a small share in world manufacturing. This share remained stable at around 7 per cent in the 1960s. Since then it has risen to 9 per cent in 1977. In the period 1970–76 their manufacturing output has indeed grown at 7.5 per cent per year – more than twice as fast as that in the industrialized countries of the OECD – though not as fast as in Eastern Europe where the growth rate was 8.7 per cent.

But industrialization in the Third World has been very uneven. Some of the middle-income countries, particularly in Latin America and South East Asia, have made spectacular advances in industry: several of them have around a quarter of their workers in manufactures, which is as much as some of the old industrialized countries have now. Other countries show little change; in many of the poorest countries less than five per cent of the work force is engaged in manufacturing.

The General Conference of UNIDO in 1975 adopted the Lima declaration which included a target for the share of developing countries in world manufacturing to reach at least 25 per cent by the year 2000. This means they would have to maintain a rate of industrial growth about 5 percentage points higher than the rest of the world. Some doubt whether this is possible, but it is not beyond reach if the industrialization of developing countries is helped rather than hindered by other countries.

The Balance between Agriculture and Industry

Some Third World countries have given emphasis to the improvement of their agricultural sector and have built up their industry on this basis. Others have used industrialization as the central instrument in developing their societies, either within the context of a conventional growth-oriented approach or within one that aims more directly at reducing absolute poverty and raising the productivity of the poor. The extent to which they succeed in their efforts is strongly related to the international environment and the reactions of other countries (we shall deal extensively with this later in this chapter). But the main responsibility for integrating a policy of industrialization in overall development activities – to increase employment and incomes, to satisfy elementary needs of the population and to promote economic independence – lies with the developing countries themselves.

Industrialization cannot be understood in purely economic terms, as it involves a profound transformation of society. The transition from the country to the city and the adoption of new lifestyles and attitudes have far-reaching consequences. But there need not be a conflict between the priorities of industry and agriculture in a nation's development. They remain closely interdependent, with the income and production from one providing the demand for the other. To manage this critical balance between industry and agriculture and provide healthy conditions in both sectors is one of the most crucial tasks for the governments of the Third World.

Promoting Industrial Exports

In the early phases of industrialization most countries try to replace imported manufactures with their own domestic products. They protect their own producers against foreign competition by tariffs, by import licences and by exchange rate practices which make imports more expensive. This import substitution process can in the long run be viable for countries with large internal markets and natural resources, which allows them to produce capital goods domestically with imported materials. Thus Brazil and India have built up sizeable and efficient machinery capacities. But sooner or later domestic markets – whether due to the size of the country, lack of efforts in the field of income distribution or other factors – and the shortage of foreign exchange for foreign inputs set limits to this approach: once they have established an industrial base they feel the need to switch or modify their policy. They cannot accomplish these changes suddenly; but since the 1960s many developing countries have moved towards strategies to promote exports and to offset disadvantages due to the insulation of their domestic markets.

A number of countries which have introduced export-oriented policies have been able to exploit their comparative advantage in world markets. They include some Latin American countries with a fairly long history of national independence, and some island and city state economies which were from the outset obliged to rely on export demand. Once industrialization has taken root, it is not only in labour-intensive industries like clothing or leather products, but also in moderately capital-intensive industries like electronics, steel and shipbuilding, that they can become highly competitive in world markets.

Manufactures Loom Larger

Although the exports of manufactures from many of the poorer countries have shown little improvement, all in all manufactures are looming much larger in the total exports of developing countries. In 1955 they made up only 10 per cent of non-fuel . exports; ten years later they were 20 per cent; and in 1975 they passed 40 per cent. Most of these exports come from only a few countries; eight of them accounted for 78 per cent of the additional exports of manufactures from the Third World to the OECD countries between 1970 and 1976; but the numbers of successful exporters are growing.

Much of this production and trade takes place within the worldwide operations of multinational corporations. Exports of industrial goods from developing countries, particularly in those industries with the best market prospects, are controlled to a substantial degree by such corporations either through subsidiaries or through sub-contracting to local enterprises. The latter procedure is growing in importance. However, locally owned enterprises account for larger overall shares and by far the greater proportion of exports of textiles, clothing and footwear.

Markets for Third World Products

The continued industrialization of the developing countries requires access to international markets. Increasingly the South itself, with its vast population, is offering a large market. In 1976,

22 per cent of the South's total exports and 32 per cent of its manufactured exports went to other countries in the South. In the first half of the 1970s these grew faster than exports to the North, which was a reversal of the experience of the 1960s. South–South trade will be particularly important if the markets in the industrialized countries grow too slowly in the coming decades to satisfy the export and import needs of the South. If, for instance, the gross domestic product in developing countries is to grow at 6–7 per cent per annum, while industrialized countries grow at 3–4 per cent, the developing countries will have to meet more of their trading needs among themselves. The better these countries manage to integrate their . industrial activities in a broad developmental effort to raise incomes and standards of living, the stronger the basis for a sustained expansion of this trade. Measures required for the encouragement of South–South trade are discussed in Chapter 8. For a long time, however, the industrial countries will remain the prime markets for manufactures from the South.

The West is not the only industrialized market. The Soviet Union and other CMEA countries take about 6 per cent of exports from developing countries, but CMEA countries have a much lower proportion of manufactures in their imports from non-OPEC developing countries about 15 per cent in 1976 than the United States (about 40 per cent), Japan (24 per cent) or the EEC (about 29 per cent). However, the imports of manufactures by CMEA countries have increased from virtually *nil* in the 1950s. There is room for much further expansion, especially if a large number of Third World countries with whom they have no trade agreements could find an entry to their markets and if CMEA countries were more willing to pay in convertible currencies.

Need for Continuous Adjustment

Nevertheless it is the OECD countries with their high purchasing power which will have to be the principal outlet for future expansion of export-oriented industrial production in the South. Such a process need not conflict with the long-term interests of the North if pursued in a way which avoids sudden disruptions and shifts in trade flows. The international division of labour is a dynamic process which calls for continuous adaptation and adjustment on the part of all countries. As developing countries accelerate the pace of their industrialization, the old industrial countries will have to deploy their capital and labour increasingly into the production of skill-intensive and technically advanced goods.

In the past fears that imports from the South would cause significant unemployment in the North have proved to be wrong. A report of the EEC covering numerous studies of the effects in the United States, the Federal Republic of Germany, Britain, France and other countries leads to the opposite conclusion: the direct impact on jobs has been small compared to that of domestic technical progress, although pressure from increased imports tends to encourage productivity improvements. This conclusion has been confirmed by a number of other investigations.

It is with clothing and textiles that developing countries have penetrated the markets of the North most effectively. In the mid-1970s their share of imports in apparent consumption in the EEC, United States, Canada and Japan reached 7.2 per cent – in a country like Sweden even substantially higher. Yet even in this area the impact on unemployment in industrialized countries is much less than that of domestic technological change. Imports of manufactures in general from developing countries have accounted for only 1.7 per cent of consumption. Here too the employment impact was small. A recent study on the adjustment problem in the UK economy showed that the increase of imports of manufactures from twenty-three newly industrializing countries from 1970 to 1977 is unlikely to have displaced more than 2 per cent of the 1970 labour force of the industries concerned. The same calculation for increase of UK exports of manufactures to the newly industrializing countries suggests a roughly similar increase in employment. No net displacement was therefore indicated. Studies for other northern countries suggest a similar balance of jobs lost and gained.

However, it is sometimes necessary to look beyond net effects. The loss of jobs in sectors affected by competition from newly industrializing countries has tended to emphasize existing difficulties in the North for economically weaker regions and groups of workers. The movement of labour out of declining industries is not always easy. Seamstresses in the clothing industry will not be able to accept jobs as lathe operators or assembly workers which engineering or electronic firms may offer in entirely different regions – not even in a buoyant economy with full employment; and in times of rising unemployment this adjustment creates difficult political and social problems which call for sensitive and imaginative handling by governments.

The Return of Protectionism

Among the greatest challenges to international economic policy for the rest of this century is the preparation for a new deployment of industrial capacity in the world economy – a shift of historic dimensions. As the economic development of the Third World progresses, newcomers will take the competitive lead in the production of many traditional goods, forcing change upon their competitors both in the South and the North. But these competitors in turn will be moving forward into other sectors and lines of activity. Contraction of employment in many traditional sectors will be required in the North in order to accommodate the new industrial capacity of the South, but this structural change of the world economy is inevitable and will bring many mutual gains in the long run. It is therefore alarming that the North has shown signs recently of turning away from adjustment towards intensified protection.

In the postwar period the industrial countries gradually reduced their barriers to trade in manufactures, mostly through the successive rounds of multilateral trade negotiations. This contributed to the steady and rapid growth of world trade for more than two decades, from which the North and much of the South benefited extensively. But by the early 1960s exports of textiles and clothing from the Third World were already subjected to 'voluntary export restraints' in order to forestall drastic unilateral restrictions. Total exports of manufactures from developing countries grew at 15 per cent annually between 1970 and 1976, and as southern competition began to enter its markets the North put up more non-tariff barriers, mostly in the form of quotas. These imports of manufactures met more and higher barriers than those from other industrialized countries.

The recession of 1974, the steep rise in unemployment in the North and continuing balance of payments problems now threaten to produce a major retreat from liberal trading principles. The Multi-Fibre Arrangement for clothing and textiles, which stipulates that import quotas should grow by at least 6 per cent per year, has been rendered less effective by unilateral restrictions. Trade in the shipbuilding, footwear, electronics and steel sectors has been seriously restricted. Governments have multiplied their subsidies to and purchases from internationally uncompetitive firms, and their complaints about foreign dumping have increased.

The pressure on governments to restrict trade may well get stronger in the years ahead. Even the threat of restriction creates a climate unfavourable to investments in the Third World and the actual imposition of such restrictions, especially through quotas, causes unemployment and losses to export producers and holds back the growth of developing countries.

The demands for protection or subsidies in the North stem from political parties, business organizations and the management and unions in industries which are threatened by cutbacks, insolvencies and losses of jobs, especially when those jobs are concentrated in regions which do not offer immediate prospects of alternative employment. In a period of general recession these demands are understandable. It is the lives of people and their families that are involved and governments may be tempted to succumb to such pressures. But it will be easier to advocate the necessary structural changes in the North if it can be shown that real benefits accrue to broad strata of the population in the countries of the South.

Dangers of Restricting Trade

In public discussions in the rich countries, the voice of consumers and manufacturers who would rather buy lower-cost imports often gets less of a hearing than that of the proponents of protectionism. Protectionism brings higher costs to consumers and long-run losses to the whole economy through keeping resources away from the dynamic sectors. The effect on price levels of a free flow of imports should not be underestimated. In industries with large imports from developing countries, retail prices have risen much less than the average price level in most of the North. A 1978 survey of all consumer goods in the United States except food and automobiles found that goods imported from Asia and Latin America were, on the average, sold for 16 per cent less than domestic products of the same quality. Imports from the Third World can play a significant part in dampening inflation in the North.

Furthermore, to limit the exports of developing countries will reduce their ability to import, thus hindering the creation of new, more productive jobs in the North and forcing the developing countries to borrow more. This in turn makes it harder for them to service their debts, which puts additional strain on an already precarious financial situation. It should be remembered in this context that most industrialized countries import from developing countries only a fraction of the manufactures which they export to them: in 1978, total imports of manufactures and semi-manufactures were $32 billion compared to trade in the opposite direction of $125 billion, while total imports of industrialized countries from developing countries amounted to $216 billion compared to $200 billion of exports to these countries.

This closing-in of the world's open trading system occurring hand in hand with the deepening economic crisis is a very serious prospect. It threatens the trade among industrialized countries as well. But the exports from developing countries meet the highest barriers. The obstacles to their expansion jeopardize the future of the more outward-looking, efficient and equitable expansion strategies which the industrialized countries and international agencies have otherwise encouraged. Much will hinge on the principles to which trading countries subscribe, in their own and in the joint interest. Protectionism by industrialized countries against exports of developing countries should be rolled back; this should be facilitated by improved institutional machinery and new trading rules and principles.

Multilateral Trade Negotiations

The developing countries have not been satisifed with the results of the most recent multilateral trade negotiations of the General Agreement on Tariffs and Trade (GATT) commonly known as the Tokyo Round, and have been slow to accept the 1979 agreement. They have found the benefits limited because of the numerous exemptions of categories of goods of special interest to them. The high tariffs restricting the processing of primary products were not significantly reduced. Existing quantitative restrictions were not subject to negotiations, preference margins would be eroded by tariff reductions; tariffs on items such as textiles and footwear have not been cut significantly. Above all, acceptable terms for the application of safeguard measures against their exports were not agreed. The negotiations have, however, produced a series of codes of conduct aimed at modernizing and liberalizing the rules of world trade. These deal with such major sources of contention as non-tariff barriers and government procurement which have become serious obstacles to free trade. The codes and regulations negotiated to cover action in these and other fields contain elaborate provisions for notification, consultation, dispute settlement, and surveillance. It remains to be seen whether this machinery will be used and sufficiently respected to provide a fairer and more predictable trading environment; but the code system opens a way to provide multilateral jurisdiction for a number of trading disputes. It should apply on a non-discriminatory basis, including as beneficiaries all developing countries.

Abuses of the Safeguard System

The Articles of GATT are based on the assumption that countries will commit themselves to liberalize their trade only if they are allowed to impose emergency restrictions when necessary. The most important safeguard allows a country to impose restrictions if an increase of imports has caused or threatens 'serious injury' to domestic producers. The importing country must first notify and consult with the exporting countries which are affected, and shall only maintain restriction 'to the extent and for such time as may be necessary to prevent or remedy such injury'.

Many countries have invoked Article 19, but more often they have put up non-tariff barriers in violation of it, whether unilaterally or by negotiating 'voluntary export restraints' or 'orderly marketing arrangements', in accepting which developing countries have had no real choice. It has thus become largely ineffective. A stricter safeguard system is clearly desirable.

Negotiations on safeguards should be pursued urgently, since there is typically a long lag between the initiation of such negotiations and their conclusion; and since these issues are of such importance, rules should be established for importing countries to consult with the affected exporting country before they resort to safeguard action, whether through unilateral, bilateral or multilateral consultation and full disclosure. Countries which wish to take safeguard action should be required to establish, to the satisfaction of a multilateral body which also consults with consumers and exporting countries, that their domestic producers are indeed threatened by serious injury.

Safeguard measures must be explicit, of limited duration and gradually phased out. They must also be non-discriminatory in their application as between industrialized and developing countries, and between developing countries themselves. Governments which resort to safeguards should also have to specify what measures they intend to take to achieve the necessary industrial adjustment, which should then be monitored by a multilateral body. In cases where a country invokes safeguards to save the jobs in an industry facing competition from other countries that is not unfair, part of the agreement with the affected countries should permit them compensation, such as commercial concessions in other fields; this would deter importing countries from invoking safeguards lightly.

Proposals which have been put forward in the North for 'orderly marketing' or 'organized free trade' seek to avoid disruptions by extending the practice of marketing agreements and quotas to more industries, such as shipbuilding, steel, petrochemicals and automobiles. But in these arrangements strong countries can take undue advantage of weaker ones, and adjustment can be blocked rather than helped. Such international accords should only be accepted if they are linked with a programme for compensation and sectoral change which is internationally agreed and achieves a fair distribution of the adjustment burden.

Retraining and Restructuring

The link between safeguards and measures for industrial adjustment is important. If governments fall back on protective industrial policies when employment is threatened, it is a matter of profound and legitimate concern to other countries. But the record of industrial adjustment policies is not very satisfactory. All too easily they take on a defensive character prolonging the life of an uncompetitive industry. Japan's experience may offer valuable lessons to other industrialized countries on how restructuring can be based on a forward planning approach, phasing out uncompetitive industries swiftly and redirecting manpower and financial resources into new sectors; nonetheless, in some sectors Japanese import policies remain a matter of concern to foreign suppliers.

There are many measures to encourage and ease structural change. While the retraining of manpower for occupations in new industries and financial aid to those who move to new locations in search of jobs is now widely practised, such efforts to increase labour mobility could be expanded. In Japan buying up and scrapping redundant capacity, rather than encouraging further investment in declining industries, has proved effective. Community and regional development plans, including the provision of jobs in new industries, also have an important role to play; for what often makes structural change difficult is the geographic concentration of the declining industries. There can be no general rules about which policies to choose, but adjustment should be tackled not defensively but positively and in a forward-looking manner; and there must be a firm timetable for whatever temporary restrictions are imposed under the safeguard rules. The aim, difficult though it be, should be a closer coordination between the plans for investment in affected industries and trade in different countries; where such plans do not exist, there should be international consultations including developing countries about investment intentions and related industrial restructuring.

The difficulties of this process are undeniable as so many interests are involved and progress can only be made step by step; but countries taking advantage of legitimate protection should provide specific time schedules, for example over a five-year period, for phasing out uncompetitive parts of an industry. Such plans should include retraining and compensation for the losses encountered by domestic workers, communities or firms. International consultations over major investments would provide adequate time for industrial restructuring and avert threats of 'serious injury'. There should be multilateral consultation and review in the relevant international organizations. Such practices would extend the principles of mutual accommodation and fairness which must guide the restructuring of the world economy.

Fair Labour Standards

When industries in the North are exposed to foreign competition which results in a loss of markets and employment, the burden falls most heavily on the workers who lose their jobs. The labour unions have in most instances resisted the natural temptation to demand protection from competition from countries where wages are low because people are poor. The international free trade union movement, which unites trade unions in the industrial countries and the Third World in a spirit of solidarity, has a progressive attitude to the liberalization of trade and cooperation for development. But unions raise questions when they suspect that wages in developing countries are being held down by exploitation of a weak and unorganized labour force, by excessive working hours, or by the use of child labour. They resent it all the more if the competition makes excessive profits – especially if it comes from multinationals, which in some cases may also be their own employers.

The World Employment Conference in 1976 stated that 'the competitiveness of new imports from developing countries should not be achieved to the detriment of fair labour standards', and in 1978 the leaders of the world's free trade unions also took a unanimous decision to request the insertion of a so-called 'social clause' in trade agreements. This clause was designed to ensure the prohibition of discrimination, child labour and compulsory labour, the protection of proper working conditions and of the right to freedom of association, and adherence to proper standards of safety and health. Exports that result from working conditions which do not respect minimum social standards relevant to a given society are unfair to the workers directly involved, to workers of competing Third World exporting countries and to workers of importing countries whose welfare is undermined. They are also unfair to business concerns and countries which encourage social progress. Just as developing countries concern themselves with the industrial adjustments of other countries, so their own domestic industrial conditions will increasingly become a matter of international concern and review.

The Need for New Trading Rules

New international rules are also needed for solving disputes that arise from world trade. Restrictive trade practices, abuses of intra-firm trade, the limitations of export controls and so-called access to supply, all require monitoring and controlling. The different pricing systems in western and eastern countries can cause unfair competition which needs to be resolved. And trade in services and in agriculture as well as intra-firm trade and state trading has remained largely excluded from the GATT.

An immediate concern is the future of the Generalized System of Preferences (GSP) which was negotiated in UNCTAD in 1968 and which initially gave preferential treatment to developing country exports for ten years. The GSP has helped developing countries – but less than it might. Its deficiencies require attention: its rules of origin, its exemptions and quota limits, for example, should now be eased. The GSP should be extended beyond 1981. It is also desirable to 'bind' it to eliminate the risk that unilateral action might cut it short. More should be done to enable the least developed countries to benefit from the GSP. The Tokyo Round agreement has recognized that preferential treatment of developing countries should be accepted as a permanent feature of the world trading system rather than as a temporary exception. On the other hand, developing countries have affirmed that as their development proceeds they will gradually be able to make negotiated concessions and assume more of the obligations of GATT membership.

The poorest countries, as we have seen, have special disadvantages in their trade: they need both finance and technical assistance to strengthen their commercial capacities, for such needs as credit facilities, insurance, freight rates, or marketing, and to help them to participate effectively in international trade negotiations.

Trade Cooperation: GATT and UNCTAD

Two world bodies, GATT and UNCTAD, now have a mandate in the field of international trade. UNCTAD was created in 1964 partly because developing countries felt that GATT did not and could not completely serve them in trying to change the trading system. Some of their reservations had in fact already been expressed at the Havana Conference sixteen years earlier, when the International Trade Organization was negotiated, only to fail to obtain ratification by the US Congress.

More developing countries are joining GATT which, despite its limitations, rests on concepts of law and economic order between nations – concepts which can be harnessed in the service of a more equitable and rational trading system. Some developing countries that have joined GATT hope that they can participate more meaningfully and have greater influence on the trade concessions made by the industrialized countries; but many remain concerned that it is too preoccupied with the interests of industrialized countries, and they criticize GATT for not being stricter with the North in trying to hold back protectionism. Furthermore, GATT does not include all of Eastern Europe, or China, and large flows of world trade – as noted earlier – remain outside its scope.

UNCTAD, on the other hand, has become a principal forum for the important international debates and negotiations about changes in the world economic system. Unlike GATT, it has universal membership. The developing countries raise their major proposals for restructuring and reform at UNCTAD; various commodity arrangements are being negotiated in UNCTAD; and the Secretariat in Geneva monitors trade relations, particularly between North and South, and between South and South. UNCTAD has been the focus for negotiations on many other issues, including the transfer of technology. At least one major international change negotiated through UNCTAD, the Generalized System of Preferences, has later been incorporated in the statutes and practices of GATT.

There have been many suggestions for bringing UNCTAD and GATT closer together; this would make it easier, for instance, to link commodity negotiations with the question of access to markets. A first small step was taken towards collaboration when the International Trade Centre was created in 1964 – under the joint control of UNCTAD and GATT – which now gives valuable assistance to developing countries in their marketing. We believe there is a definite need in the short term to coordinate these two bodies more closely, and to prevent duplication. This could be achieved by a small coordinating body, the creation of which should not be difficult, since both organizations have an interest in concerting their negotiations and research.

A New Trade Organization?

In the longer term we believe that a new attempt should be made to create an International Trade Organization which would encompass the functions of both GATT and UNCTAD. GATT is an agreement covering tariffs and trade to which a limited number of countries have subscribed. The possibility of international agreements in other areas, such as trade practices of transnational corporations, international investment, double or multiple taxation and tax havens, rules governing mutual accommodation of industrial policies, state trading practices and transfer of technology are being explored. The signatories of any agreements should not be confined to those who subscribe to the GATT. On the other hand, for each such agreement to stand in isolation, serviced by its own Secretariat, would lead to an unnecessary proliferation of international institutions with overlapping spheres of jurisdiction and possibilities of working at cross-purposes with each other. The need for an Organization for Trade Cooperation to serve as an umbrella for such efforts had been accepted by the GATT signatories during the review of its Articles in 1954–5. But, like the International Trade Organization, the OTC never came into being.

The role of UNCTAD as a forum for dialogue, debate, and increasingly for negotiation, where new ideas pertaining to trade, finance and development emerge, is a distinct one which needs to be preserved. Proposals which command agreement in UNCTAD may in their actual implementation necessitate action not only in the GATT – as with the GSP – but also in other international agencies such as the World Bank, the IMF, FAO and UNIDO. For some years to come UNCTAD and GATT will continue to have different interests and viewpoints, which should not be concealed: but the restructuring of the trading system to ensure fairer treatment for all nations would necessitate in the end an organization which can represent all interests.

Recommendations

The industrialization of developing countries, as a means of their overall development efforts, will provide increasing opportunities for world trade and need not conflict with the long-term interests of developed countries. It should be facilitated as a matter of international policy.

Protectionism threatens the future of the world economy and is inimical to the long-term interests of developing and developed countries alike. Protectionism by industrialized countries against the exports of developing countries should be rolled back; this should be facilitated by improved institutional machinery and new trading rules and principles.

Adjustment to new patterns of world industrial production should be accepted as a necessary and desirable process. Industrialized countries should vigorously pursue positive and time-bound adjustment programmes developed through international consultation and subject to international surveillance.

Safeguard measures must be internationally negotiated and should be taken only on the basis of established need. They should be non-discriminatory, of limited duration and subject to international surveillance.

The Generalized System of Preferences should be eased in respect of its rules of origin, its exceptions and its limits. It should be extended beyond its present expiration and not be liable to unilateral termination.

Financial support and technical assistance should be given to the poorer countries to facilitate their establishment of improved commercial infrastructure and their participation in international trade negotiations.

Fair labour standards should be internationally agreed in order to prevent unfair competition and to facilitate trade liberalization.

An international trade organization incorporating both GATT and UNCTAD is the objective towards which the international community should work. Meanwhile, there is need for improvement in existing arrangements including wider development of trade cooperation in such matters as the establishment and administration of rules, principles and codes covering restrictive business practices and technology transfer.

12 Transnational Corporations, Investment and the Sharing of Technology

The transnational corporations, or as they are also called, multinational corporations, are closely involved in many of the areas which are dealt with in this Report: with minerals, commodities, industrialization, food, and energy. Many of them have played a large role in bringing technology and capital to developing countries. Oil and food companies have been operating globally since the early years of the century. But in the postwar years the scale and sophistication of their operations have greatly increased, and they have become politically much more visible and have frequently been the centre of controversy. They are now major actors in the world's political economy. They control between a quarter and a third of all world production and are particularly active in processing and marketing. The total sales of their foreign affiliates in 1976 were estimated at $830 billion, which is about the same as the then gross national product of all developing countries excluding oil-exporting developing countries. In addition to oil, the marketing, processing or production of several commodities – including bauxite, copper, iron ore, nickel, lead, zinc, tin, tobacco, bananas and tea – is dominated in each case by a small number of transnational corporations.

In 1975 the total stock of direct foreign investment in the developing countries was about $68 billion, about one-fourth of world foreign investment. The annual flows in the mid-1970s were about $8 billion, which is about 12 per cent of the total flow of resources to the Third World. Foreign investment has moved to a limited number of developing countries, mainly those which could offer political stability and a convenient economic environment, including tax incentives, large markets, cheap labour and easy access to oil or other natural resources. Purely financial investments have gone to tax havens in developing countries, which the UN lists as Bahamas, Barbados, Bermuda, Cayman Islands, Netherlands Antilles and Panama. Of the rest, 70 per cent of the investment in the Third World has been in only fifteen countries. Over 20 per cent is in Brazil and Mexico alone and the rest in other middle-income countries in Latin America – Argentina, Peru, Venezuela – or in South East Asia – Malaysia, Singapore, Hong Kong. About one-quarter is in oil-exporting developing countries. In the poorer countries foreign investment is mainly in plantations and minerals, or in countries with large internal markets – like India. Private investment can supplement and complement aid, but it cannot substitute for it: it tends not to move to the countries or sectors which most need aid.

A foreign company need not always bring capital with it, for it can borrow in local markets. It is mainly technology, management or marketing that it provides. In some cases developing countries, particularly if they are rapidly industrializing, want not only capital from abroad, but the technology, management and marketing skills which transnational corporations also own. The role and influence of foreign companies produce very different government reactions in different developing countries. Some countries have based much of their pattern of growth on the inputs of foreign companies; others have chosen not to take this path. Foreign investment or technology can bring disadvantages and costs, both direct and indirect, and many developing countries believe that they greatly reduce, if not even outweigh, the potential benefits. Many of these costs are closely linked to the operations of the transnational corporations.

Tensions between Corporations and Countries

Much of the international trade which these corporations conduct goes on within their own organizations, between the parent firm and its affiliates; and this extensive 'intra-firm trade', according to one estimate, makes up over 30 per cent of all world trade. Other transactions also take place extensively between the different parts of these enterprises, for example the granting of loans, the licensing of technology and the provision of services. In all such transactions, transfer prices may be settled which are different from the price which would have been the case between independent parties operating at arms length. Such differences may reflect the legitimate business concerns of the companies but are also capable of being used in order to shift profits from high to low tax countries or to get around exchange or price controls or customs duties. The ability of multinationals to manipulate financial flows by the use of artificial transfer prices is bound to be a matter of concern to governments. The monitoring and control of transfer prices involves intergovernmental cooperation and measures to secure due disclosure of relevant information by companies. This is necessary to make effective the tax laws covering transfer prices which exist in many countries. Intra-firm trade also opens up the possibility for corporations to impose restrictive business practices within their own organization; they can limit the exports of their affiliates, allocate their markets between nations or restrict the use of their technology or that developed by their affiliates. Such practices, although pursued in the best business interests of the companies, may conflict with the developmental objectives and national interests of host countries.

Multinational corporations have also been heavily criticized for unethical political and commercial activities. The attempt to bring down the Allende regime in Chile; the illegal payments by oil companies to governments in different parts of the world; the support given by certain corporations to illegal regimes in Africa: such cases have exposed the corporations to scrutiny and criticism in the United Nations and elsewhere. This is not to suggest that as a class transnational corporations have been guilty of such practices. Many of them have believed in maintaining legal and ethical standards and have been free of blame. In some cases governments may be as much to blame as the corporations, and the distinction between bribery and extortion can be a fine one. But these cases have all underlined the potential political power of the multinationals, in addition to their commercial power. Tension between the companies and developing countries has been an important element in North–South relations. The investors in the corporations have been worried by nationalizations and contract disputes, and want protection and predictable conditions for their investment; while many developing countries have reservations about the character and good faith of the corporations. The establishment of the UN Centre for Transnational Corporations (UNCTNC) is an expression of international recognition of these issues.

Underlying many of the fears about multinational corporations, both in the South and the North, is the concern that they have been able to race ahead in global operations out of reach of effective controls by nation-states or international organizations; that they have been able to benefit from economic disorders at a time when many nations have suffered from them; and that they constitute a network of transnational power which has provided a new element in the struggle of political and economic forces.

Both developing and industrialized countries have obtained benefits from the management and the worldwide technology of these corporations, but are often ambivalent in their attitudes. The challenge is whether it is possible to reconcile the different interests from the outset. The removal of the causes of distrust is important to the prosperity of both sides in the relationship.

The Need for Regulation

There is always a triangular relationship between the home country, the host country, and the transnational corporation which originates in the first and operates in the second. Clearly, a corporation which aims to maximize its worldwide profits will not have the same interests as a country which seeks to derive the maximum national benefit. But there are also strong mutual interests which can reconcile the concerns of home and host governments with those of the investors. Both North and South have an interest in the effective transfer of capital and technology, which can bring great benefits in terms of expanded production, trade, and jobs. The home governments are themselves increasingly aware of the problems posed by the corporations, since about three-quarters of overseas direct investment is made within the industrialized countries. The international trade union movement is also concerned to ensure that the flows and functioning of private capital are beneficial; increased cooperation among trade unions in different countries can create a better equilibrium in the relations between transnational corporations and governments. Although the overwhelming part of direct foreign investment in the Third World comes from developed countries, in recent years firms in Latin America and Asia have also begun to invest in other developing countries. CMEA countries too have formed a number of trading and manufacturing companies abroad, some of them in developing countries. Industrial cooperation between eastern enterprises and western transnationals has grown rapidly in the 1970s. The issues involved in foreign investment are becoming broader and call for participation of all countries in their discussion. We believe, therefore, that it is essential and possible to find the means both to promote and regulate private investment, with measures that would be mutually reinforcing.

More effective regulation is essential for achieving global objectives of maximizing benefits and minimizing costs from transnational investment. For instance, the restraint of restrictive practices by transnational corporations, alongside the reduction of protectionist barriers by governments, will lead to greater benefits from freer trade. In the commodity sphere, prices, improved marketing arrangements and monitoring of transfer pricing are necessary if the share of incomes going to producers and workers engaged in the production of primary commodities is to be improved. Providing greater security and trust will stimulate private investment.

Increasing Bargaining Strength

To obtain full benefits, the developing countries, particularly the smaller and poorer ones, need to improve their bargaining strength. This would lead to a more stable relationship with corporations as it would help to dispel distrust and increase confidence. In addition to improved access to international development finance, these countries need to have more information about the choices and relative merits of different technologies, about the rival merits and skills of corporations, and information about their worldwide contracts. The services provided by the UN system and other international bodies should be developed to strengthen the capability of developing countries to negotiate effective and durable agreements with transnational corporations, and to assist them in the interpretation and implementation of agreements.

Developing countries are likely to obtain better terms if they pursue more selective policies in admitting foreign investments and if they can promise stability in dealing with them. This means that they must carefully evaluate the costs and benefits, and they must have clear national codes for investment which seek to ensure a predictable climate for investment. Many developing countries have already benefited from this approach.

As developing countries acquire more technological skills of their own they should be in a better position, where appropriate, to unpackage the 'technology-investment package', separating out the components of investment, technology, management and marketing, and importing only what they need and using their domestic inputs wherever they can. There are signs too that corporations are becoming more flexible in negotiating conditions for ownership and concluding licences for pure technology, joint

191

ventures, production-sharing and other looser forms of technology transfers. These trends should be encouraged.

A Regime for International Investment

There is now much interest in trying to formulate international codes of conduct for the transfer of technology, for restrictive business practices and transnational corporations. Definite progress has been made in some of these negotiations. Any code, of course, will only work if it can influence the actual behaviour of home and host governments and of investors. The major elements of any effective code should be capable of being eventually translated into agreements between governments. Such an overall regime will have to have elements of both persuasion and effective implementation, with flexible approaches and attitudes on all sides. The participating governments will have to consult with labour and business to find the means to reconcile interests and to monitor and implement the agreements. The ILO has created a committee for consultation and monitoring its Code of Conduct relating to multinational enterprises. This offers one model.

In our view the principal elements of an international regime for investment should include:

1 A framework to allow developing countries as well as transnational corporations to benefit from direct investment on terms contractually agreed upon. Home countries should not restrict investment or the transfer of technology abroad, and should desist from other restrictive practices such as export controls or market allocation arrangements. Host countries in turn should not restrict current transfers such as profits, royalties and dividends, or the repatriation of capital, so long as they are on terms which were agreed when the investment was originally approved or subsequently renegotiated.

2 Legislation promoted and coordinated in home and host countries, to regulate the activities of transnational corporations in such matters as ethical behaviour, disclosure of information, restrictive business practices, cartels, anti-competitive practices and labour standards. International codes and guidelines are a useful step in that direction.

3 Cooperation by governments in their tax policies to monitor transfer pricing, and to eliminate the resort to tax havens.

4 Fiscal and other incentives and policies towards foreign

investment to be harmonized among host developing countries, particularly at regional and sub-regional levels, to avoid the undermining of the tax base and competitive positions of host countries.

5 An international procedure for discussions and consultations on measures affecting direct investment and the activities of transnational corporations.

Fair Contracts Are More Stable

Investors and their governments in the industrialized countries constantly stress their concern with the security of their investments, the need for predictable policies, and for compensation in the event of nationalization. We recognize that sovereign states have the right to nationalize investments, including foreign investment. But nationalization must be accompanied by fair and effective compensation, under internationally comparable principles which should be embodied in national laws.

It is important to recall that when multinational corporations have at the outset made inequitable contracts with developing countries – particularly in minerals – the result has often been that the contracts have run into trouble. We believe strongly that there is a close connection between the equity and stability of investments. If a developing country can offer stability, it can get better terms from investors; and equally if the initial terms are tilted in favour of the investors they will tend in the end to make the investment less stable. Contracts should aim at fairness and ensure stability, and conditions for renegotiation could usefully be included in the original contract.

The insurance of investments and the settlement of disputes are issues which affect security. Many national schemes in investor countries for investment insurance already exist, and host countries who wish to give confidence to foreign investment should participate in them, through bilateral agreements with home countries. They could also agree to make use of multilateral bodies to settle disputes, in addition, or as an alternative, to national tribunals.

Sharing Technology

The sharing of technology is a worldwide concern, since all

193

countries have much to learn from others. But clearly it is most important to the developing countries; and it can even be argued that their principal weakness is the lack of access to technology, or of command of it. The acquisition of technology is crucial, not only to growth, but to the capacity to grow. The planning priorities and the economic and social objectives of a developing country will both determine the choice of technology, and be determined by it; a country will only be able to benefit from additional technology if it can absorb and adapt what it has already received, and if it can provide the 'welcoming structure' which can connect up new technology to old societies. The developing countries' efforts towards greater technological self-reliance need to be fully supported through international cooperation.

Technology is transmitted in many ways. While some spreads through published literature, personal exchanges, imitation and copying, most is transmitted commercially. It comes with the sale of machinery and knowhow, through training and technical assistance, or through participation in the construction, operation and management of a foreign firm. The market for technology is very imperfect. To the seller, the marginal cost in the sale of an already developed technology may be small although the use may be very profitable to him; the cost to the buyer of doing without it, or developing it on its own, could be very high. The range between the two is so wide that it is relative bargaining strength which essentially determines the price; and in this market the developing countries find themselves in an inherently weak negotiating position because of their overwhelming dependence on technology from the North. Almost all advanced technology originates in industrial countries and most of it continues to be developed by them. The North accounts for about 96 per cent of the world's spending on research and development. The scientists and engineers, the advanced institutions of education and research, the modern plants, the consumer demand and the finance are all found mainly in the richest countries.

Public Interest in the Use of Patents

Nearly all of the world's patents are registered in the industrial states and most of them are in the hands of the transnational corporations. Most patents granted by developing countries are to foreigners, and studies show that they are not used for production in these countries and that they then have the effect of creating import monopolies. Patents are also used to exclude competitors from investment in developing countries. Developing countries are therefore concerned that many restrictive clauses in the present industrial property system tend to strengthen monopolistic and oligopolistic practices among the corporations. The World Intellectual Property Organization (WIPO), which deals with patents, and UNCTAD are now discussing possible revisions in the Paris Convention and model laws to secure greater recognition on the part of patent holders of the public interest in developing countries, for example by limiting the duration of patents for certain products.

'Appropriate Technology'

In international discussions on the transfer of technology there has been an increasing concentration in the 1970s on the above aspects of the structure and characteristics of the market in commercialized technology. Earlier enthusiasm for the unqualified transfer of technology from the industrialized to the developing countries and optimism and faith in its beneficial effects have given way to increasing scepticism and criticism. There has been vigorous questioning of the 'appropriateness' of the technology and critical scrutiny of the various costs associated with the transfer. Linked to this is a shift from the earlier emphasis on the promotional or developmental role of private foreign investment to a demand for the regulation of transnational enterprises. These concerns are reflected in the effort to formulate codes on the transfer of technology in UNCTAD, in the UN Centre for Transnational Corporations and in discussions in several other international fora, notably UNIDO, ILO and WIPO.

The call for appropriate technology does not prescribe any particular type; much less does it imply that the technology should not be the latest or the most sophisticated. It means that the choice of technology should be a conscious one, taken in the knowledge that it can affect the character and direction of development. The South may wish to choose machines very different from those automatically offered by the North. Appropriate technologies can include cheaper sources of energy; simpler farm equipment; techniques in building, services and manufacturing processes which save capital; smaller plants and scales of operation which can permit dispersal of activity. Appropriate technologies also take account of the special nature of the problems in each area, for example human diseases or agricultural pests which may be unknown to industrialized society where most research is concentrated. Some technologies can conserve scarce materials and save on imports; some are much better suited to the skills, management and industrial organization of developing countries. An appropriate 'consumption technology' can choose products which suit local incomes and objectives.

Only the developing countries themselves can decide which machines and systems will suit their own local needs; how far they should move towards technologies which can save resources, or which use more workers and less capital, taking into account the need for modernization, technological advance and efficiency. But international cooperation can help to develop new technologies and to disseminate them.

The multinational corporations and other commercial firms which control most technological developments are unlikely, of their own accord, to direct their research into areas which do not promise high returns to themselves. There is an urgent need to provide new incentives to develop appropriate technologies and, almost equally important, to make them known to everyone. There is a need for more research into adapting existing machines; a need to know more about which technology is most useful to a particular territory; a need to see case studies of where and how different systems have worked; and the international aid agencies need to take more account of appropriate technology, particularly as it is developed in the Third World, in their loans for projects.

The question of appropriate technology is relevant to both rich and poor countries. Industrialized countries too need more appropriate technologies which conserve energy and exhaustible resources, which avoid rapid job displacement and which do not damage the ecology. It is quite possible that rising energy costs, afflicting both North and South, will eventually compel corporations in the North to concentrate more on new kinds of techniques which may be appropriate to many parts of both North and South. It is a question of enabling the inventiveness and enterprise of scientists and engineers everywhere to give the fullest possible benefit to mankind. To achieve this will require developing countries to be more adaptable, and to assimilate appropriate technology effectively. It will require from the industrial world a greater awareness of the needs of the rest of the world, and greater incentives to extend and adjust their own inventiveness.

How to Transfer More Technology

We believe that much can be done, through more effective organization, to increase the transfer and development of technology:

1 It is essential, in the first place, that information about technology should flow more freely, both between and within nations. Many international organizations including FAO, UNIDO, UNEP, UNESCO, ILO, WHO, and UNCTNC now operate systems which collect, store and make available information on the technological possibilities of interest to developing countries; private commercial systems are also becoming a valuable source. But the potential users are often at a loss to know where to go for what. The speed, relevance and up-to-dateness of the existing systems need to be carefully evaluated, to make them more usable and better used: where possible they should be consolidated and complemented with national institutions which can explain their own needs and transmit their own information.

2 There should also be greater support for technical assistance, including the UNDP and its participating agencies, which provide an important channel for transmitting technology; they need to be enlarged and made more effective. In particular, more support should be given to provide the local basis for research and evaluation of needs.

3 Special international support should be given to research into more efficient production, development and marketing to defend and improve the market competitiveness of those raw materials mainly produced in developing countries – including rubber, jute, cotton and hard fibres, most of which are threatened by synthetic substitutes. The activities of the Second Window of the Common Fund in this area could be of major significance.

4 Serious study should be undertaken of the implications and ways of coping with major technological breakthroughs in the North – notably micro-electronics – which may not only reduce the demand for labour in the North but also deprive the South of its comparative advantage in low wage costs.

5 The situation should be changed whereby – according to recent UN studies – at present barely one per cent of spending on research and development in the North is specifically concerned with the problems of the South; whereas 51 per cent is devoted to defence,

atomic and space research. The importance of disarming as a possible means of promoting development is nowhere more evident than in the field of research.

6 The aid agencies should make more use of local consultants and skilled people in preparing their projects and programmes. At present they rely largely on experts from the advanced countries, who can easily perpetuate the dependence of the receiving country, and sometimes are insufficiently aware of local problems. The lending agencies could do more to encourage local engineering and advisers, and they could promote the techniques of learning-by-doing, which can help to reduce costs, can diffuse the understanding of new technologies, and can provide a feedback in the developing country for better planning and better bargaining.

7 Countries providing aid should give freedom to the recipients to make their own choice of imported technology. When they tie aid to their own sources the donor countries greatly limit choices and discourage local initiatives; and corporations normally insist on a technology-investment package which further restricts the choice. If aid has fewer strings, if there is more lending for programmes rather than projects, and if financing can cover local costs, it can be more effective and the receivers can have a better chance to develop their own future potential. Donor countries should give more aid to activities traditionally 'reserved' for private investment, and should provide funds for developing countries to import technology of their own choice.

8 Last but not least, there should be more effective coordination in the many areas of technology which affect countries all over the world. Many of the technological challenges of today are not local needs of single countries, but are part of the basic problem of the survival and conservation of the world's resources; these tasks serve the enlightened self-interest of the North as well as the immediate needs of the South; and their solution depends on imaginative cooperation and feedback. The management of the oceans and river basins, of the weather and natural catastrophes, is part of this common challenge. The rescuing of regions which are being ruined by deforestation, soil erosion or creeping deserts is part of the common need to protect the world's ecology and the human environment. And the need to increase food production, to stimulate industrial growth, to abolish poverty and to improve the health of the poorest populations, as we have seen, involves the security of the whole world.

Connecting Skills to Problems

In all these tasks, technology will play a critical role; often in ways that cannot be predicted. The poorer and smaller countries which bear the brunt of the difficulties lack the funds and the experts to tackle these problems on their own; and it is essential that the most effective pooling and coordination should be achieved, to connect the right skills to the right problems, on both international and regional levels. One hopeful model has been provided by the Consultative Group for International Agricultural Research, which is financed by lending agencies and foundations: it has supported research on rice in the Philippines, tropical agriculture in Nigeria, potatoes in Peru, maize and wheat in Mexico, and semi-arid tropical crops in India, all for use on a worldwide basis. This kind of research should be supported and extended, with more regional cooperation.

Developing countries should themselves cooperate more closely in their research and development: the UN Conference on Technical Cooperation Among Developing Countries in 1978 has identified several important areas. But there is a need for more effective funding and coordination in all areas where local problems – whether of food, industry, health or ecology – are part of broader experience; and it is in meeting these essential requirements that the sharing of technology is most urgent and most valuable.

It was proposed at the UN Conference on Science and Technology for Development (UNCSTD) in 1979 that 20 per cent of the world's research and development should take place in the Third World by the year 2000, as opposed to 3 per cent today. The developed countries were invited to make funds and information available to strengthen the scientific and technological capabilities of the Third World. A study was proposed to define a mechanism for financing scientific and technological work in support of development; and an interim fund was proposed of $250 million to cover the 1980-81 period before the study is completed. These are important initiatives, although there has been disappointment that the results of the conference were not as far-reaching as originally expected. The North–South discussion of the sharing of technology must continue on many fronts. It is vital to the objectives of a new order.

Recommendations

Effective national laws and international codes of conduct are needed to govern the sharing of technology, to control restrictive business practices, and to provide a framework for the activities of transnational corporations.

The investment regime we propose would include:

1 Reciprocal obligations on the part of host and home countries covering foreign investment, transfer of technology, and repatriation of profits, royalties and dividends.

2 Legislation, coordinated in home and host countries, to regulate transnational corporation activities in matters such as ethical behaviour, disclosure of information, restrictive business practices and labour standards.

3 Intergovernmental cooperation in regard to tax policies and the monitoring of transfer pricing.

4 Harmonization of fiscal and other incentives among host developing countries.

In addition to improved access to international development finance, the bargaining capacity of developing countries, particularly of the smaller and least developed countries, *vis-à-vis* the transnational corporations should be strengthened with the technical assistance now increasingly available from the UN and other agencies.

Permanent sovereignty over natural resources is the right of all countries. It is necessary, however, that nationalization be accompanied by appropriate and effective compensation, under internationally comparable principles which should be embodied in national laws. Increasing use should also be made of international mechanisms for settling disputes.

Greater international, regional and national efforts are needed to support the development of technology in developing countries and the transfer of appropriate technology to them at reasonable cost.

There should be increased efforts in both rich and poor countries to develop appropriate technology in the light of changing constraints regarding energy and ecology; the flow of information about such technology should be improved. The international aid agencies should change those of their practices which restrict the recipients' freedom to choose technology, and should make more use of local capacities in preparing projects.

13 The World Monetary Order

The prospects in all areas of world trade, whether in commodities or manufactures, in energy or in the activities of multinational corporations, are greatly influenced by the functioning of the world monetary system. Predictable rates of exchange encourage investment as well as trade: erratic and fluctuating rates discourage both. Stable rates increase the confidence of asset holders, whether surplus oil producers or other potential investors. An adequate flow of international liquidity likewise smooths out cyclical fluctuations, makes protection of domestic markets less necessary and enables commodity producers to ride over deteriorating terms of trade. The events of the 1970s have made the industrial countries much more aware of their dependence on a stable world monetary system; what is less often realized is the particular vulnerability of the developing countries to the uncertainties and fluctuations of the major currencies.

The rate of exchange between national currencies of two sovereign states closely concerns both of them, for it pervades their mutual trade and investment. To provide an orderly and agreed way to establish and, where necessary, change exchange rates, is therefore the first task of an international monetary system. Since the end of the Second World War, the dominant international monetary system has been that constructed at Bretton Woods in 1944 centred on the International Monetary Fund, a system of which many features broke down in the early 1970s. There is also the Comecon-based system which was initially built around bilateral settlements, but in 1964 was made multilateral with the introduction of the transferable rouble issued by the International Bank for Economic Cooperation (IBEC). The only link between the two systems, but an important one, is that much of Eastern

Europe's trade with the rest of the world is carried on through western convertible currencies, especially dollars.

The Bretton Woods System

In the Bretton Woods system, the rules guiding the relations among states were intended to prevent the repetition of the international economic conflicts of the 1930s: competitive devaluation, discrimination in foreign exchange dealings and tariffs, lack of convertibility, disorderly flows of capital. For unique historical reasons the United States and the United Kingdom had an unusually large influence in establishing the system and subsequently controlling it. Europe was in ruins; Germany, Italy and Japan were enemy countries. Most developing countries were still colonies; only India, Egypt, Ethiopia and Liberia and the independent countries of Latin America attended the Bretton Woods conference. The Soviet Union and other East European countries participated at Bretton Woods, but the Soviet Union eventually chose not to join. Poland resigned its membership in 1950 and Czechoslovakia was required to withdraw from the IMF in 1954. After the revolution of 1949 the China that then retained membership did not represent the mainland. East European countries gave their main reasons for not adhering to the Bretton Woods system as (a) the procedure adopted for allocating votes among members of the IMF in accordance with their subscriptions; (b) the requirement to report their national gold and foreign exchange holdings and transfer part of them to the US where the IMF and the World Bank have their headquarters; (c) the terms on which members were allowed credits to correct their balance of payments. An unstated reason was the deterioration of international political relations.

Under the Bretton Woods system, each member undertook to maintain the par value of its currency, that is, a central value in terms of gold, the ultimate standard of value of the system. In practice, the United States came to play a unique role in managing this system. That was not only because it retained gold convertibility for dollars held by foreign central banks and had initially (with Britain) half the total votes, but also because of the overwhelming strength of the dollar. In the immediate aftermath of the war, the crippled economies of Europe and Japan needed vast imports and could export very little. The United States had emerged from the war with an immense productive capacity and national wealth, including its reserves of monetary gold. Through the Anglo-American Financial Agreement of 1945 and the Marshall Plan it provided resources to reconstruct Europe. Most countries of the world wanted to hold dollars even more than gold, since dollars were readily exchangeable into gold and also earned interest for the holders. Thus the dollar became the world's principal reserve asset and the United States could create international money by expanding its short-term liabilities to the rest of the world. The stability of the monetary system came to depend on the management of the United States' monetary policy and, by implication, her economy.

Postwar Growth and Currency Stability

For about twenty-five years after the Second World War economic growth and living standards improved, especially for the industrial countries, at a rate unprecedented in history and in a climate of relative economic stability. It is impossible to demonstrate, much less measure, how much of that achievement was due to the orderly relationships between currencies. But it is reasonable to suggest that the Bretton Woods system reinforced the rapid and yet relatively stable economic expansion which a combination of favourable factors allowed governments of major financial powers to encourage. The rules of the IMF together with the GATT delineated the permissible in monetary and trade behaviour and erected the predictability and security that is essential for long-term investment.

While this postwar growth was continuing, there was a gradual but inevitable change in the balance of power between the United States on one hand and Europe and Japan on the other. Between the end of the war and 1975 the United States' share of total OECD production declined from 60 per cent to 40 per cent. But the growing importance of the Federal Republic of Germany and Japan, for example, was not formally matched by the increase in the role of their respective currencies. The dollar today still accounts for over 80 per cent of that part of international liquidity which consists of national currencies. At the same time the transnational corporations, most of them originally based in the United States but now with other bases as well, were growing to a scale that was quite unforeseen. The restoration of currency convertibility and the growth of domestic liquidity in the industrial countries, which was substantial in the 1970s, increased the volume of funds which could be shifted quickly from one country to another. The new freedom to do so directly as well as indirectly through the Euro-market, the increased knowledge of short-term investment opportunities and of the channels for moving such funds, and the increased interpenetration of these economies through transnational activity – all these factors augmented the potential for short-term capital movements and tested the stability of the Bretton Woods system.

The Breakdown of Bretton Woods

The relatively smooth functioning of the Bretton Woods system was disrupted in the 1970s for reasons which were related to these changes. Disagreements emerged between countries with balance of payments deficits, notably the United States, and countries enjoying balance of payments surpluses as to the responsibility for adopting policies which could return them to payments balance. The surplus countries had few incentives, under the Bretton Woods arrangements, to undertake the necessary adjustment. Normally, adjustments therefore had to be made by the deficit countries. Since the balance of payments deficits of the United States had become the principal source of growth in world liquidity, however, it seemed to have, in General de Gaulle's words, the 'exorbitant privilege' of continuing to finance its deficits through the provision of still more dollars. The required orderly adjustments of United States deficits and others' surpluses were therefore not undertaken, while nervousness increased.

As the United States' gold reserves ran down and foreign holdings of US dollars increased, there was less and less confidence in the United States' capacity to honour its obligation to convert dollars into gold. Declining confidence manifested itself in the speculative selling of dollars and increasing private demand for gold, in anticipation of a dollar devaluation in terms of gold.

Anticipation of changes in exchange rates increasingly generated enormous speculative flows of capital across international frontiers. The multinational corporations and other large holders of liquid assets augmented such flows, as they sought to avoid losses by placing their cash wherever currency devaluations were least likely.

Attempts had been made to patch together the system in the late 1960s through *ad hoc* intergovernmental credit arrangements, and the abandonment of official intervention in private gold markets. Special drawing rights (SDRs) were created by the IMF as a first step towards the creation of an alternative source of expansion in international liquidity. But the pressures upon the world monetary system proved too great. After further major capital flows out of the United States into other currencies, the United States finally suspended the convertibility of the dollar into gold on 15 August 1971. An attempt was made to restore the old monetary order through a formal dollar devaluation against gold negotiated at an international conference at the Smithsonian Institution in Washington in December 1971. By March 1973, however, the par value system had finally broken down.

Current Monetary Disorder

Since then the world's monetary and economic relations have been under increasing strain. All countries are worried about this disorder. Developing countries and small industrialized countries find themselves buffeted by the unpredictable ups and downs of the major currencies. They have been faced with major new problems in the management of their own exchange rates, foreign reserves and debt. The major industrial countries are also affected by the increased uncertainties of the new regime, not least through their effects upon their growth and inflation. Short- and medium-term fluctuations in their exchange rates have far exceeded those generally considered necessary for balance of payments adjustment and that adjustment has itself proceeded only very sluggishly. The surplus oil revenues which accumulated at the end of the 1970s added to these difficulties, as we discuss in Chapter 15.

Proposals for reform of the international monetary system were prepared by the Executive Board of the IMF in 1972. The Committee of Twenty formed in the same year with nine developing country members negotiated a set of reform proposals with respect to the adjustment process, the convertibility system, the management of global liquidity and the transfer of real resources to developing countries. Unfortunately, there was no agreement on some of these proposals. Subsequent negotiations on reform were carried out in the Interim Committee of the Board of Governors of the IMF. The fifth meeting of the Interim Committee in Jamaica in January 1976 set the seal on the Second Amendment of the IMF articles that limited reform to those areas on which consensus had been reached. But on the central aspects of reform – the exchange rate regime, convertibility of official balances and the reserve system – the Jamaica agreement virtually accepts the *fait accompli* that had followed the breakdown of the Bretton Woods system. Thus members are permitted to adopt the exchange arrangements of their choice; the IMF is given the role of exercising firm surveillance over the exchange rate policies of members and adopting specific principles for the guidance of all members with respect to those policies.

The current monetary disorder, together with the growing tide of protectionism and persistent inflation and recession, could have increasingly dangerous consequences for all countries. Without clear rules to govern the conduct of monetary relations, governments could be more and more tempted to take unilateral actions – whether for damage limitation or for national advantage – that would lead to greater political friction and growing nationalistic sentiments. There is thus an urgent need to establish a mutually agreed international monetary order which would take into account the changes in the world environment since 1944. But we must face the fact that there are great conflicts of interest, since different monetary regimes will benefit nations in different degrees.

Towards a New Monetary Order

Proposals for monetary reform must take full cognizance of the existing international environment as well as future prospects. Firstly, they must take into account the great expansion of private international money and capital markets – for instance, Eurocurrency and Eurobond markets and the Asian and Middle Eastern currency markets. Secondly, they must provide for a broader-based and fully representative management of the international economic system. Thirdly, they must take note of the potential consequences of East–West *détente*. The economic policy of eastern countries during the period of confrontation tended to be inward-looking, but their economic policy in a time of *détente* can be expected to lead to increased participation in the international division of labour. In proposing reform the options open to the international community include: continuing with the prevailing situation with the role of the dollar reduced, with an increased role for other currencies and private financial markets and with all governments trying to reduce their exposure to exogenous events; or moving in the direction of regional monetary blocs, which would each work out their own relations with other monetary areas; or advancing to a better-organized world system.

We have pointed out that the prevailing situation is not a healthy one. As for regional blocs, they could contribute to important monetary reforms. The main aim of the European Monetary System (EMS), as we see it, is to permit trade expansion within Europe on the basis of fixed though adjustable rates of exchange between the currencies of the European Community. The EMS provides many pointers for the future of the international monetary system. It suggests for example that there must be strict but fair rules for adjustment between surplus and deficit countries, and that in a world of unequals, consideration must be given to the problem of the weaker countries. But the regional option only makes sense eventually in the context of a reformed monetary system in the whole world.

The Commission believes that reform of the world monetary system is urgent and must address itself to the following issues: the exchange rate regime, the reserve system (the creation and distribution of the international means of payment or liquidity); and the adjustment mechanism as it affects the countries issuing reserve currencies, surplus countries and deficit countries.

The Exchange Rate Regime

Since the major currencies began to float, the changes of exchange rates have not only been large but also erratic. The significant appreciations of the yen, the Deutschmark and the Swiss franc *vis-à-vis* the US dollar since 1973 are in keeping with the requirements of balance of payments adjustment. But the wide fluctuations up and down over shorter periods, in spite of official intervention in exchange markets, have served no constructive purpose. In particular periods such as in October 1978 speculative capital flows have dominated the markets and driven exchange rates far beyond levels which can be related to real economic adjustment needs Governmental interventions in foreign exchange markets have been motivated by the same basic objectives as those of primary exporting countries seeking stabilization in world commodity markets.

While some developing countries have floating or 'crawling' exchange rates, most are pegged to the major currencies, or to a basket of currencies, because their own money markets are very rudimentary and their economies are vulnerable. The floating of the major currencies introduces uncertainties about real earnings from exports and real costs of imports since exports and imports are often invoiced in currencies which move against each other in unpredictable ways. This kind of uncertainty discourages allocation of resources to producing goods for export or for competition with imports, and introduces complications in external debt management.

We believe that any serious reform must aim at a greater

measure of stability in international currencies. This can only be brought about if there are simultaneous reforms of the reserve system and the adjustment mechanism, which we discuss below. Measures must be designed to assure holders of reserves in national currencies that their assets are not only secure but are also accessible in accordance with international law. Further consideration should be given to the role and working of private international money and capital markets in relation to offshore activities presently beyond the jurisdiction of central banks. Last but not least there is need for national policies which both curb inflation and achieve adequate rates of growth and rising employment levels, policies which have proved difficult to find. It is in the context of such an overall set of reforms and policies that the IMF 'surveillance' mechanism can be made to work. Exchange rate stability requires both discipline at home and international cooperation to maintain it.

The Reserve System

When gold reserves are officially valued at free market prices, as is done in some countries, they become a major element in most industrialized countries' official reserves. IMF figures for July 1979 suggest that under such valuation gold reserves could be SDR 210.7 billion as contrasted with foreign exchange reserves (SDR 233.4 billion), reserve position in the IMF (SDR 12.4 billion) and SDRs (12.4 billion). Because of the historical circumstances, developing countries have unfortunately not held much gold and therefore have not profited from the recent price increases. These increases have been a most erratic and inequitable element in expanding world liquidity.

The main source of expanding liquidity in the past three decades has been growth in official foreign exchange reserves, particularly in the form of US dollar assets. Between 1947 and 1967 when the dollar was fully convertible, the foreign exchange reserves held by national monetary authorities increased at a moderate rate – by $24 billion over the entire period. During the 'dollar flood' of 1970–71, these reserves grew by substantially more than they had grown in the previous twenty years; and over the remainder of the 1970s they grew by about a further $150 billion. Liquidity in the form of IMF-related assets has expanded, but its size is still quite limited. In mid-1979, reserve positions in the IMF and SDR allocations, as shown above, were about one-tenth of total reserves excluding gold.

While the aggregate value of world reserves has risen, their distribution has been highly concentrated and does not accord with any measure of reserve needs. The massive growth in commercial bank financing of short-term balance of payments requirements and of reserve creation is also concentrated in its distribution; the poorest countries have been insufficiently creditworthy to benefit from it.

The SDR: Advancing towards International Currency

The present reserve system is unsatisfactory. Expansion of world liquidity is erratic in both its volume and its distribution. The objective of the creation of Special Drawing Rights in 1968 was to begin to provide for an orderly increase in official reserves, which would reduce dependence on the dollar. But SDRs became only a small addition to, rather than a substitute for, reserve currency holdings. From 1970 to 1972 modest SDR allocations ($9.5 billion) were undertaken, while official foreign exchange reserves increased from $33 billion at the end of 1969 to $104 billion at the end of 1972.

An SDR is essentially a line of perpetual credit in the IMF on which member countries can draw, under certain conditions, to obtain the foreign currencies they need to settle their payments deficits. Its use is limited to central banks and treasuries, as well as the Bank for International Settlements (BIS). A participant in the SDR scheme cannot give foreign aid to another participant in SDRs, and until recently (1979) a participant could not lend SDRs to another or pledge its SDRs as security for a loan. But an SDR has one outstanding feature: it is the only means of meeting international payments which has been established through international contract; for gold and reserve currencies as reserve assets are created by unilateral action (production and sale of the metal, US running balance of payments deficits) and their status is based primarily on custom. The SDR therefore represents a clear first step towards a stable and permanent international currency.

After all the experience of the gold exchange standard for sterling and for the dollar, there is broad agreement today that the future international monetary system should not be reconstructed on the basis of any dominant national currency. Only if the participating countries agree on the means of creating world monetary reserves can they make possible the non-inflationary expansion of liquidity necessary to meet the needs of the expanding world economy. To this end, the Amendment of the IMF articles agreed to in Jamaica in 1976 enjoins each member to collaborate with the IMF and its other members in 'making the Special Drawing Right the principal reserve asset in the international monetary system'. But the SDR can only be the centrepiece of the international monetary system if it becomes the principal means of increasing global liquidity and if it is itself used to improve the adjustment mechanism. These changes, which in our view are desirable objectives, imply reducing the role of national reserve currencies and of gold, and improving the characteristics of the SDR. An SDR system would enable a broader and more equitable sharing among countries of the benefits and costs that accompany an international reserve currency. It would also avoid the danger of instability that comes from a multiplicity of reserve currencies.

By making the SDR the principal reserve asset, holders of international reserve currencies, especially the dollar, will have greater freedom to diversify the composition of their portfolios. This would avert the risk which countries run, when holding their external assets denominated in other currencies, of having those assets frozen. The countries with strong currencies (Federal Republic of Germany, Japan and Switzerland) are reluctant to assume the role of reserve currency countries. It is under these circumstances that the IMF has been exploring the idea of a 'substitution account', to enable private or official holders of unwanted dollars to swap them for SDRs or liquid SDR-denominated assets. The major issues that require ironing out are: how to share exchange risks, how to harmonize such substitution with the main aims of monetary reform, the size of the account and the technical characteristics regarding its operation, e.g. the relationship between new SDR assets and ordinary SDRs, their rate of interest, etc. For the substitution account to enhance the role of the SDR, it must be established in such a way that it avoids a possible future national reserve currency 'overhang' by ensuring a steady means of 'asset settlement'; thus imbalances of payments of any country should not in future be settled by using its own currency. At the 1979 annual meeting of the IMF at Belgrade these issues were discussed and the Interim Committee asked the Executive Board to continue to give priority to designing a Substitution Account.

Demonetizing Gold

The strengthening of SDRs as the principal reserve asset will also require a further demonetization of gold. At Jamaica in 1976, the

IMF agreed to abolish the official price of gold, to eliminate gold from all transactions between the member countries of the IMF and to dispose of one-third of the gold stock of the IMF; one-sixth of this gold was sold and one-sixth restored to members. Recent events in the gold market imply that the further demonetization of gold will depend upon more stable currencies and reducing inflation in the major countries. It will also be assisted by utilizing for the purpose of development the remaining IMF gold stock, which amounts to about 100 million ounces. This stock can be used as collateral against which the IMF can borrow from the market. Such borrowed funds could then be made available to developing countries in need of them, particularly the middle-income ones. At the same time, further staggered sales of some of the gold could be undertaken and accruing profits of such sales used as interest subsidy on loans to low-income developing countries. This will not affect the reserve value of the gold subscription since such gold is entered in members' reserve positions at the IMF book-value, and this valuation will be credited to the members' gold quota account.

The SDR should be made a more attractive reserve asset. A number of steps need to be taken into consideration. Its valuation will have to be put on a basis which will assure predictability and stability. In addition, present limits on its use should be relaxed, by making it as freely usable as other forms of reserves which central banks use. Such changes would encourage the valuation of oil, raw materials and other major international contracts in terms of SDRs, which some of the members of the Commission advocated.

Allocating SDRs

A system dominated by SDRs should be accompanied by a change in the IMF rules governing the distribution of liquidity. At Bretton Woods, a multipurpose quota was agreed upon which determined (a) the subscription or contribution of each member to the Fund, (b) the entitlement of each member to draw reserves and (c) the members' voting power and representation. Quotas were distributed on the basis of the perceived economic and political importance of countries rather than their demand for reserves as such; they were based on trade and international reserves including gold holdings. Only a small proportion of the quotas is available as unconditional liquidity such as SDRs provide. A more functional and equitable formula for SDR allocations is now required.

Reserves are generally held as a precautionary stock of international purchasing power; they are a means to finance future temporary balance of payments deficits. It is in the international interest – indeed it is a purpose of the IMF – that countries should be provided with adequate short-term resources so that they are not forced into measures which may be harmful not only to themselves but also to others by balance of payments pressures which are only temporary in their incidence. For this reason new reserves should be allocated to those countries which are most likely to experience balance of payments deficits and high domestic costs of adjustments, and least likely to be able to finance them from alternative sources. Many developing countries fit into these categories: a low level of development and a high concentration of primary production tend to increase both their export earnings instability and their costs of adjustment. At the same time, they have limited access to international capital markets, and relatively high opportunity costs of reserve acquisition. There is therefore a strong case based on efficiency as well as equity for a larger share of new unconditional reserves to be distributed to the developing countries than is achieved through allocations proportional to the IMF quota system. This is the underlying rationale for what is often referred to as an 'SDR link'.

Unfortunately the link with development assistance has often conjured up the spectre of increased liquidity creation with accompanying inflation. Our concept of a link would not involve creating any more SDRs than would be warranted by the *total* reserve needs of the world economy; nor does it mix aid with monetary issues. Given the prevailing rate of interest which is paid by users of SDRs, the concessional element of an SDR allocation is low. In response to fears that the distribution of SDRs such as we propose might tempt developing countries to demand a greater amount of SDRs allocated to them than would be warranted by prudent needs of world liquidity, it may be recalled that an 85 per cent majority in the IMF is at present required to allocate SDRs. But distributing SDRs more equitably, in a way which is not circumscribed by existing quotas, would provide the developing countries with more of the liquidity which they need and which others can acquire from other sources.

Financing Deficits

Some have argued that there is little need to increase official reserves as the market can play a key role in financing deficits. They see the 'invisible hand', in the form of the private banks, as providing the necessary additional discipline and pressures for adjustment as well as a responsive mechanism which automatically meets any legitimate demands for international credit and reserves. They regard official action as having only a secondary role as a supplement. We reject this view. We recognize that countries that are regarded as creditworthy by the market have received timely and substantial funds from the international capital markets. But the market has some major shortcomings. First, it adds to reserves, in the form of liabilities of national monetary authorities, through a mechanism which is very imperfectly subject to international monitoring let alone control, and is easily affected by crises of confidence. Consequently it has sometimes lurched from the provision of too much finance to particular countries to the provision of too little. Secondly, it is not easily accessible to the poorer developing countries. Thirdly, it tends, because of its terms, to exacerbate the problem of servicing and refinancing debt. Lastly, there are growing doubts as to the continuing availability of adequate private bank financing in the future, as banks' exposure in this kind of foreign lending increases.

It is noteworthy that the ratio of IMF quotas to world imports, which averaged about 10 per cent in the period 1960–65, is now down to little more than 4 per cent, though the sixth review of quotas has raised the level of quotas to SDR 39 billion and the proposed seventh review will increase them even further to SDR 58.6 billion. The ratio of official reserves to imports is below that of the 1960s; indeed, it is lower than in 1969 when one of the grounds for activating the SDR was the anticipated reserve shortage. This is in spite of the IMF decision to allocate SDR 4 billion per year for a second period, 1979–81. We therefore urge that the creation of SDRs should be continued in accordance with non-inflationary demand for world liquidity, in addition to the establishment of the substitution account.

The Adjustment Process

A reformed international monetary system must provide incentives and mechanisms for adjustment by both surplus and deficit countries. The world economy will always display payments imbalances and in the immediate future they are likely to be more severe because the costs of energy and grains are likely to go up and the terms of trade for other primary producers will worsen in recessionary conditions. Since deficits have their counterpart in surpluses, a reformed system must ensure that both surplus and deficit countries have some obligation to adjust. In the past it was only when deficit countries turned to the IMF for credit that adjustment mechanisms were internationally enforced. Means should therefore be devised, through the IMF or otherwise, to encourage countries in current account surpluses to make long-term loans to deficit countries that are undertaking needed adjustment. The IMF could also take the needs for international adjustment into account in future distribution of SDRs by reducing those distributed to surplus countries and assigning them instead largely to developing ones. This would enhance the SDR link – a link that assists the process of adjustment. The establishment of an SDR-based system, including a satisfactory mechanism for asset settlement, would provide the necessary discipline for the reserve currency countries.

The Resources of the IMF

One purpose of the IMF, in terms of its statutes, is to 'give confidence to members by making the general resources of the Fund temporarily available to them under adequate safeguards, thus providing them with opportunities to correct maladjustments in their balance of payments without resorting to measures destructive of national or international prosperity'. These general resources of the IMF are made up of several regular 'facilities', including since 1974 the Extended Fund Facility, the specialized facilities (the Compensatory Financing Facility and the Buffer Stock Facility), the Supplementary Financing Facility and the Trust Fund. During the emergency period between 1974 and 1975 there was also an Oil Facility, and a Subsidy Account to reduce interest charges for the most seriously affected countries was established. These facilities can be regarded as different 'windows' of the Fund. Some of them – the Oil Facility and the Supplementary Financing Facility – are a result of official borrowing; the Trust Fund receives profits from the gold sales. The remaining facilities get their resources from members' subscriptions, which are augmented periodically through quota increases. In financial terms, as of 31 December 1978, the total cumulative use of the Fund's resources by all its members since it began in 1946 was as follows: the regular facilities – about SDR 37 billion; the oil facilities – SDR 6.9 billion; the specialized facilities – about SDR 4.4 billion; and the Trust Fund – SDR 0.84 billion. In recent years, non-oil-exporting developing countries have drawn relatively large amounts from the Fund's specialized facilities, particularly the Compensatory Financing and Oil Facilities, which together accounted in mid-1979 for over half of their total outstanding drawings on the IMF. It will be apparent that the resources of the Fund are modest. In 1977 and 1978 members actually repaid more than they borrowed. Access to these resources, however, requires considerable justification. The 'conditionality' of the IMF governs not only the circumstances of borrowing but more significantly the policies which a country is required to pursue during the loan period.

The IMF's Policy Conditions

It is necessary and legitimate for the IMF to lay down conditions for the members who borrow from it. There must be normal bankers' prudence and, in the IMF's case, the need to ensure the 'revolving character' of its resources. Any banker must satisfy himself that borrowers will be in a position to repay and, when a country borrows a large sum relative to its reserves, its ability to pay may depend considerably on its macro-economic policies. Many IMF loans, especially to members with small quotas, provide only a small proportion of a country's requirements. A degree of conditionality is inevitable and would generally be acceptable to borrowers. But over the years the IMF has imposed such rigorous conditions that deficit countries have failed to make use of their quotas or made use of them too late, preferring the private international banks instead. The conditional resources that the Fund can make available – limited as they are – have been greatly under-utilized. The drawings on special facilities such as the Oil and Compensatory Financing Facilities which accounted for so much of the Fund's provision of credit in the period 1973–8 are subject to relatively little conditionality.

The developing countries – and also on occasion some industrial member countries including Italy and the United Kingdom – have been critical of the IMF's conditionality. They feel that the Fund has tended to impose conditions which go beyond its legitimate interests of ensuring that it gets its money back on the due date within the framework of the Fund's Articles, since these can be satisfied by far less rigorous programmes. Many member countries find that the IMF has used its unique position in a paternalist way – proposing policies which it sees as likely to be effective. The IMF has formulated these policies on the basis of a monetary approach to balance of payments analysis, an approach which generates too uniform and rigid conclusions on the required timing and content of programmes. In practice the Fund often seems to assume that

215

any country that needs to borrow conditional liquidity must have been incompetent or careless at running its affairs and is therefore likely to benefit from some guidance from a disinterested party. But many borrowing countries do not accept this assumption.

The credit conditions of the IMF thus normally presume that balance of payments problems are a result of too much domestic demand and can be solved by balancing the budget, curbing the money supply, cutting subsidies and setting a realistic exchange rate. Sometimes these measures are appropriate and have been effective. But in many cases these measures reduce domestic consumption without improving investment; productive capacity sometimes falls even more sharply than consumption. This is because many developing countries with deficits have a shortage of food or of basic consumer goods or cannot readily shift resources in line with their new needs. Indeed, the Fund's insistence on drastic measures, often within the time framework of only one year, has tended to impose unnecessary and unacceptable political burdens on the poorest, on occasion leading to 'IMF riots' and even the downfall of governments.

Needing Time for Adjustment

Many developing countries now face many pressures on their balance of payments which are outside their control. The unprecedented prices of oil, grains and capital goods, the slackening of business activity and hence of import demand in the industrial countries, and the protectionism of industrial countries against imports from developing countries have all affected their balance of payments. The deficits for which a government can be held responsible should surely be distinguished from those that are due to short-term factors beyond its control. Where external influences impose the need for longer-term adjustments, as in the case of oil prices, special consideration must be given to the poor countries, since they will experience greater difficulties in undertaking them.

We are aware that the IMF itself continues to give attention to these issues. In 1979, new guidelines were issued, authorizing the liberalization of its conditions in order to 'pay due regard to the domestic, social and political objectives of member countries', and permit longer periods of adjustment. At its annual meeting in Belgrade in October 1979 the Development Committee requested the Executive Board to give further consideration to raising the repayment period of the Extended Fund Facility from eight to ten years and to introduce arrangements that will provide subsidies against the interest cost of resources drawn on the Supplementary Financing Facility. While the new IMF lending guidelines already seek to limit the imposition of performance criteria to those necessary for adjustment programmes, we believe that the Fund should generally restrict detailed regulation and endeavour to place the process of adjustment (including the rate of adjustment) in the context of maintaining long-term economic and social development.

This implies, among other things, that conditions for lending requiring deflationary adjustment – including devaluation policies – should not be imposed by the IMF unless it justifies such action in detail by assessing the probable consequences of deflationary policies for income distribution, employment and social services; and that programmes of adjustment should be more often formulated for periods longer than one year. Because adjustments in developing countries often require more time than the Fund's relatively short-term lending facilities now provide, we suggest later a substantial expansion in programme lending by other international institutions. We also think that the IMF should increase the level of its lending relative to the member's requirements. This might attract members to approach the Fund at the onset of their problems. If the IMF is truly to take broader domestic development objectives into account, it should also recruit and promote more people from developing countries with appropriate qualifications and sensitivity to the problems involved.

Enlarging Compensatory Financing

An important proposal in support of the adjustment of deficit developing countries is the further expansion and improvement of the Compensatory Financing Facility, which assists countries over problems which are clearly not of their own making. This facility has been recently reviewed by the IMF Executive Board. Nevertheless, the Commission urges the IMF to consider the removal of quota-based limits to drawings on this facility because the entitlement of members to draw on it should be a function of their need to compensate for export shortfalls. In addition to export shortfalls, the IMF should also take into account movements in import prices as the rationale for balance of payments lending is in fact to forestall the need for harmful cutbacks in the flow of imports which may otherwise adversely affect development plans. This is particularly important at those times when there are sharp changes in the prices of major imports and there is persistent world inflation. Coverage should also be expanded to take care of cases of harvest failure. There is also need to make repayment terms flexible, so that they are linked to the changes in the borrowers' capacity to repay.

If quota limits are removed, if the coverage is enlarged to include food import requirements or other major causes of deficits beyond the country's control, if shortfalls are measured in real terms and if repayments are more flexible, the IMF Compensatory Financing Facility might require much greater funding, which we estimate at about $12 billion, three times its present size.

Power Sharing

The Bretton Woods international monetary system reflected the economic and political relations of the time. Since then much has changed – and the new system should reflect the changing political and economic circumstances of nations. The new international monetary system should have a pluralistic basis, in which no single political entity or small group of entities plays a predominant role. The EEC, the United States and the developing countries already constitute groupings within the IMF. Fairly soon one might expect China to take its rightful place. It is also not unreasonable to expect the Comecon countries to have an interest in joining a global monetary system since these countries increasingly use western convertible currencies and the international market as a basis for the pricing of important transactions among themselves – thus in effect participating in the IMF system without any opportunity of influencing its further development. This means that a broad-based leadership should be established to manage the international monetary system, including provision for a growing role for the developing countries in the decision-making process.

Such a collective leadership can be established if there are clear, fair and explicit rules for managing the system – rules which will protect the interests of all members of the system including the weaker ones. Such rules must ensure that the Fund is not wholly administered on the basis of shareholding. There is hardly any central bank today which is so administered. This is an inevitable consequence of entrusting the role of issuing international means of payment to the IMF. The proposals presented above provide the framework within which such a system of rules – flexible enough to meet changing circumstances but strong enough to assure predictability – can be undertaken. The reform process must be urgently reinitiated.

Recommendations

The reform of the international monetary system should be urgently undertaken by all interested parties building on the large measure of consensus which emerged in the Committee of Twenty, and taking account of current difficulties and dangers. Reform involves improvements in the exchange rate regime, the reserve system, the balance of payments adjustment process; and the overall management of the system which should permit the participation of the whole international community.

Mechanisms should be agreed for creating and distributing an international currency to be used for clearing and settling outstanding balances between central banks. Such a currency would replace the use of national currencies as international reserves. It could take the form of an improved Special Drawing Right, and could be facilitated by an appropriately designed 'substitution account'.

New SDRs should be created to the extent called for by the need for non-inflationary increases in world liquidity. The distribution of such unconditional liquidity should favour the developing countries who presently bear high adjustment burdens. Such a distribution – often referred to as an SDR link – would also assist the adjustment process of the international monetary system.

There should be agreement on an adjustment process which will not increase contractionist pressures in the world economy. The adjustment process of developing countries should be placed in the context of maintaining long-term economic and social development. The IMF should avoid inappropriate or excessive regulation of their economies, and should not impose highly deflationary measures as standard adjustment policy. It should also improve and greatly extend the scope of its compensatory financing facility, for example by relaxing quota limits, measuring shortfalls in real terms and making repayment terms more flexible. Surplus countries should accept greater responsibility for payments adjustments, and IMF measures to encourage this should be considered.

Increased stability of international exchange rates, particularly among key currencies, should be sought through domestic discipline and coordination of appropriate national policies.

The participation of developing countries in the staffing, management and decision-making of the IMF should be enlarged.

In furthering the demonetization of gold, the bulk of the IMF gold stock should, after the completion of the present sales arrangements, be used as collateral against which the IMF can borrow from the market for onward lending particularly to middle-income developing countries. Staggered sales should also be undertaken and accruing profits of such sales should be used as interest subsidy on loans to low-income developing countries.

14 Development Finance: Unmet Needs

The developing countries obtain finance from a number of sources: government-to-government aid programmes and export credit agencies; international financial institutions, including the World Bank Group and Regional Development Banks, the IMF, the UN agencies and other multilateral funds; private investment, much of it by multinational corporations; and commercial banks. The creation and expansion of the system of financing development in recent decades amounts to a major change in international economic cooperation.

The Third World will have enormous financial requirements in the next few decades. We have surveyed the large unmet needs, particularly in the poorer countries, in food production, industrialization, development of energy and minerals, transport and communications, education and health. The developing countries' economic growth has slowed down from 6 per cent a year during 1967–72 to 5 per cent in the mid-1970s, and probably below that in the last three years. However great their own efforts, huge sums will be needed to enable the countries of the South to regain their momentum, to provide the jobs and incomes to overcome poverty, and to enable them to become more self sufficient and to take a fuller part in the world's trading system.

The Channels for Aid

For the transfer of official funds there are two main channels: one flows directly between the countries concerned, and the other goes through the multilateral institutions. UN agencies receive their funds from donor governments. The World Bank gets some of its funds directly from governments, particularly those for its soft loans through the International Development Association (IDA) window; the rest of its money is borrowed on the world's capital markets, under guarantees provided by the subscriptions of the member governments. The Regional Development Banks have a similar structure.

A very big change has occurred in the composition of the total flows to the developing countries. In 1960, 60 per cent came from concessional aid or Official Development Assistance (ODA). By 1977, more than two-thirds was commercial, mainly from private bank loans, direct investment and export credits. The debt burdens of a number of countries have become extremely heavy. Both the amounts and types of available finance are now clearly inadequate. And the uncertainty of future flows threatens progress in development.

Most official assistance, whether bilateral or multilateral, covers the foreign exchange cost of specific investment projects: dams, power stations, railway and road systems, industrial projects, rural development schemes. Little is made available for 'programme lending', for national development programmes as a whole, which can support the entire set of projects and activities of a country in the face of low savings and fluctuating fiscal revenue and foreign exchange. The developing countries as well as many experts – including the Pearson Commission – have laid great stress on the need for this type of finance, which gives more flexibility and certainty to overall economic management. Similarly lacking is support for financing exports, particularly capital goods; and for economic integration between developing countries, through financing of payments arrangements. The issue of adequate finance for commodity price stabilization is still not fully settled; the refinancing of debts is handled in an *ad hoc* manner.

Growing Debts

The better-off developing countries have been able to overcome a number of these problems with funds from commercial sources, mainly loans from banks and export credits. One of the most dramatic changes in recent years has been the increase in the loans of the international private market, which now account for nearly 40 per cent of the outstanding debt of developing countries, compared to only 17 per cent in 1970. Most of the private loans have gone to a few middle-income countries, helping them increase rapidly their investment, output and exports, giving these countries the freely usable foreign exchange which they need – not tied to individual projects, to orders from particular countries, or to any specific economic policy. But there are also drawbacks to these private loans as a method of financing. Their terms (though they improved in 1977 and 1978) have meant that the countries have to meet heavy debt-servicing burdens. In the three-year period 1979–81 the aggregate payments for servicing the debts of all developing countries excluding OPEC are estimated at $120 billion – on top of the sharply rising trade deficits. As we show below, the borrowing needs of these countries are likely to rise considerably further in the 1980s. As the loans fall due, they need to borrow more in order to repay and service them. The debtor economies and the entire international credit structure are now very vulnerable to any disruptions in the flows of capital, which can be caused by a greater demand for credit in the North, by a borrowing country being regarded as less creditworthy, by insufficient bank capital, or by the actions of regulatory authorities.

The heart of the debt problem is that a very large proportion of funds are lent on terms which are onerous for borrowers from the point of view of both the repayment capacity of the projects they finance and the time debtor countries need to correct structural imbalances in their external accounts. The debt servicing record of developing countries has been excellent on the whole and payments crises have been rare. But there are likely to be more difficulties with payments in the future. Already between 1974 and 1978 many more countries were in arrears on their current payments, or were renegotiating – or trying to renegotiate – their debts with private banks. These banks may be able to expand their credit still further; but the risks and constraints of the present unbalanced structure of debts will mean that developing countries must look for new sources of long-term finance. As we discuss in the next chapter, with trade deficits rising sharply and with the leading banks already highly exposed, there is great concern that the international banking system, which has played a crucial role in channelling OPEC and other surpluses to the deficit countries in the last five years, should be able to perform the same role in the future.

Relationships

It is not only the volume and kinds of finance which are inadequate: it is also the relationships between borrowers and lenders. The developing countries do not have an adequate share of responsibility for decision-making, control and management of the existing international financial and monetary institutions. The latter have made significant contributions to development through their lending and technical assistance. At the same time, they have been hesitant to engage in some of the activities of critical importance to developing countries, as we shall describe. Many countries also have misgivings about the involvement of some of these institutions in the determination of their domestic policies and priorities, which has in some cases gone beyond what could be justified by the need to protect current loans and guarantee their responsible use. Further, the major international financial institutions have not been able to secure universal membership. The USSR and most of the countries of Eastern Europe are not members, and the People's Republic of China has so far not taken its place in these institutions. The lack of universality, in addition to its political cost, deprives countries of the benefits of learning from each other's development experience and curtails the scope of international assistance.

Official Aid: A Disappointing Record

The poorer and weaker countries have not been able to raise much money on commercial terms. For them, Official Development Assistance or aid is the principal source of funds. While the needs for concessional finance have been growing, the actual flows have faltered. It was a decade ago that the United Nations resolved on the objective of one per cent of the gross national product of developed countries for the net transfer of resources to developing countries, including private flows, and within it 0.7 per cent as a target for official development assistance. The ratio between these two figures reflected the relative flows at that time and the ODA target was largely a political goal. At the time this target was discussed, most of the industrialized countries accepted it, some with a time frame (e.g. Belgium, the Netherlands, Sweden) and others in principle (e.g. Federal Republic of Germany). But some others, most notably the United States, did not commit themselves to the target.

While the one-per-cent norm for overall net flows (including private investment and commercial lending) has been reached, the hopes aroused for the ODA target have been dashed. The average performance in this respect of the industrialized countries in the OECD was only 0.35 per cent of GNP in 1978. This is a deeply disappointing record. At the same time, we must point out that a number of individual countries, such as the Scandinavian countries and the Netherlands, have exceeded the target. It is very encouraging that the OPEC countries have, with their increased oil revenues in recent years, contributed nearly 3 per cent of their

GNP. Their effort is specially noteworthy because, in their case, aid does not result in export orders to the donors. On the other hand, the United States contribution has fallen from 0.5 per cent in 1960 to 0.27 per cent. Japan at 0.23 per cent and the Federal Republic of Germany at 0.38 per cent also remain at low levels, although they had accepted the target in principle. Also disappointing is that the average performance of the Soviet Union and other CMEA countries, according to OECD estimates, has been only of the order of 0.04 per cent of their GNP.

Relative performance between different countries in meeting this target is a matter on which hard and fast comparisons may not be in order. Some donors have argued that while their aid performance has been low, their trade policies are liberal; some who have shown better performance also include expenditures on overseas commitments which in a proper reckoning should not qualify as aid; some donors allocate their aid as far as possible on need-based criteria; others concentrate theirs on countries with whom they have special historical, commercial or other ties. Assistance from the eastern countries has been available for public sector, industrial and resource sectors for which aid from other sources has been unavailable and they take goods in repayment of debt. These clarifications are important but they do not contradict the position that the industrialized countries as a whole, and the major ones among them, have failed to fulfil expectations and commitments.

This failure points to a marked lack of political will. We must face this issue squarely. In the annual aid reviews in the Development Assistance Committee (DAC), governments with poor aid performance often plead budgetary constraints and balance of payments difficulties, but it is clear that these are not insuperable obstacles. When GNP in industrial countries increases by 3 to 4 per cent a year, the allocation of one-fortieth to one-thirtieth of the annual *increase* in GNP to foreign aid would close the gap between 0.3 and 0.7 per cent in only five years. The pressure on public funds is always intense, as our experience makes us well aware, but what the neglect of foreign aid expresses is ultimately the lack of political priority attached to it.

Why More Aid Is Essential

We have been informed that in many countries the political climate is at present unfavourable to an increase in aid, with a range of serious domestic problems looming large. But this climate must be changed. Citizens of rich countries must be brought to understand that the problems of the world must be tackled too, and that a vigorous aid policy would in the end not be a burden but an investment in a healthier world economy as well as in a safer world community. International development issues must be given the attention at a high political level that their urgency entitles them to.

Public opinion in industrial countries has often been critical of aid. Some developing countries are highly inegalitarian, and there have been doubts whether aid was getting through to the poor. The mass media have given much publicity to cases of waste, corruption, and extravagance, and the resulting scepticism creates resistance to the aid-giving intentions of governments. There is no doubt that the use of aid can and should be made more effective. At the same time it would be wrong not to recognize that the overwhelming proportion of aid money is usefully spent on the purposes for which it is intended, and aid has already done much to diminish hardships in low-income countries and to help them provide a basis for progress in rural development, health and education. For the poorest countries, aid is essential to survival.

Fortunately there have recently been signs of a more favourable attitude to aid in some major countries as the importance of the Third World is slowly beginning to be more clearly perceived. Japan not long ago announced a doubling of its aid programme. The Federal Republic of Germany is increasing its aid. The French government is raising some parts of its multilateral assistance. A new and important source of aid in the 1970s has been the OPEC members which supplied about 20 per cent of all Official Development Assistance in 1978. This represents an average of 1.59 per cent of their GNP; but individual countries such as Saudi Arabia, Kuwait, the United Arab Emirates and Qatar have provided between 6 to 15 per cent of their GNP in past years, and between 4 and 5 per cent in 1978. Besides OPEC a number of other developing countries have in recent years provided assistance. So far most of this has taken the form of scholarships and the provision of technical assistance experts, but India, Yugoslavia and some Latin American countries are also extending financial assistance. The People's Republic of China although itself a developing country has also given significant aid to several other developing countries.

We argue below that an increase in total aid must remain a high priority for alleviating the worst deprivation in the developing world. The spreading practice of development aid makes us think the time has come to consider a universal system of contributions, based on present targets for the richest countries but also providing for contributions from all other countries, except the poorest, on a sliding scale related to income. This would be an expression of shared responsibility for international development. We return to this proposal later.

Gaps in Financing Development

As we have suggested, there are a variety of shortcomings in the network of development finance which taken together show the need for a number of fundamental changes. The overall flow of finance must increase, in the interests both of the Third World and the world economy. The poorest countries urgently need more concessional aid; the middle-income countries need loans on longer maturities. Types of finance which are currently difficult or impossible to obtain must become available in significant volumes. Loans for development need to be in more flexible forms and on a longer-term basis. Developing countries need better access, if necessary through intermediaries, to capital markets. And relations between borrowers and lenders must be improved. Multilateral institutions need to be restructured to enable the Third World to participate effectively in their management and control.

It is also urgent to fill the serious gaps in the existing financial flows to the developing world. We analyse these gaps from three perspectives: the needs of different groups of countries; sectors of activity; types of lending. The Commission has taken into account reliable estimates that have been made by international institutions. These requirements do not all add up to a total. There is a considerable area of overlap between needs related to country-groups and those identified in sectoral terms. Types of lending are a separate dimension. Our main purpose in this review of gaps is essentially to illustrate the nature, magnitude and high priority of unmet needs and to argue that a massive global effort is necessary to meet them. In the light of this analysis we go on to discuss, in the following chapter, which institutions and measures are most appropriate to meet the needs and fill the gaps.

Country Needs

Least developed, low-income and lower middle-income countries
The low-income countries, which contain most of the world's poor people, have a very limited capacity, as we have seen, to participate in the world economy. They depend on exports of primary

commodities; their agriculture is frequently threatened by drought; they have a thin margin between income and consumption; and their domestic savings are necessarily low. Looking into the future, the prospects for their food supplies are alarming. They need massive investments in irrigation and agriculture to avoid dangerous food deficits towards the end of the decade; and large outlays for improving health, nutrition and literacy.

The poverty belts of Asia and Africa need long-gestation projects for such purposes as water management, hydropower, transport, mining, afforestation, the prevention of soil erosion and desertification, and the elimination of diseases. These tasks alone will require extra finance of at least $4 billion a year over at least twenty years.

Whatever criteria are used, existing assistance to the poorer countries is inadequate, in both investment and recurrent spending. If present levels of assistance are merely continued, there cannot be much progress in meeting essential needs, and an annual growth in income per head of only one per cent in low-income Africa and only 2.8 per cent in low-income Asia would be possible. This, according to the World Bank's 1979 *World Development Report*, would actually widen the gap in living standards between the poor and the rich countries (from 1:40 in 1975 to 1:47 by 1990) even if the poor countries were to increase their savings sharply – an unacceptable situation. The aggregate needs of all the least developed countries for external capital are estimated by UNCTAD at $11 billion annually during the 1980s, and $21 billion during the 1990s, to support a 6.5 per cent rate of GDP growth (3.5 per cent *per capita*). For the poorest countries the assistance should be highly concessional.

According to a study for the Overseas Development Council in Washington, countries with an income per head of below $520 (least developed, low-income and lower middle-income) will need annual aid in the 1980s in the range of $40–54 billion (in 1980 dollars), either for achieving a 3.5 to 4 per cent growth in *per capita* income, or for obtaining resources equal to half the costs of meeting essential human needs, the other half being borne by the countries themselves. If 1980 aid were no higher in real terms than in 1977, it would fall short of adequacy for such objectives by $21–35 billion. If this shortfall could be met in the early 1980s low-income and lower middle-income developing countries could tackle the worst forms of poverty, and they could finance industrial and agricultural projects, imports of raw materials, fertilizers, equipment and spare parts. Such assistance will have to be concessional but it need not be all in the form of grants, except for the least developed countries. Depending on circumstances, the transfers can be a blend of different types of finance – soft loans like those provided by IDA, bilateral long-term low-interest development loans, interest-subsidized market loans, export credits. Food aid may also play an important part. Developing countries will need project loans, which where appropriate can finance local currency costs; and also programme loans, to complement project lending and to meet maintenance needs.

Middle-income and higher-income countries

The middle-income and higher-income developing countries need development loans on terms and in forms which suit their stage of development. Their total borrowing requirements will be affected by the growth and openness of markets for their exports. They need improvement in the maturity structure of their debts. They need longer-term programme finance. Some lower middle-income countries will also need interest subsidization.

According to World Bank projections (which assume annual inflation of 7.2 per cent), borrowing by these countries from commercial banks and other private sources will be needed at a level of $155 billion in the year 1985 (in current dollars) compared to less than $40 billion annually in 1975-7. By 1990 it will be as much as $270 billion. Even this may turn out to be an underestimate: the projected rate of growth of exports in the 1980s (6.3 per cent) may be too high in the light of the present prospects for the world economy, and oil prices have been assumed constant at their 1975 levels in real terms, although this assumption is already out of date. In any case, much more official lending is needed to reduce the pressure on the international credit structure and the associated risks; and to reduce the difficulties of the middle-income countries in servicing their debts. Their financing problems should also be tackled through other means, including better access to the bond markets of industrialized countries. Their debt service ratio (the proportion of their exports absorbed by servicing debts), which in 1977 averaged 9.2 per cent and already exceeded 20 per cent for a few countries, is now projected almost to double from 1975-7 to 1990. If these countries are to receive adequate funds, at the right time and on terms that they can reasonably repay, there can be no substitute for a major expansion of public lending, mostly in the form of programme loans.

Sector Needs
We now turn to the financial needs of the different sectors in the developing world, giving specific estimates for the capital needs in some sectors – agriculture, industry, energy and minerals – which also form part of the aggregate needs of countries which have been discussed above.

Food and agriculture
Rural development has already received much support, but the low-income food-importing countries need urgent assistance. The International Food Policy Research Institute (IFPRI) has estimated that, without more help, the gap between the production and consumption of cereals, which amounted to 37 million tons in 1975, may reach 120–145 million tons by 1990. Such huge shortages could cause mass starvation, besides seriously adding to world inflation. It is estimated that foreign aid to support half the capital spending, and 20 per cent of the recurring costs, for increasing agricultural production in low-income countries with food deficits should amount to $12 billion (1975 dollars) annually in the 1980s, calling for additional foreign aid of $8.5 billion (or $13 billion in 1980 dollars). Of this, 70 per cent would be for producing staple foods, and the balance for other agricultural spending. Some of the finance, particularly for financing recurring costs of imports of fertilizers and pesticides, should be in the form of programme loans on concessional terms.

Industry
To reach the Lima target for industrialization in the Third World would require an annual growth rate in manufacturing value added of 10–11 per cent: UNIDO has estimated that this would need a total annual investment of $40–60 billion between 1980 and 1990, and $120–140 billion between 1990 and 2000. Approximately 60 per cent of these sums would finance the imports of capital goods, technology and engineering services, including 10 per cent to finance training and technical assistance. If foreign financing is to meet fully the foreign exchange component of the projects, industry in the Third World would need $25–35 billion from abroad annually over the next decade. At present it obtains (as estimated by UNIDO) about $10 billion annually.

A large part of these extra funds will have to be borrowed from official agencies. Only some ten to fifteen developing countries in Latin America and South East Asia have received major direct investment by multinational corporations. Most countries in the past have financed industrial investment through export credits from the industrialized countries and by borrowing from the market; but the repayment terms have been short, and credit has frequently been very expensive. The poorer countries, as noted, have had only limited access to private funds. Most official aid has gone to such purposes as agriculture and infrastructure, and industry has not received adequate support. For a long time the multilateral development banks refused to finance government-owned industry altogether; they have recently made more finance available for industry, but still not enough to cover rising needs.

Energy and minerals

The need to finance exploration and development of energy and minerals is now increasingly recognized. The World Bank and Regional Development Banks are expanding or planning to expand in these fields, but there remain large gaps. For oil and gas alone the non-OPEC developing countries need additional annual capital of roughly $14 billion in the 1980s (at 1980 prices). This investment would need official multilateral loans of at least $3.3 billion a year, to finance two-thirds of the exploration costs and 20 per cent of the production costs. For coal, annual lending of $0.4–0.6 billion might support investment in exploration and production of $2–3 billion a year. The total extra finance required from multilateral sources for oil, gas and coal would thus be at least $4 billion per year: the balance would have to come from domestic sources and from the private capital market, supported through co-financing. Further large-scale finance is required to develop renewable sources of energy, particularly hydro-electric and solar.

For non-fuel minerals there are no precise estimates of investment needs, whether present or future; but the gap in external financing may be about $9 billion to enable the balance of the funds to be raised. Thus oil, gas, coal and minerals between them will need external finance of at least $6.5 billion per annum, plus finance for renewable sources of energy which are so far unquantifiable, but still vital for the future.

These projects will be spread between different groups of countries – least developed, other low-income and middle-income – but many would be in the poorer countries which contain both minerals and large populations, and they will thus help to alleviate poverty. Financing exploration will generally need to be concessional, perhaps with grants for unsuccessful exploration; finance for investment will have to take into account the country's capacity to repay; market loans, interest-subsidized lending and official assistance will need to be appropriately blended.

Missing Types of Finance

For reasons which are partly historical, partly based on the self-interest of donors and partly due to an inadequate understanding of the role of external resources in helping development, most of the official finance which developing countries get is earmarked for the purchase of capital goods from outside. In the initial stages aid was no more than an extension of credits which industrialized countries were providing to promote the export of their capital goods, taking the shape of additions to such credits and the improvement of credit terms. The popularity of monumental projects, both in donor and recipient countries, further strengthened the trend. What was overlooked was that the shortage of domestic capital which creates the need for external resources is not identical with the gap in the capacity to pay for imported capital goods. The poorer developing countries need external finance to cover their local currency expenditure if they are to avoid inflationary pressures and balance of payments difficulties.

We now turn to the types of official finance which are lacking or difficult to obtain: programme loans, which provide long-term capital not specifically linked to projects and improve the structure of debt; export credits for capital goods; support of economic integration; finance for stabilizing commodity prices. They are the means of meeting some of the needs of countries and sectors which we have discussed. We discuss each type of finance below.

Programme lending

The most serious gap is in programme lending – that is, providing flexibly usable funds which are not tied to specific investment projects. Most bilateral and multilateral financing is available only for projects, as we have said; but project loans on their own are inefficient in facilitating an adequate transfer of resources. They are disbursed very slowly. In the experience of the World Bank, there is almost a ten-year cycle on average from the first identification of a project to its completion.

An exclusive reliance on project lending also produces certain important biases: firstly, it favours large projects over small, since lending agencies have a minimum threshold size of operations, to keep down their administrative costs. Secondly, it favours new fixed investment, rather than using existing capacity more efficiently, since working capital (labour and raw materials) is not normally eligible for project finance. Thirdly, the specification of projects and the tying procedures of agencies may encourage capital-intensive processes, which may not suit the developing country. Fourthly, the industrialized countries and the lending agencies from time to time change their views on development priorities; this leads to changing preferences for the type of projects they want to finance, often irrespective of the developing countries' own priorities.

Project and programme lending are in fact complementary. Programme lending corrects some of the distortions which come from relying exclusively on project lending. Firstly, programme loans are disbursed quickly, normally over two or three years. When these loans finance imports which are sold on the domestic market, they generate local currency for the government. Thus they can help to finance the local costs of projects and accelerate their execution. Secondly, programme lending, by providing more flexible funds, can encourage self-reliance. A country may have its own industrial plants which may make it unnecessary to use scarce foreign funds on importing capital goods. Or a country may have a large excess industrial capacity from previous investments, which it cannot put into full production because it lacks foreign exchange; and this need cannot be met by project lending, which aims to create new capacity. In both cases, programme loans help to provide jobs and raise incomes throughout the economy. Thirdly, developing countries also need the long-term support of programme loans for undertaking changes which cannot be achieved through project lending alone – including building up their social infrastructure, administration and management, or diversifying economies which depend too heavily on a few commodities or minerals.

Expanded programme loans would help to lighten the debt burden especially if it involves the lengthening of maturities. Developing countries need foreign exchange to adjust to balance of payments difficulties which can arise from a variety of causes outside their control. These cannot be treated as projects; but if they are not adequately met, the whole development programme will be jeopardized. The distinction between temporary support for 'adjustment', which should normally be provided by the IMF, and longer-term borrowing is often blurred. In real life, a country's needs for short-, medium- and long-term external finance do not fall into tidy compartments; the line of demarcation is a shifting one. If finance for adjustment is available too little and too late, the only solution for a developing country is a quick correction, which curtails growth, lowers wages, reduces employment and worsens income distribution. It is particularly serious for the poorer and weaker countries who cannot borrow from commercial banks, and who need long-term programme lending. What is needed essentially is a bridge between the long-term project financing available from such institutions as the World Bank and the short-term adjustment finance available from the IMF. Without this kind of bridge, in the form of long-term programme lending, developing countries have often slid back on their development programmes or have depended too heavily on commercial loans, jeopardizing their future capacity to borrow.

In highlighting these aspects of programme *vis-à-vis* project lending, we are not unaware that the industrialized countries of the North and the East have preferred to lend money to identifiable projects whose successful completion can be monitored and benefits from which can be clearly discerned. They have been apprehensive that general-purpose lending for balance of payments support might enable, if not encourage, diversion of foreign exchange to arms purchases, waste or misuse. They feel that the monitoring of the use of programme loans will raise very sensitive questions in borrower-creditor relationships, questions which both parties would prefer to avoid. The receiving countries, on the other hand, see the overwhelming emphasis on project loans as a constraint on their self-reliant development, and worse, as one more instance of lack of trust. We recognize this difference in perceptions but we believe that it should be possible to avoid this conflict. It should be feasible for programme lending to supplement and complement project lending, and for it to be related to well-conceived, clearly defined development programmes, the fulfilment of which can be monitored. In many developing countries, domestic public financing institutions such as industrial and agricultural development banks could be more extensively used as channels for external support to sectors and programmes. Later, we also deal with changes in international institutional structures that are necessary to build greater trust and confidence between borrowers and lenders.

Export finance
The developing countries need support for providing export credits, particularly for capital goods. The market for capital goods is highly competitive: not only in the price, quality, after-sale service and speed of delivery of the goods, but also in the availability and cost of export credit finance. A number of developing countries are now exporting capital goods and others are developing the potential to do so. To sell them, the exporters

have to extend medium-term credit for which, being deficit countries, they need refinancing. Some developing countries in recent years have provided export credit finance, but further rapid growth of their capital goods exports would strain their institutions.

There have been many initiatives for refinancing schemes, but they have not been followed up. Only the Inter-American Development Bank can refinance export credits for capital goods, mainly within Latin America; and a new Latin American Export Credit Bank, with a modest equity participation of the International Finance Corporation, plans to refinance short- and medium-term credit for non-traditional goods. One effect of giving broad support to export credit finance would be to stimulate trade among developing countries and their economic cooperation.

Economic integration

Developing countries need financial support to increase trade among themselves. Economic integration has long been a principal objective, intended to ensure closer cooperation and expansion of trade. But many integration schemes have achieved only slow progress, or have retrogressed. This has sometimes been due to political causes, but is also partly due to the balance of payments difficulties of the participants. Liberalizing trade under such schemes often creates payments deficits for one or more members vis-à-vis other partners. The difficulty can be overcome by expanding mutual credit through payments arrangements, but external assistance is needed when the partners, despite intra-group surpluses, have difficulty with overall payments and have individually little access to external finance. More generally, there is need for the periodic settlement of balances from intra-trade, and such payments will require outside finance. This can be provided by programme lending if it is on an adequate scale.

Commodity stabilization

In the chapter on commodities we have argued the case for more commodity agreements and for financing national stocks. Finance is urgently needed to stabilize the prices of primary products of developing countries, and to assure a price floor. Without this they cannot improve their external economic situation, and stable commodity export prices for the poor countries would also help to sustain their demand for manufactured goods and promote assured supplies of raw materials. This need has been recognized for a long time but no decisive action has been taken and unstable prices and earnings still dislocate the world economy. The weak economies which are heavily dependent on a few primary exports are especially vulnerable. This will entail larger capital support to the Common Fund in the course of time, or increased programme lending.

Relationships and Institutions

We are not the first to have drawn attention to the missing elements in the structure of financing. Their common feature is that they involve difficult and sensitive policy issues in the economic and political relationships between North and South. Whether it is programme lending, or commodity stabilization, or promotion of developing countries' exports, or finance to enable them to cooperate with each other more effectively – all of these, in their several ways, singly and together, are forms of finance which would enable the poor countries to become more self-reliant and independent participants in a more equitable exchange with the rich countries. Thus they all call for a new approach to decision-making.

These gaps have persisted, partly because the governments of the North have been reluctant to change their practices adequately; partly because the developing countries have not been able to influence critical decisions in international institutions. The quality of the relations between borrowers and creditors is vitally important to the character of financial institutions, and their ability to provide for the needs of their clients; the inequality between borrowers and lenders has made it harder to reach joint agreement and to generate mutual trust. Greater equality and participation by the developing countries can help to overcome these difficulties; it is with these ends in view that we make our proposals for reform.

15   A New Approach to Development Finance

We have outlined the workings and shortcomings of the present system for financing development, and the growing needs of the Third World. We believe that these can and must be met, and that measures can be taken which will not only accelerate development in the South, but will also stimulate exports from the North and thus help to restore the health of the world economy. Taken together, such measures could produce a fundamental change in the relations between North and South and lay the basis for a more peaceful and prosperous world.

The most urgent need is for the programme of large-scale transfer of funds from North to South to be stepped up substantially from year to year during the final two decades of this century. Such an effort effectively directed towards the solution of the major problems discussed in this Report will benefit the South and turn back the rising tide of world poverty, it would also provide important benefits to the North.

Looking first at the North, we see advanced industrial countries in the midst of their worst recession since the end of the Second World War. Six per cent of the labour force in the OECD countries – about 18 million people – are now unemployed. Allowing for part-time workers and under-employment, roughly twice this number in the labour force do not effectively contribute to production. Productive capacity is under-used to the extent of at least $200 billion, in terms of the annual potential output. In the present recession the OECD countries are expected to grow by at most 2 per cent during the next twelve months, thus making still less use of their productive capacity; the 2 per cent growth rate would be the lowest since 1960 except for 1975, and the average growth for the 1975–80 period at 3.6 per cent would be considerably below the 4.9 per cent average for 1960–70. At the same time, the current account deficit of developing countries, which amounted to $21 billion in 1977 and $32 billion in 1978, is now estimated to have reached $50 billion in 1979 and to rise to perhaps $60 billion in 1980. The coexistence of the great needs in the South and the under-used capacity in the North suggests the scope for large-scale transfer of resources based on mutuality of interests.

Facilitating Recycling

Over the last few years, economic activity in the industrialized countries has been sustained by a major recycling of financial surpluses through the commercial banks particularly to middle-income developing countries; this has helped to prevent further unemployment, under-utilization of capacity and even inflation. The Commission of the European Communities pointed out that:

Had developing countries followed the example of industrialized countries after 1973 by cutting back both their growth and imports to adjust to the oil price increases, the recession in the industrialized world would have been far more serious. The figures for 1975 when the Community economies reached their lowest point are particularly striking. While Community exports to the US fell by 17 per cent and those to EFTA countries by 3 per cent, Community exports to the developing countries increased by 25 per cent and those to ACP countries alone by 33 per cent.

If the developing countries outside OPEC had cut their imports of manufactured goods to meet the increased oil prices of 1973–4, there would have been three million more unemployed in the OECD countries. In fact, by maintaining their trade in manufactured goods with the newly industrializing countries alone the industrialized countries (according to OECD estimates) have gained on average 900,000 jobs in each of the years 1973–7. This indicates how critically the North has come to depend on the South for its markets.

The result of increasing borrowing in the 1970s has been a rapid growth of the indebtedness of developing countries. Their combined debts rose from $70 billion at the end of 1970 to an estimated $300 billion at the end of 1979. Much of it was concentrated in a relatively small number of middle-income countries. The greater role of private commercial lending was reflected in an increasing share of short-term debt at interest rates which have recently risen steeply. Unless oil-importing countries are to check their imports and growth in the 1980s it is clear that their debts will have to increase further. Between 1980 and 1985 as much as $300–500 billion may have to be added to developing countries' debts if their financial needs are to be met – provided the funds can be found.

We face, therefore, not merely one, but several crises: the crisis of relentless inflation and increasing energy costs, the crisis of dwindling energy availability, the crisis resulting from mounting financial requirements, and the crisis posed by constraints on world trade and on the growth of export earnings to meet increased debt service commitments. Taken together, they threaten the whole structure of our political, industrial and financial institutions, unless we move urgently and adequately to deal with the basic causes.

As an immediate step, we recommend that the various international institutions begin immediately to study and articulate the range of likely debts and debt servicing problems as they emerge, particularly in the various categories of developing countries, and the likelihood of existing private and public institutions being able to meet these needs. In this connection it is important to consider the relative roles in the recycling process of the private banking system of the developed countries, multilateral financial institutions, jointly shared guarantees by developed countries and capital-surplus oil exporters, and direct lending by the oil-producing countries themselves.

It is far from certain that the process of recycling mainly through commercial lending can continue. The European Communities' *Annual Report* of 1978 summarized the position as follows:

The present equilibrium of the world economy depends to a considerable degree on a continuing flow of private lending to the non-oil-producing developing countries (and to the Soviet Union and Eastern Europe) on a scale unheard of before 1974 and would be called in question by any impediment to that flow.

Any disruption in financial flows would not only reduce economic activity, but would seriously affect banks and other major institutions. Against this worrying background the world economy is now being called upon to deal with the further deflationary impact of growing external surpluses, particularly those of the major oil-exporting countries.

A series of oil price increases at the end of the 1970s, which promises to continue into the 1980s, led to a new spate of oil revenue surpluses. At the same time, the developing countries which had played so important a part in the post-1973 recycling process faced very serious debt management problems because of their past borrowing and increasing current account deficits – the latter also due in part to the increased cost of oil imports. Debt grew two and a half times as fast as exports for more than half the oil-importing developing countries during 1973–8. For all these countries together current account deficits also grew, at the rates already mentioned. The commercial banks were under pressure to restrain further lending to them as a result both of national regulatory action in some countries and of their own exposed positions – many major banks having a very large share of their funds placed in the middle-income developing countries.

World Economy Slowing Down

The recycling process in the post-1973 period was itself incomplete, which contributed to the slow-down in growth in the industrialized countries. A further factor causing difficulties for the post-1979 round of recycling is that governments in the industrialized countries are even more concerned with controlling inflationary pressures, several of them employing monetary policies which restrict domestic expansion. These factors together lead to increasing concern that the international capital market and the private commercial banks, in the absence of intermediation by public institutions, can no longer be counted on to conduct the recycling process unassisted. It becomes a matter of urgency that positive measures be taken by governments and international institutions to ensure that the surplus funds are re-lent to borrowers who are willing to spend them; the alternative would be a further decline of world economic activity and the threat of a serious crisis in the capital markets.

The danger is not only in the short run. The world economy has been slowing down for a considerable time and it is possible that the previous trend has broken: we may have entered a new long-term phase characterized by a lack of investment in general and a decline in the growth of productivity. In our view these bleak prospects underline the urgency of a programme for international action that would simultaneously assist the Third World and alleviate economic difficulties in the industrialized countries. Fundamentally, we require a set of measures which are designed to sustain effective demand in the world and promote an expansion of world trade. Such measures will help to ensure that deflation, balance of payments difficulties and default on debt are not widespread in the Third World. A programme of transfers to the developing countries should be designed to increase output and productivity, to raise agricultural yields and to expand production of energy, minerals and other commodities. The programme would thus help to ease bottlenecks, to create jobs through low-cost labour-intensive industry and to create the necessary social and economic infrastructure. It should provide special benefits to the low-income countries and be linked with the structural changes we propose in the international financial system.

The Need for 'Massive Transfers'

Suggestions for 'massive transfers' have ranged from $10 to $50 billion per year. The effect of an increase in the transfer of resources to non-oil developing countries of $20 billion annually has been analysed in an econometric study. This shows an increase in developing country imports which would raise exports from industrialized countries by about 3 per cent a year in the first three years. After three years the level of OECD exports to these countries would be 9 per cent higher than they would have been without the transfers. The simulation analysis only covered a three-year programme; if the higher transfers are maintained the ultimate effect will be even greater.

There has been reluctance in the North to take such an initiative partly because of the fear that it would be inflationary. In our view, this fear is overstated. The present continuing high unemployment causes uncertainty about future levels of demand and employment, and generates cumulative reactions in ways which may result in greater cost-push and inflationary tendencies, rather than less. The growth in developing countries and the North's trade with them have in fact helped to hold back inflation in recent years. The OECD has also recognized that imports from the newly industrializing countries have moderated inflationary pressures within the industrial countries both in the short run and, by encouraging productivity and efficiency, over the long run. We therefore feel that the fear of inflation cannot be a reason to hold back from a major initiative towards the South. As the Managing Director of the IMF said at the 1979 UNCTAD meeting in Manila:

It is paradoxical that industrialized countries, most of which are not using their productive potential to the full, are hesitating to increase their financial aid to poor countries. This is despite the fact that such aid could result in increased global demand and thus contribute to reactivation of world trade in a recovery of production. There is nothing in the present state of deflationary chain reactions in the industrialized world (stagnation feeding inflation) which would argue against such an increase in financial aid.

Increased and Improved Aid

The attack on world poverty should involve all countries in a truly universal joint enterprise. While we think the most urgent step is for developed countries to reach the 0.7 per cent of GNP target for official aid in the near future, we believe there is a case for enlarging the scope of such a target by making the development assistance effort universal. All countries could be involved in raising development finance based on income levels, with a progressively lower proportion of GNP as the aid target for countries at lower income levels. The poorest countries could be exempt and many other developing countries which provide aid under this scheme would still be net recipients of aid. Acceptance of such a system of contributions could be a valuable step towards creating a genuine community of nations. It should be noted that the developing countries themselves, including the poorest, have made a step in the direction of more universality: through the system of financial contributions to the Common Fund for commodities. Contributions to UNDP are also based on this principle of universality.

A large-scale transfer of resources must include increased aid. We recommend that those countries which have not met the target of 0.7 per cent of GNP should now adopt timetables requiring them to reach it. If this target were reached in 1985, it would produce an additional \$30 billion in aid, and \$37 billion in 1990 (both at 1980 prices), as compared with what would be the case if aid were to remain at the 1978 level of 0.35 per cent of GNP. This sounds very large, but is not in fact unrealistic: if aid appropriations were raised by only 2.5 per cent of the annual *increase* in GNP (assuming it grows at 4 per cent), overall aid would go up from 0.3 per cent to 0.7 per cent of GNP in five years. If GNP were to grow more slowly, at 3 per cent annually, it would take 3 per cent of the yearly increase to reach the same aid target. We also recommend that the Official Development Assistance target be raised to one per cent of GNP before the end of the century.

We believe also that there is a case for looking again at the reporting systems and definitions of aid and development performance. At present the OECD Development Assistance Committee, UNCTAD and the World Bank all produce figures of aid flows with differing coverage of recipient countries and differing definitions of aid. It would be helpful to have a single internationally agreed reporting system. It should also be considered whether, for example, transfers to countries with *per capita* income above, say, $1000, or to dependent territories, should be classified at all as aid.

Increasing 'Absorptive Capacity'

The quality of aid must be improved. It can be made more efficient by lengthening the period of assured flow, by untying aid-financed purchases from aid sources to permit procurement in the most economic manner; by increasing the grant component of total aid flow; and by allowing the financing of recurrent expenditures and local costs. For example, the untying of aid could be progressively implemented with surplus countries untying aid forthwith, and deficit countries in stages but with liberal provision for purchases from the Third World. Aid can be more fairly allocated, with less consideration of politics and strategy, if it is largely channelled through multilateral institutions. Nearly 40 per cent of total aid in 1975–7 was directed to countries with *per capita* incomes above $400. More aid should be directed towards the poorest countries and to programmes attacking the roots of poverty.

We are aware that many people have argued that the low-income and least developed countries cannot absorb larger amounts of capital or aid, which would therefore be wasted. But a lack of 'absorptive capacity' should be viewed as a development problem in itself: it should neither become an excuse for continuing stagnant levels of aid, nor be dismissed as a non-existent problem. Absorptive capacities have to be increased at the same time as levels of aid. The terms and procedures of aid have to be improved and made more flexible. Countries will be able to absorb more assistance if the funds are more closely related to their needs, and if they can be relied on for a longer term, without being subject to year-by-year appropriations. The expansion of programme lending, alongside project lending, would speed up the effective use of aid. Absorptive capacity should also be improved with more purposeful technical assistance to identify, prepare and implement projects, and to help to operate plants and installations already

243

established. The difficulties with absorptive capacity thus cannot be accepted as a reason for not increasing aid: they can be largely overcome by careful deployment of funds and manpower.

Advantages of 'Automatic Revenues'

An important concept which has attracted growing interest is that of raising revenues for development by 'automatic' mechanisms, which can work without repeated interventions by governments. We believe that over time the world must move to a financial system in which a progressively larger share of such revenues is raised by these means. The fact that revenues are raised automatically does not, of course, imply that their transfer should be automatic; on the contrary, they should be channelled through an appropriate international agency or agencies as we discuss below.

At present, the amount of aid depends on the uncertain political will of the countries giving it, and is subject to the shifting priorities of annual appropriations, and the vagaries of legislatures. With more assured forms and methods developing countries could plan on a more predictable basis, making aid more effective; the donor governments should welcome the possibility of avoiding annual appropriations for a continuing cause. Automatic forms would not evade or avoid the political process; but once there is the initial will to set up the international arrangements, annual reiteration will be unnecessary. There is mutual interest in making aid continuous and predictable. We believe that there should be a worldwide effort to raise such automatic funds, which would make a beginning in mobilizing international resources with a built-in growth potential. In the welfare states taxes are progressive in incidence, social expenditures are redistributive and the links between taxpayers and beneficiaries are indirect. It may seem ambitious to internationalize this model, but the concept itself is intelligible and already accepted on a national scale. Even if the first results at the international level are modest, they will have a profound value in demonstrating global solidarity and partnership in the process of development. The international progressive aid target discussed above would be one possible step in such a direction.

A Levy on International Trade?

Various proposals to raise the international revenues have been outlined in recent years. These include placing a levy on international trade, on arms trade, on international investment, on hydrocarbons and exhaustible minerals, on durable luxury goods, on military spending, on the consumption of energy, on internationally traded crude oil, on international air travel and freight transport, or on the use of the 'international commons' – ocean fishing, offshore oil and gas, sea-bed mining, the use of space orbits, radio and telecommunication frequencies and channels. The yield would vary widely, from about $250 million from a one-per cent levy on international passenger and freight transport, to about $7 billion from a 0.5 per cent levy on international trade. In devising any tax measures it is often hard to reconcile administrative simplicity, fairness, potential revenue and desirable economic effects; this is much harder with international schemes involving all countries.

Among these proposals international trade offers some attraction as a basis for raising revenues both because of its volume – about $1300 billion at present – and because the levy and collection of a small surcharge on imports would not be too difficult to administer and universal participation would be possible. Such a levy should be seen as a means of taxing countries' GNP by proxy; built-in adjustments would ensure that its incidence on different countries was equitable in relation to their GNP. A trade levy would bear heavily on countries whose foreign trade is a high proportion of their income, such as Japan or the Federal Republic of Germany, compared to countries like the US and USSR with a more limited external trade. Appropriate adjustments would limit the levy to a certain maximum proportion of national income for all countries.

Profits from new global enterprises could yield further funds. Sea-bed mining is one promising possibility, particularly the exploitation of the manganese nodules lying mainly in the deep ocean area outside the 'exclusive economic zones' assigned to nation states. Manganese nodules are potato-sized lumps consisting principally of iron, manganese, silica and lime, plus smaller amounts of nickel, copper and cobalt. The profits from mining them are difficult to estimate but there might be an annual revenue of about $500 million by the middle or late 1980s.

Another proposal that can be considered is for donor countries to fund repayments and interest they receive on development loans for further lending. These funds could be augmented if they could be matched by equivalent budgetary contributions. In this way, an element of automaticity and predictability could be introduced, besides the additional resources raised.

Use of IMF Gold

There are ways of raising more automatic resources through the monetary system, which we discussed in Chapter 13. These measures could be implemented relatively quickly. The continued creation of Special Drawing Rights consistent with the total reserve needs of the world economy and a more equitable allocation of SDRs to developing countries would be one such measure. Another measure lies in the use of gold holdings with the IMF. One possibility would be to use these gold holdings as collateral for raising resources in financial markets which can be re-lent to developing countries. Another would be to use profits from gold sales for development assistance in ways to be decided by the member countries of the IMF. The profits from the progressive sale of the remaining two-thirds of the IMF's gold holdings – about 100 million ounces – could amount, on the basis of a market price of $300 to $400 per ounce of gold, to a sum in the order of $30 to $40 billion over a period of time. Such a sum could yield annual revenues in the order of $2.4 to $3.2 billion, assuming a return of 8 per cent. If these resources are used to subsidize interest, they could enable a substantial volume of semi-concessional finance to be made available to developing countries. Members could decide in negotiation the proportion of the profits which would be devoted to development lending as well as the purposes for their use. Even if member countries insist on keeping a part of these profits, they might agree to keep their share of the profits on deposit, and to permit the annual return from these deposits to go to development uses.

All Countries Must Share the Burden

The Commission believes that with all these possibilities it should be feasible to find efficient and fair methods of raising revenues, through a small surcharge, or levy, on items of income, production, consumption or trade. If the will is there, the ways can be found. Any such international taxation must be universal; all countries must share the burden. There is already mutual cooperation, including aid and technical assistance, among developing countries themselves. A fully international effort to raise development resources would formalize and extend this process. Those automatic resources attributable to individual countries could count towards aid targets.

We do not discount the difficulties in the way of agreement on international taxation and the use of automatic resources, but those who argue that the concept of international taxation is unrealistic in the light of public opinion should recall that the same was said about national income tax in nearly all western countries a century ago. We believe the arguments in favour of international automatic resources, whether practical, political or philosophical, are very powerful; any future system of international public finance will have to include such revenues as a source of secure and long-term funds.

Other Ways to Transfer Capital

There have been many proposals to help developing countries to obtain more long-term capital, which we put forward for consideration.

1 They should have easier access to bond markets in the North. The bond market can be a stable source of funds, at fixed and reasonable rates of interest, once a country has established itself in it. One obvious instrument to promote such access is the guarantee power of the World Bank and of Regional Development Banks. Another possibility is a collective guarantee system, on the lines of proposals made by the Mexican Government to the Development Committee of the World Bank in 1978, with such modifications as may be necessary.

2 Individual countries should as far as possible ease legal restrictions on access for developing countries to their capital markets; particularly the restrictions now limiting foreign investments by US institutions such as insurance companies, pension funds and savings institutions.

3 Non-bank institutions and smaller banks could lend more to less developed countries by buying participations in Eurocurrency syndicated loans from larger commercial banks or by syndicating such loans among themselves. Existing loans on the books of large banks could be packaged and interests in the package sold to non-bank institutions or smaller banks in the form of 'participation bonds'. The 'participation bonds' or 'packaged loans' may need guarantee arrangements from an international lending institution to be marketable.

4 Adequate arrangements are needed to provide independent assessment of sovereign (country) risk and advise investors in order that smaller, non-traditional lenders to developing countries can evaluate credits and make loans to institutions in those countries

without a very large investment in skilled sovereign-risk analysis.

5 Portfolio capital in the North could be tapped more extensively to provide investment on terms acceptable to developing countries. This will be particularly relevant in the area of minerals and energy investments.

The World Bank: Responsibilities and Reform

The World Bank is the leading development lending institution. In recent years, it has given assistance to development over a broader front and expanded and liberalized its operations. It has placed great emphasis on anti-poverty programmes. Its policy statements and the analyses of its staff have had great influence, particularly among donors of aid. Its successive Presidents have given valuable leadership to the world development effort, often ahead of opinion in the major shareholding countries. A problem in the eyes of some is whether the World Bank is not too big and too concentrated: at present it has a professional staff of about 2400, of which over 95 per cent work in its headquarters in Washington. This concentration may help to achieve a unified approach, but it tends to make the staff more remote from the problems and attitudes in borrowing countries.

The Bank's Articles of Agreement anticipated a decentralizing of its activities, but this has not happened. As the Bank acquires extra funds it will grow further, making it all the more necessary to locate a larger part of its operational staff in regional centres in the different continents. This should also enable the Bank to attract and retain a wider range of staff from developing countries. Such regional offices will be better placed to assess and respond to the problems in the field; and they should be encouraged and underpinned by Regional Advisory Councils, which were also provided for in the Bank's Articles. The relationship between the Executive Board and the central administration in Washington and the Regional Advisory Councils and regional operating staff will have to be such as to encourage autonomy and genuine decentralization.

The developing countries are entitled to responsive attitudes, both from the World Bank and the IMF, in the operations that so closely concern them; and they should have more of their own people in these institutions. In 1978, only eleven of the sixty-five principal officers of the World Bank and IDA were nationals of the developing countries and the same proportion of the twenty-four principal officers of the IMF. We recognize that nationality does not necessarily imply any particular bias; an officer from the Third World may have little empathy for the problems of the poor and one from the industrialized countries may be very sensitive to Third World situations. But adequate representation of developing countries in staff and management, consistent with objective standards of quality in recruitment, will be an important step in building confidence.

The World Bank is now in the process of increasing its capital subscription from $40 billion to $80 billion. It is a tribute to the Bank's reputation that it will acquire this extra capital. But in the light of the huge capital needs that we have outlined above, this expansion will not in itself be sufficient. We believe that there is a strong case for the Bank's modifying the conservative regulations by which, at present, it is restricted to a gearing ratio of 1:1 – that is, the total outstanding borrowings cannot exceed total capitalization. The record of the Bank's borrowers has been excellent; there have been no cases of default in its whole history. Indeed it has been safer to lend money through the Bank than to some domestic institutions within the United States or Europe. With this history, it would be quite possible for the Bank to expand its gearing ratio to 2:1 or more without really increasing the risks; such a change would of course make very large extra funds available to the developing world. The expansion could be gradual, so as not to disturb the present high rating of Bank bonds. It should go hand in hand with the reforms we have proposed.

IDA and Regional Development Banks

The process of IDA replenishment also requires reform. Governments currently make their contributions on a three-year basis. This is too short: work on the next replenishment has to begin even before arrangements have been concluded for the previous one. The cycle should be extended, at least to five years. It is also important that contributions to IDA should be free of political conditions attached to their use. The United Nations Development Programme has an even shorter cycle of budgetary provision, reviewing its annual budget every year; it needs to be much longer to be effective.

The Regional Development Banks (the Inter-American Development Bank, the African and Asian Development Banks, and the Arab Fund for Economic and Social Development) should play a more important role in development lending. They should be ready to lend for programmes no less than for projects and give more importance to strengthening domestic and regional capabilities. At present the regional banks provide about one-fourth of multilateral lending to their regions, while the balance comes mainly from the World Bank. They are in many ways modelled on the World Bank, but being situated in their regions they are in a position to have a closer awareness of the needs of their borrowing members. However, they lack the funds and the long expertise of the World Bank, and they need to be strengthened, particularly the African Development Bank, if they are to become broader sources of finance. Provided that they are appropriately reformed, the objective should be to achieve a more equal position for regional banks *vis-à-vis* the World Bank in the next decade. They need more capital and (like the World Bank) they should consider gradually increasing their borrowing-capital ratios. They might also, where necessary, obtain lines of credit from the World Bank and other worldwide financial institutions to build up an international network of development institutions. In turn, they should lend to sub-regional institutions such as the Caribbean Development Bank, the Bank for Central American Integration, and the East African Development Bank.

A More Equal Partnership

The relationships between borrowers and creditors and between members of international financial institutions are crucial. The voting pattern in these institutions reflects this relationship. Over time voting shares and the management structure of the IMF and the World Bank have changed to some extent but they need further revisions. Many members, especially the borrowers in the Third World, resent the unequal balance of power and influence in working relationships. The United States in particular has a 'blocking minority' on major decisions with its voting strength of more than 20 per cent, and it has used its special position to influence operating policies of the Bretton Woods institutions. On their side, not only the United States but the industrialized countries as a group want to maintain sufficient control over the institutions which depend on them for funds.

Whatever the precise distribution of voting power all operating and policy decisions in lending institutions have to be based on genuine consensus to be effective. A genuine as distinct from an illusory consensus calls for more equal representation. In this situation, what is essentially needed is a move towards greater equality and partnership, which should be reflected in revisions in the voting pattern no less than in the structure of the top management. This will in time break down mistrust and build confidence. The existing institutions should move in this direction and any new institution adopt a decision-making process where votes will be more evenly shared between industrialized and developing countries.

Monitoring the Aid-giving Organizations

Confusion and overlapping between different sources of development finance can be ineffective and wasteful. At present economic cooperation is financed by several different channels. The UN is the main source for funding technical assistance, through the UNDP, its participating agencies and special funds The development banks, together with bilateral and multilateral agencies, are the main channels of capital. In recent years agencies have proliferated both inside and outside the UN system and their policies, programmes and procedures need to be much more effectively coordinated and concerted. Technical assistance should be more clearly related to capital aid. The longer cycle of budgetary provision which we have suggested for the UNDP would permit long-term programming.

Inter-sectoral coordination of assistance and country programming can make foreign aid much more effective. There should be greater thrust to mobilize and allocate resources. For all these reasons, there is need to monitor the entire assistance system, to reduce the dispersion of effort, to identify shortfalls, to promote initiatives, to fill gaps, and to recommend institutional reforms A first step might be the pooling of UN special funds in a UN Development Authority as recommended by the Group of Experts on the Structure of the UN System in 1975.

Many of us are concerned about the need to oversee, audit and coordinate the whole complex of aid-giving organizations, and to make them more accountable to governments and to a wider public. Precise steps in this regard will have to be decided by governments but we stress the need to make aid-giving organizations more accountable, and comprehensible, to politicians and publics in all countries. We discuss possible measures in the following chapter.

The Gaps and How to Fill Them

We have identified the major gaps in development finance: the need for increased concessional aid to the poorest countries and programme lending. In Chapters 9 and 10 we have dealt with mutual interests in financing the exploration and development of mineral and energy resources in ways which will ensure the developing countries' control over their own resources and reduce investors' uncertainties.

We have also identified the sources of funds. We have called for increased ODA moving towards the 0.7 per cent target, a greater redirection of aid to the poorest countries, a universal effort in raising development finance, and the beginning of a system of international taxation. We have drawn attention to the possibility of increased share capital and borrowing powers for the development banks; of the non-inflationary creation and more equitable allocation of SDRs; of utilizing profits from IMF gold sales; and to the need for greater access to market borrowing for developing countries. These measures, we believe, will constitute the basis for a substantial augmentation of international resources for development to meet the unmet needs which we have discussed.

The Case for a New Institution

The creation of a new institution, which might be called a World Development Fund, has played a major role in the Commission's discussions as an innovative approach to institutional reform. A large share of the unmet needs, in particular a substantial level of programme loans, support for trade between middle-level and less-developed developing countries, and the financing of mineral exploration, according to a widely held view, can be met by such an institution. It would offer an opportunity for developing and developed countries to cooperate on a basis of more equal partnership, and would make universal membership possible.

There are those who argue that existing institutions, suitably enlarged and reformed and with greater resources, would meet the above needs; that their experience and expertise make them more effective than any new institution; that this would avoid further proliferation; and that it would be easier to find the required additional funds if they were administered by proven existing institutions in which major donors have confidence. They have felt that the proposal would be academic if major governments were not receptive to it. It has also been argued that the establishment of new structures should be postponed until it becomes clear that existing institutions are not prepared to meet the gaps.

We wish to make it clear, however, that the proposal for a new institution is not an alternative to the reform and restructuring of existing institutions. On the contrary, it could be a catalyst for change in the entire system of development finance. In putting forward this option, it is not our intention to suggest an institution that will overlap, much less work at cross-purposes, with existing ones; rather, it is intended to complement and complete the existing structure. Indeed, the logic of a new system of universal and automatic revenues for world development points towards an institution established by all countries – West, East and South – and which can serve as a channel for such revenues. The relative economic strength of countries, both in the North and in the South, has changed since Bretton Woods; and unless a new institution is created which reflects these changes, it may not be feasible to mobilize efficiently all the resources that can be made available for development.

The quantitative and qualitative gaps in the present development finance structure are such that there will be both need and room for the existing institutions and for a new one which could relate in a number of ways to those now existing. The qualitative gaps – the missing types of finance – are more fundamental. The new institution can meet these gaps and at the same time complement the lending of the World Bank and the IMF. Its long term programme lending should help the disbursement of World Bank projects held up by the shortage of domestic resources, and help also to keep countries from reaching a crisis situation in which they have to go to the IMF for balance of payments adjustment finance. The new institution would have to cooperate with the Bank and the Fund and the Regional Banks in discussions both on individual borrowing countries and on broad policy issues. The World Development Fund's lending should mainly go through regional and sub-regional institutions and should be undertaken in full cooperation between industrialized and developing countries. It need not have a large staff; many of its operations could go through co-financing arrangements with the World Bank and Regional Development Banks.

We are aware that any new proposal such as this will be viewed with caution. More than three decades have passed since the Bretton Woods Conference which established the World Bank and the IMF. Many of the reforms we have suggested to the existing institutions would themselves call for a comprehensive review of their working in the context of the gaps in the international financial system. Such a review should also include serious consideration of a new institution on the lines of the World

Development Fund, which would strengthen the structure of development lending and represent a new start in North–South relations.

An Immediate Action Programme

We are aware that proposals for changes in existing institutions, and much more so the creation of a new institution, will involve complex and time-consuming negotiations. In the interim, the urgent tasks we have identified cannot and should not wait. We believe that the present predicament of the world economy can be resolved only with a major international effort for the linking of resources to developmental needs on the one hand and the full utilization of under-utilized capacities on the other. This process of recycling and linkage has taken place so far largely through the international commercial banking system, resulting in short maturities, uncertainty about continued flows and increasing risk to both borrowers and lenders. In this context there is scope for an immediate action programme based in part on direct lending by surplus countries and their monetary authorities and in part on borrowings from the market guaranteed by governments, complemented by a measure of additional official assistance. The size of the effort, the scope of the programme, the pattern of participation and the institutional arrangements necessary are all matters to be worked out in detail and settled in negotiation. But we would like to underline that the effort will have to be a large-scale one; that it should extend special benefits, with subsidized interest and extended maturities, to the poorest countries; that it should give a key role to quick-disbursing programme loans; and that it should be undertaken in full cooperation between industrialized and developing countries. Such an action programme can help to meet the most urgent needs of the Third World and prepare the way for more basic and constructive reforms of the world economy.

Recommendations

There must be a substantial increase in the transfer of resources to developing countries in order to finance:

1 Projects and programmes to alleviate poverty and to expand food production, especially in the least developed countries.
2 Exploration and development of energy and mineral resources.
3 Stabilization of the prices and earnings of commodity exports and expanded domestic processing of commodities.

The flow of official development finance should be enlarged by:

1 An international system of universal revenue mobilization, based on a sliding scale related to national income, in which East European and developing countries – except the poorest countries – would participate.

2 The adoption of timetables to increase Official Development Assistance from industrialized countries to the level of 0.7 per cent of GNP by 1985, and to one per cent before the end of the century.

3 Introduction of automatic revenue transfers through international levies on some of the following: international trade, arms production or exports; international travel; the global commons, especially sea-bed minerals.

Lending through international financial institutions should be improved through:

1 Effective utilization of the increased borrowing capacity of the World Bank resulting from the recent decision to double its capital to $80 billion.

2 Doubling the borrowing-to-capital ratio of the World Bank from its present gearing of 1:1 to 2:1, and similar action by Regional Development Banks.

3 Abstaining from the imposition of political conditions on the operations of multilateral financial institutions.

4 Channelling an increasing share of development finance through regional institutions.

5 A substantial increase in programme lending.

6 The use of IMF gold reserves either for further sales, whose profits would subsidize interest on development lending, or as collateral to borrow for on-lending to developing countries.

7 Giving borrowing countries a greater role in decision-making and management.

Resource transfers should be made more predictable by long-term commitments to provide ODA, increasing use of automatically mobilized revenues, and the lengthening of the IDA replenishment period.

Consideration should be given to the creation of a new international financial institution – a World Development Fund – with universal membership, and in which decision-making is more evenly shared between lenders and borrowers, to supplement existing institutions and diversify lending policies and practices. The World Development Fund would seek to satisfy the unmet needs in the financing structure, in particular that of programme lending. Ultimately it could serve as a channel for such resources as may be raised on a universal and automatic basis.

There is need for major additional multilateral finance to support mineral and energy exploration and development in developing countries. Some of this will come from existing institutions, but we believe there is a case for a new facility for this purpose.

The flow of lending from commercial banks and other private financial bodies to developing countries must be strengthened. Middle-income countries need special measures to lengthen the maturity of their debt structures and poorer developing countries should be enabled to borrow more easily in the market. The World Bank and other international financial institutions should assist this process by co-financing, by the provision of guarantees, and by using concessional funds to improve lending terms and reduce interest rates.

Measures should be adopted to facilitate the placing of bonds by developing countries in international markets. These should include the removal of restrictions and the provision of guarantees and adequate arrangements for the assessment of risks.

16   International Organizations and Negotiations – An Overview

An Indispensable System

We have been impressed as a Commission by the extent to which the various parts of the United Nations system and its affiliated organizations such as the World Bank and the International Monetary Fund have become central to the task of world development. As we discussed in several other chapters of this Report, they are increasingly the channels by which, with greater or less effectiveness, the development process is assisted and monitored. Therefore, while a critique of the United Nations system as such does not lie within our mandate, we consider that our work would be incomplete if we did not comment on the working of the system as it came to our notice and suggest ways in which, through further work, it might be improved.

The survival and expansion of world institutions to preserve peace and to promote development in the postwar decades make a hopeful contrast to the disarray and chaos of the prewar period of the nineteen twenties and thirties. The world is now used to the system of the United Nations which has universal membership, including both the Soviet Union and China. At the same time, the UN system is frequently the subject of criticism, for its weaknesses and compromises. An organization which embraces so many nations with such differing views, and which provides a framework for cooperation and communication between them, is both a uniquely valuable and an inherently complex and delicate one, and crucial to world action. The UN is the only such system we have; everyone has a stake not just in keeping it alive and active, but in strengthening it as an indispensable force for peace and development.

National politicians and media are inclined sometimes to

criticize the UN and its agencies as if they were something quite separate from their own country's responsibilities. But the effectiveness of the UN is no more than the member governments make it – through their political support or neglect at home, and through the quality of the contribution of their delegations at meetings. At the same time, the tendency of large international bureaucracies to acquire and develop a style of their own, increasingly unrelated to the real world, cannot be underestimated; such, indeed, is the case even with large national bureaucracies.

The Emergence of World Bodies

The earliest world organizations arose in fields where the common interests were clearly visible, such as communications, meteorology and health. But the interplay of economic and political relations in today's world gives rise to a much more complex interdependence, involving the growing impact of domestic policies on other nations and of international developments on the domestic economy. In this pattern of convergence and conflict mutual adjustment is burdensome and often requires not only rules but, what is more difficult, tact and restraint. This calls for a steady perception and enlargement of mutual interests, which can only be achieved by relationships over a period of time.

The principal world bodies were established before most of the Third World countries had emerged as independent states. To reflect the diversity of the present-day world and to accommodate the aspirations of the new nations will require both reform and innovation.

The United Nations and its principal organs provide opportunities for universal international deliberations. For the developing countries, who are in a majority in the General Assembly, the principle that each state, big or small, has one vote makes it a forum where they can make themselves heard in the world. But, of course, the decisions which are taken in United Nations bodies do not by themselves change the policies of governments. All governments have to realize the risk for further international cooperation if there is no political basis for real consensus on major issues through appropriate mechanisms within the UN system; without this consensus there can only be ritual discussions and resolutions without obligations for consequent action.

Educating Public Opinion

Above all, it is essential that the distrust and lack of confidence which pervades international conferences should be reduced and dispelled. International institutions mainly deal with governments; but they should increasingly involve other important social groups in their dialogue. The consultation mechanisms of ILO and UNIDO with representatives of industry and trade unions are in the right direction. The effort to create a new international economic order in particular necessitates the involvement of important groups within societies that are affected by such changes and which have to be persuaded to support them.

The Commission considers it essential that the educational aspects of improved North–South relations be given much more attention in the future. It is imperative that ordinary citizens understand the implications for themselves of global interdependence and identify with international organizations that are meant to manage it. It is no accident that those countries in the North which score high in official development assistance also provide an outward-looking education to their people and particularly to the younger generation.

Also, international institutions need to communicate to an audience wider than the community of persons which participates in their discussions and negotiations. Resolutions and declarations will only be effective if they influence the public at large. Youth and their organizations should be among the more important non-governmental organizations with which international institutions should intensify contacts.

Proliferation and Reform

There is much concern about the seeming proliferation of international organizations. Most of the growth in international organization has been a normal response to new or increased needs, reflecting the consensus of member governments to devote more attention or resources to solving an urgent or emerging problem. The original base of international institutions was found inadequate to meet the diverse needs of economic cooperation in the postwar period: and in the meantime the membership of the United Nations grew from 51 countries in 1945 to 152 in 1979, with the arrival of newly independent developing countries. These changes called for greater flexibility in the institutions, and developing countries have sometimes wanted to supplement inherited institutions with new ones (like UNCTAD) in which they could have a greater voice. Yet, as the UN Secretary-General said recently:

> We also have to accept a certain degree of institutional escapism as the Governments of the world grapple with new and overwhelming problems. By this I mean that it is sometimes easier to call a conference, or even found a new institution, than to confront a complex problem directly.

Growth in organizations and members has not been without its costs. On the institutional side, it has led to fragmented and diffused activity, overlapping responsibilities, and organizational rivalries: issues which ought to be dealt with in an integrated manner are continually shifted from one forum to another, each organization seeking to preserve its status even if its original task has been achieved. The very large number of international meetings – about 6000 every year in New York and Geneva – and the connected documentation – about a million pages a year – have put an enormous burden on member governments, particularly on the smaller ones, when they try to contribute effectively to international cooperation; and the permanent secretariats of UN organizations have been saddled with burdens which they were not originally called upon to shoulder. The question may validly be asked whether the existing negotiating mechanism serves to facilitate the development or emergence of the political will that is necessary for major decisions.

The volume of meetings and documentation partly reflects the growing number of subjects on the international agenda as the world becomes more inderdependent. Changing international relations is always a slow process; governments need to have long discussions before they move at all, and more for them to move together. But we believe that many international institutions need to define their objectives much more clearly, to have more purposeful agendas, to relate their discussions to specific results, and to coordinate more closely between themselves. They need to be more economical in their use of time, staff and paper, and they should be more accountable to their member governments and to the general public. While much of the responsibility for improvement must lie with the secretariats of the organizations, the ultimate responsibility lies with the member governments.

The UN itself has been aware of many of these shortcomings. In 1969, a major study was undertaken and consequential reforms were made to the United Nations Development Programme. In 1975 the General Assembly appointed an Expert Group which made a number of recommendations to increase the UN's effectiveness in economic development, including appointing a Director-General for Development and International Economic Cooperation, which is one of the few changes realized so far. We express the hope that institutional rationalization and reform will be seen as a dynamic process responsive to changing needs and to the inadequacies which experience of the working of institutions reveals.

A High-level Monitoring Body?

It is clear that the present channels of coordination, of which there are many, are not working as efficiently as is necessary. We therefore see the need for the United Nations hierarchy, and for member governments at a high political level, to pursue more vigorously this difficult but essential task of streamlining the system, with a view to achieving better coordination of budgets, programmes and personnel policies. It is only if progress is made in these fields that the United Nations system will command the public confidence and support which are necessary for the performance of its tasks in relation to world development.

We believe that this process might be reinforced by an external body to monitor the work of the different international bodies in the development field. It would aim to streamline the institutions, to define their objectives more clearly, and to achieve them more economically and effectively. In this connection we have been attracted by a proposal made in 1968 to the UN Committee for Development Planning for the creation of a body of 12 members: a third of the members would be citizens of developing countries, a third would be from the industrialized countries and the remaining third selected for their experience and independent judgement. The group would be constituted by the UN Secretary-General in consultation with governments and others, and with due regard to regional and political balances, but members would act as individuals, not as government representatives. They would be essentially a 'brains trust', rather than an organization with a large staff of its own, and they would rely mainly on the statistical, analytical and reporting services of UN agencies and on independent consultants. Their basic function would be to act as an Advisory Body to governments and to the UN General Assembly and its organs, to improve the effectiveness of the UN and other international institutions engaged in development and international economic cooperation in achieving their global objectives. They should make their reports available to the public, to stimulate interest in the workings of the international system, as the reports of Parliamentary and Congressional committees do in many countries. They would have no executive functions. Their effectiveness would derive from their standing and the quality of their work. The Commission is convinced that monitoring and evaluation should be built into the system of international cooperation; and we endorse the concept of a high-level independent body for this purpose.

Improving the Negotiating Framework

There is also a case for improving the negotiating framework in the North–South dialogue. UNCTAD and many other fora have been moulded by the Group system, which comprises three groups of countries – the 77, Group B and Group D – as well as China. The Group of 77 (which now has 117 members) consists of developing countries. Group B consists of the western industrialized countries, and Group D of East European countries. This division has consolidated itself as a pattern of alignment, and the Group of 77 represents the solidarity of developing countries which is of historic importance, enabling them to present a common stand, and bring to bear their combined strength in North–South negotiations. The Group system has its merits in deliberations where the South has needed to articulate and publicize its problems and positions; and the Commission fully recognizes its validity and value.

However, such deliberations have often ended in resolutions which exhort everyone, without binding or committing any of the parties; the differences are drafted away to create an appearance of agreement, but they persist in reality. One result of this process is that the language of international resolutions has become inbred, specialized and coded.

Genuine progress in international relations depends on painstaking negotiations to reach agreed principles or legal instruments; only these processes can produce a common language to provide a basis for action. In this context the Group system has been criticized as tending to crystallize extreme positions on either side, which delays and sometimes defeats practical progress in resolving conflicting interests. The process of reconciling differences within each Group has often led to extreme positions driving out moderate ones: maximum demands elicit minimum offers. It has become necessary to carry each Group along as a whole at every stage, without neglecting differences, so that the negotiating process becomes unwieldy, cumbersome and time consuming. The time has come to examine whether a negotiating format can be devised which is more functional, while fully respecting the concerns of developing countries for maintaining their solidarity.

Solidarity Goes beyond Bargaining

Wherever possible, negotiations should look for joint gains, rather than slowly wresting uncertain 'concessions'. The starting point has to be some perception of mutual interests in change. In North–South negotiations immediate or short-term reciprocal benefits cannot always be expected, and greater equity will sometimes require non-reciprocity. Mutual interests are often longer-term and overall; they need to be supplemented with considerations of forward-looking solidarity which go beyond strict 'bargaining'. All sides have an interest in a framework which is designed to enlarge their common ground and the dialogue must be structured to allow the participants to perceive their specific mutual interests clearly on each issue. The agenda should be balanced, or synchronized with other negotiations, to allow 'trade-offs' and 'packaging'. At the same time, the mechanism of negotiation should be able to accommodate the principles of universality and joint responsibility. These considerations could be reconciled within a framework somewhat on the following lines, essentially extending and formalizing existing procedures.

The agenda should be based on previous consultation between different governments, subgroups and regions, reflecting the preparedness of major interests to work towards final agreements. All countries should be represented at the plenary sessions of the negotiating forum, but on each separate issue (like commodities, or trade) each Group should nominate a limited number of countries most seriously interested in that issue to the negotiating group, the number varying with the scope of the issue, and maintaining an appropriate balance between developing and industrialized countries. These representatives would then naturally maintain close and continuous contact with other members of their Group. On issues such as money and finance, which interest all countries in one or more of their aspects, participation could be by representatives of regions or sub-regions. Negotiations would thus take place in smaller, but self-chosen groups; but any agreements should be endorsed, after full discussion, by the plenary session. Our world society has grown to the point where we must now consciously apply to its institutions, particularly its decision-making ones, the principles of the Committee system. And there may be other ways and other techniques of dialogue that should be explored. The dangers from a foundering of the human dialogue are so great that every effort must be made to avert it.

Building on UN Consensus

The valuable and unprecedented basis for consensus in the UN system, for communicating between North and South, and between East and West, must be preserved. It is vital to get the best out of it, to strengthen it, and to build on it, utilizing the experience of the last three decades and the benefits of wide participation. An increasingly interdependent world must organize itself for the different and more difficult tasks of the future, which will call not only for political will and wisdom, but for a framework of institutions and negotiations which can convert policies and ideas into action.

Injecting New Purpose into the Dialogue

In earlier chapters we have drawn attention to the common interests of all countries – North, South, West or East – in peace and disarmament, in the attack on poverty and hunger, in achieving an orderly energy transition and in protecting the environment. We have pointed to the strong mutual interests of all countries in worldwide economic growth, control of inflation and promotion of employment. We have underlined the need for solidarity and for a more equal relationship between rich and poor nations in the councils and institutions of the world.

We were conscious, throughout our discussions, that many negotiations on these issues had ended in stalemate, although there had been progress on specific fronts to a greater or smaller degree. What was missing as we saw it was a sense of purpose, a feeling of urgency, an appreciation of priorities, an understanding of common interests and the political will to achieve concrete results in at least some areas. How can these be injected into the dialogue among nations?

There is no alternative to dialogue itself and to further negotiation. The task will be to bring about a genuine and meaningful exchange. We felt that if this is to happen, it cannot be on the basis of well-worn rhetorical or technical positions. Political commitment and statesmanship has to take over in a process where the leaders of the world give their mind to the central issues.

In the OECD and in Comecon, political leaders of the North – West as well as East – exchange views and harmonize policies. In the Non-Aligned group and in OPEC the developing countries have similar fora. Would it now be possible to envisage a summit for all groups of countries? Would not the interests be too divergent and the process so cumbersome that it would be doomed to fail?

We feel that the issues that face the world in the 1980s and beyond are such that risk of failure should not stand in the way of urgent attention being given to them at the highest political level.

Recourse to Occasional Summits

It is clear that no nation can decide for any other; universal participation within the UN framework is a *sine qua non* for international decision-making. But the process can be started and prepared for, by a limited summit of heads of governments from the North and the South, and hopefully including the East and China. The numbers must be small to make progress possible but large enough to be representative and credible.

Such a summit cannot negotiate because it is not universal; nor will it be an appropriate forum to discuss details. But it can reach an understanding on what is necessary, and what is feasible, and how to harmonize the two. It can forge commitments and give guidelines for detailed negotiations in the appropriate inter-national fora, settle the parameters and the format for such negotiations, and decide upon timetables for results to be reached.

As the Commission was concluding its work, we received the resolutions of the Non-Aligned Conference in Havana, of the Group of 77 and of the Thirty-third Session of the UN General Assembly calling for global negotiations. Our proposal is not inconsistent with these calls. The summit we propose would be a step in the same direction and can prepare for such negotiations. In the next and final chapter of our Report, we outline the programme of priorities which such a summit might consider.

Recommendations

Policies, agreements and institutions in the field of international economic, financial and monetary cooperation should be guided by the principle of universality.

The UN system, which faces ever expanding tasks, needs to be strengthened and made more efficient. This calls for more coordination of budgets, programmes and personnel policies, to avoid duplication of tasks and wasteful overlapping.

The performance of the various multilateral organizations in the field of international development should be regularly monitored by a high-level advisory body.

There needs to be a review of the present system of negotiations to see whether more flexible, expeditious and result-oriented procedures can be introduced without detracting from cooperation within established groups.

Increased attention should be paid to educating public opinion and the younger generation about the importance of international cooperation.

The occasional use of limited summit meetings should be considered to advance the cause of consensus and change.

17 A Programme of Priorities

In this Report we have considered several of the major changes which have taken place in international relations and in the world economy in recent decades, and their influence on development issues. This process of change is continuing: mankind already faces basic problems which cannot be solved purely at the national or even regional levels, such as security and peace, development goals, the monetary system, protection of the environment, energy, and the control of space and ocean resources. The international community has begun to tackle these problems but, to date, very inadequately.

At the beginning of the 1980s the world community faces much greater dangers than at any time since the Second World War. It is clear that the world economy is now functioning so badly that it damages both the immediate and the longer-run interests of all nations. The problems of poverty and hunger are becoming more serious; there are already 800 million absolute poor and their numbers are rising; shortages of grain and other foods are increasing the prospect of hunger and starvation; fast-growing population, with another two billion people in the next two decades, will cause much greater strains on the world's food and resources. The industrial capacity of the North is under-used, causing unemployment unprecedented in recent years, while the South is in urgent need of goods that the North could produce. Rapid inflation, erratic exchange rates, and unpredictable interventions by governments are seriously disrupting the trade and investment on which an immediate return to world prosperity depends.

What limits our response to this challenge, on which the destiny of mankind depends? Not primarily the technical solutions, which are largely already familiar, but the non-existence of a clear and generalized awareness of the realities and dangers and the absence of political will to face up to them and take corrective action. Only in a spirit of solidarity based on respect for the individual and the common good will it be possible to achieve the solutions that are needed.

It is undeniable that these solutions will call for readjustment on various planes of the domestic and external life of each nation; there will be some inevitable sacrifices in the short run and these will doubtless be greater for those with more power and resources to bear them. It will not be possible for any nation or group of nations to save itself either by dominion over others or by isolation from them. On the contrary, real progress will only be made nationally if it can be assured globally. And this global approach cannot be limited to economic problems: it must also take into consideration the great complexity of human society.

In a sense, the world is a system of many different components interacting with one another – changes in one affecting all the rest. Among the major components, apart from sovereign states, are international and regional institutions, transnational corporations, public opinion (both national and worldwide) and diverse religious, ideological, social and political forces. With so complex a world system, due consideration has to be given to each of its central elements in responding to the challenges of the future. Viewed in this light, the new international order itself can be seen as a continuously changing process in which forethought and negotiation operate constantly to establish an overall balance between all its elements, whether individual or collective.

Approached with such an understanding, the necessary political decisions would more likely be taken; but they will not be possible without a global consensus on the moral plane that the basis of any world or national order must be people and respect for their essential rights, as defined in the Universal Declaration of Human Rights. Only if these ideas are sincerely accepted by governments, and especially by individuals, will the political decisions be possible and viable. This requires an intensive process of education to bring home to public opinion in every country the vital need to defend the values without which there will be no true economic development and, above all, no justice, freedom or peace.

In our terms of reference we said that we would keep the need for a new international order at the centre of our concerns. The present world economic and political environment only adds urgency to this task. We are convinced that the world community will have to be bold and imaginative in shaping that new order and it will have to be realistic in its endeavours. Change is inevitable. The question is whether the world community will take deliberate and decisive steps to bring it about, or whether change will be forced upon us all through an unfolding of events over which the international community has little control. It is the joint responsibility of all countries and peoples to act without further delay.

A Dangerous Future

Prospects for the future are alarming. Increased global uncertainties have reduced expectations of economic growth, and the problems of handling surplus oil revenues are accentuating the threat of a grave financial crisis. There is serious doubt as to whether adjustments to international balance of payments problems and the management of world liquidity and debt can be achieved adequately by the existing machinery. Those middle-income countries which are rapidly increasing their industrial exports are generating anxieties and uncertainties among competing industrialists and workers in the North, and governments are failing to agree about rules to allow access to their markets. Investment in exploration for energy and minerals in the South, which is critical for industrial growth in both North and South, has slowed down to a trickle, as a result of political and economic uncertainties. The abolition of poverty is itself not only a moral obligation. It is against everyone's interests to allow poverty to continue, with the insecurity, suffering and destruction which it brings. In the meantime military spending, now at a pace of over $400 billion a year, is wasting still more resources and energies which could be devoted to world development.

With the prospect of even higher unemployment and slower long-term growth many people will instinctively want to protect themselves from the harsh realities of foreign competition, turning instead to their purely domestic responsibilities; this withdrawal has already begun. But there can be no doubt that such a defensive reaction will be disastrous, as it was in the years before the Second World War. Since that time the nations of both the South and the North have become far more interdependent and actions taken by one country can seriously affect countries at the other side of the world. The self-interest of nations can now only be effectively pursued through taking account of mutual interests.

We realize that much of the responsibility for averting

catastrophe must lie within nations and regions, both in the North and the South; their governments must set their own programmes based on long-term survival and justice rather than temporary expediency. While developing countries call for social justice internationally, they must not neglect such values at home; nor must they let slip the opportunities at hand for greater cooperation among themselves. The North for its part must not pursue selfish policies, depleting the world of precious resources; it too must find new patterns of growth, more sensitive to the world's needs.

We are also aware that long-term world security and development will depend on the participation of both the East European countries and of China, each of which have their own important experiences of rapid development. Only a reduction of the distrust and fears between East and West can establish a sound and permanent basis for North–South cooperation, and we therefore hope that the eastern governments and their peoples will participate more fully with the rest of the world in joint endeavours to find solutions to the world's problems.

Each of us on the Commission, coming from countries in five continents with very different political systems and principles, has our own perspective and historical experience. But all of us have become convinced that the world community will have to work out dynamic new approaches, both immediately and for the longer run. The debate between North and South has been continuing for some years: it is urgent that both sides should now work together in a programme based on action for a rational and equitable international economic order.

The journey will be long and difficult, but it must begin now if it is to meet the challenge of the next century. We have to set clear goals for solving the most serious and dangerous problems if we are to concentrate our minds, and prevent a retreat into the dead-end which results from the pursuit of short-term self-interest. We must do so as a matter of common humanity, and also of mutual survival. The poor will not make progress in a world economy characterized by uncertainty, disorder and low rates of growth; it is equally true that the rich cannot prosper without progress by the poor. The world requires a new system of economic relationships that acknowledges these mutual needs and human interests. The challenge for the next decades will not be met by an adversary system of winners and losers – North versus South or East versus West – but only by one founded on human solidarity and international cooperation amongst all.

A new international order will take time to achieve: we have set out the full range of our proposals in our Summary of Recommendations on all the subject matter we have discussed. Here, we outline first the principal tasks for international negotiation and action over the next two decades. But the present world crisis is so acute that we have also felt compelled to draw up an emergency programme, one which would go far to overcome the present *malaise*, while working towards the long-term structural reforms.

Tasks for the 80s and 90s

All countries must be able to participate fully in the world economy in a way which assists genuine development. This will come about in the long run only in an economic environment which enables all developing countries to achieve self-sustaining growth.

Priority Needs of the Poorest

Priority must be given to the needs of the poorest countries and regions. We call for a major initiative in favour of the poverty belts of Africa and Asia. We recognize that the removal of poverty requires both substantial resource transfers from the developed countries and an increased determination of the developing countries to improve economic management and deal with social and economic inequalities.

Abolition of Hunger

The world must aim to abolish hunger and malnutrition by the end of the century through the elimination of absolute poverty. Greater food production, intensified agricultural development, and measures for international food security, are essential. These too require both major additional external assistance and revised priorities in many developing countries.

Commodities

Earnings from commodities must be strengthened so that they can contribute more adequately to the development of Third World countries, most of which are still heavily dependent on primary commodity exports. They should be enabled to process their own raw materials locally and to participate in their international marketing, transport and distribution. Commodity prices should be stabilized at a remunerative level to become less vulnerable to market fluctuations. For these purposes the proposed Common Fund and other relevant institutions need adequate resources. Existing schemes for compensating against instability should be improved and expanded.

Manufactures

The North should reverse the present trend towards protecting its industries against competition from the Third World and promote instead a process of positive, anticipatory restructuring. Industrial adjustment policies affect other countries closely and should be subject to international consultation and surveillance. The codes established by the GATT Tokyo Round which concluded in 1979 will be useful if they are acted upon forcefully, but further work is necessary to link temporary safeguard restrictions to genuine adjustment policies. Developing countries should beware of their own protectionism, which affects the competitiveness of their exports, and curtails the opportunities for trade among themselves which is an essential element in their mutual cooperation.

Transnationals, Technology and Mineral Development

International codes of conduct and effective national laws should be agreed to ensure the broader sharing of technology, to control restrictive business practices and to provide a framework for the activities of transnational corporations. A better international investment regime should both enable developing countries to benefit from the expertise and resources of multinational corporations, and promote stable relationships between these corporations and host governments. It would also encourage greater initiatives and investments for the exploration of minerals and oil in the Third World which are essential for the prospects of world supplies. The weakest countries will require special assistance to permit them to participate effectively in such a regime.

Reform of the Monetary System

The disarray of the international monetary system is one of the key problems of the world economy. A system is needed which will establish more stable exchange rates, symmetry in the burden of adjustment to balance of payments deficits and surpluses, and an orderly expansion of international liquidity. A key element in international policies to increase monetary stability must be to make Special Drawing Rights the principal reserve asset. The issuing of SDRs must be geared solely to the agreed need for international liquidity, and will not create any additional element of international inflation. But we think that the distribution of those SDRs that are issued should also be related to the financial requirements of developing countries.

A New Approach to Development Finance

The objectives we have defined above, together with others we discuss in our Report, will call for a transfer of funds on a very considerable scale. The dangers and hardships which will occur without it are unprecedented. There are pressing needs in food, in mineral and energy exploration and development – needs in the South whose satisfaction is important to the North. The plight of the poorest countries is desperate. A large range of other low-income developing countries need major support from concessional finance to accelerate growth and cope with balance of payments deficits. The middle-income countries have relied extensively on commercial borrowing, and measures are needed to ensure that they can continue to borrow from the market and manage their heavy debt burdens. Basing ourselves on the best available estimates made by a variety of agencies, we have concluded that the achievement of goals with which we could be satisfied will require sums equal to more than a doubling of the current $20 billion of annual official development assistance, together with substantial additional lending on market terms.

Such a substantial stepping-up of the financing of imports that are vital for world development would also serve to maintain and promote world trade on which the welfare of all countries depends. The economies of the North need to regain economic vitality but their intimate dependence on world markets makes it impossible for them to do this by trying to put their own house in order while forgetting about the rest of the world. Public and political leaders in all countries must be aware of the need to take determined action and to mobilize the political will. We envisage a new approach to development finance incorporating the following elements:

1 Funds for development must be recognized as a responsibility of the whole world community, and placed on a predictable and long-term basis. We believe all countries – West and East, and South, excepting the poorest countries – should contribute. Their

contributions would be on a sliding scale related to national income, in what would amount to an element of universal taxation. There is an existing aid target for rich countries to provide 0.7 per cent of their gross national product as aid. For a country with average incomes of $6000, this would amount to $42 per person. The rich countries should commit themselves to a definite timetable for reaching the target, and for advancing towards one per cent before the year 2000.

2 We also believe more funds should be raised from 'automatic' sources. We have examined a number of possibilities including levies related to international trade, military expenditures or arms exports, and revenues from the 'global commons', especially sea-bed minerals. Funds accruing from some of these new sources, insofar as they can be attributed to individual countries, would count towards aid targets. We believe that a system of universal and automatic contributions would help to establish the principle of global responsibility, and could be a step towards co-management of the world economy.

3 The World Bank and Regional Development Banks should take new steps to increase their lending. The World Bank is already doubling its capital to $80 billion. We urge that the statutes of the World Bank be amended to change its gearing ratio from 1 to 1 to 2 to 1 which would raise its borrowing capacity to $160 billion. With the record and prestige the Bank has built up, we believe that the change' would not affect its market standing. We also call for a higher proportion of financing to be channelled through the Regional Development Banks, which should be similarly strengthened for this purpose.

4 Borrowing for on-lending to developing countries should take place against the collateral of the retained portion of the gold reserves of the IMF, which represents a large resource worth upwards of $40 billion at market prices prevailing towards the end of 1979. The profits from such further sales of this gold as may be agreed should be used to subsidize the cost of borrowing by developing countries.

5 The serious gaps which our Report has found in the present range of financing, particularly the lack of programme lending, must be filled. We believe a different type of relationship and policy discussion is required between borrowers and lenders to permit much greater amounts of such lending side by side with the funds available for specific investment projects. Consideration should therefore be given to the creation of a new institution – a World

Development Fund – based on broader sharing in decision-making and able to attract universal membership. Further, we have expressed our hope that a growing consciousness of worldwide responsibility to bridge the gap between the rich and the poor will eventually be expressed in a system of international taxation to which all countries contribute. The new institution could ultimately serve as a channel for such resources, but need not wait for them before it is established.

6 Major additional multilateral finance is required to support mineral and energy exploration and development in developing countries. Some of this will come from existing institutions, but we believe there is a case for a new facility for this purpose.

7 The commercial banking system should continue to lend to the developing world, and on an adequate scale. Other private financial bodies should also be encouraged to participate. Measures are needed to ensure that middle-income countries receive funds on terms which permit them to manage their indebtedness; and concessional funds should be used to subsidize interest rates so that poorer countries can also take advantage of such loans. The World Bank and other international financial institutions should provide guarantees and play their part in ensuring a continued flow of commercial funds.

Power Sharing

While these specific tasks require major transfers of finance, we believe that the power and decision-making within monetary and financial institutions must also be shared more broadly, to give more responsibility to the developing world. This calls not only for the willingness of member governments to join in a revision of voting structures, but also for a style of management which exhibits closer understanding of and sensitivity to Third World problems, such as we put forward in our new institutional proposal.

A special responsibility falls on the World Bank, which has already done much to adapt itself to a fast-changing world. We are very conscious of its high standards and expertise; but, in order to represent more fully the interests of its clients, we are convinced that it should widen representation of Third World countries in its management and decentralize its operations and operating staff. We believe that the regional and sub-regional banks should play an increasingly important part in development finance, and should be well qualified to maintain closer links with countries in their own continents; therefore they should be adequately funded and should achieve a uniformly high standard of management.

We are aware that the IMF has recently become more sensitive to the wider objectives of nations with balance of payments difficulties, and that it is often consulted at a late stage when drastic measures are required. But we emphasize that the IMF should give practical expression to its desire to (in its own words) 'pay due respect to the domestic, social and political objectives of member countries'. The repercussions of the rigorous conditions of IMF loans on developing countries can have very serious effects on these objectives, and we recommend that the IMF should provide for a longer period of adjustment by borrowers. Like the World Bank, the IMF should also pay attention to proper representation of Third World countries in its management and the upper echelons of its staff.

In the United Nations and its agencies it is essential that proliferation, duplication and waste be eliminated. We believe that in particular there is a need for new ways of monitoring and evaluating the performance of world institutions of quite different kinds, in order to make them more accountable to governments and publics. Both industrialized and developing countries have a strong interest in ensuring that the flow of funds, the expertise and the awareness of problems should be as effective as possible. It is important too that all sides have an effective machinery to develop and elaborate their positions in international negotiations.

An Emergency Programme: 1980–85

We believe, however, that the world cannot wait for the longer-term measures before embarking on an immediate action programme for the next five years to avert the most serious dangers, an interlocking programme which will require undertakings by all parties, and also bring benefits to all. Its principal elements – all of equal importance – would be:

1 A large-scale transfer of resources to developing countries.

2 An international energy strategy.

3 A global food programme.

4 A start on some major reforms in the international economic system.

We see the resource transfers as having as their most urgent objectives:

– assistance to the poorest countries and regions most seriously threatened by the current economic crisis

– provision for financing the debts and deficits of middle-income countries.

The energy strategy must aim at ensuring:
– regular supplies of oil

– rigorous conservation

– more predictable and gradual price increases in real terms

– development of alternative and renewable energy sources.

The food programme would aim at:

– increased food production, especially in the Third World, with the necessary international assistance

– regular supplies of food, including increased emergency food aid

– a system for long-term international food security.

The start on reform of the international economic system must concentrate on:

– steps towards an effective international monetary and financial system, in which all parties can participate more fully

– acceleration of efforts to improve developing countries' conditions of trade in commodities and manufactures.

Such an emergency programme is not a substitute for or in any way inconsistent with the longer-term programme of priority reforms that we recommend; but it is essential to undertake it if the world economy is to survive the threatening crisis of the years immediately ahead – a crisis which could itself immeasurably diminish the prospects of achieving results from that programme of priorities. It can only be undertaken, of course, if it commands wide support, and agreement will need to be reached upon it through international negotiation of an appropriate package of measures. All parties have a positive role to play in that process; all will benefit from its results.

Resource Transfers

In relation to the transfer of resources, some major needs demand urgent global responses. There must be, for example, a major effort to assist the poverty belts of Africa and Asia. Immediate aid must be accompanied by long-term plans to set these regions on the path to lasting growth which can eventually be self-sustaining. We estimate the minimum cost at $4 billion annually in addition to current aid.

The borrowing needs of the middle-income countries must be met. This will be facilitated if adequate measures are taken to provide programme lending and to ensure the recycling of surplus funds. Co-financing, or guarantees by international financial institutions, should be used to support commercial lending to these countries.

These purposes and the others discussed will require large additional aid together with an improvement in its quality. The rich countries must commit themselves to a timetable for reaching the 0.7 target, starting with an increase in 1980 and reaching the target by 1985. This will provide by 1985 additional aid of $30 billion annually, most of which must go to the poverty belts and other low-income countries. The East European countries and the better-off developing countries should commit themselves to making an early start with contributions on the basis we have proposed.

Our assessment is that increased lending by commercial institutions on a co-financing or guaranteed basis, increased official aid, expanded lending by the World Bank and the Regional Development Banks, use of IMF gold, and other resource-transfer mechanisms could provide an additional flow of funds to the developing world through public channels rising to a sum of the order of $50–60 billion annually by 1985.

Energy

These transfers would be a major part of a global agreement such as we have in mind. Another major part must deal with the worldwide energy problem, and the exceptional role of oil. There must be an accommodation between oil-producing and consuming countries which can ensure more secure supplies, more rigorous conservation, more predictable changes of prices and more positive measures to develop alternative sources of energy. This accommodation is essential to arrest the slide towards economic disaster and to prepare for the inevitable transition to the new energy era. An international strategy for energy in the emergency programme should include these elements, many of which already command a measure of acceptance:

– Oil-exporting countries, developing and industrialized, will assure levels of production and agree not to reduce supplies arbitrarily or suddenly unless the circumstances are beyond their control. Special arrangements will ensure that the poorer developing countries receive the amounts of oil they need.

– All major energy-consuming countries will specifically commit themselves to agreed targets to hold down their consumption of oil and other energy. More ambitious targets than those agreed in 1979 by western industrialized countries at the Tokyo Summit, and by the twenty members of the International Energy Agency, should be accepted and monitored. Countries should set conservation standards for the use of energy, covering for example the insulation of buildings and the consumption of petrol for automobiles; and they should work towards internationally agreed standards on such matters.

– Oil prices should be set in such a way as to avoid sudden major increases, and at levels which give incentives for production and encourage conservation. An eventual agreement could include price indexation related to world inflation, denomination of the price in a basket of currencies or SDRs, and guarantees of the value and accessibility of financial assets which oil producers receive.

– There must be major investment in oil and natural gas exploration and development in Third World countries, as well as in known and available alternative energy sources such as coal and hydro-electric power; planning and funds are also required for research and development of new types of energy use, especially solar and other renewable forms. All countries should share to the greatest extent possible in these research and development activities, both the consumers and the producers of traditional energy.

We have shown how the 1980s will inevitably see massive increases in the deficits and debts of the developing countries. Further studies are badly needed of the range of those debts and deficits by 1985 and of the resources – both private and public – potentially available to meet them. But it is already apparent that special measures are needed. The industrialized and the oil-exporting countries should reach agreement on their respective additional roles and additional lending capacities, both directly by each and in the form of jointly shared guarantees. Given the new sense of the interdependence affecting all parties, it is essential that these two groups of countries join forces to transform this potential crisis into a new opportunity for cooperation – in the common interest.

Food

A broad programme of increased food production and agricultural development must be launched with intensified efforts in the South and increased aid of some $8 billion annually. (A part of this is included in the $4 billion for the poorest countries mentioned above.) These efforts are essential to overcome food deficits in poor countries and to ease inflationary pressures in the world food market. As a start to the programme of international food security, we call for an early conclusion of the International Grains Arrangement, and increases in emergency food supplies.

Reforms

The large-scale transfer of resources we call for should be organized in partnership between developed and developing countries. Our proposal for a new financial institution should be examined by the international community. Those on the use of IMF gold, international taxation and power-sharing in existing institutions must also be examined, and joint efforts must be made to restore international monetary stability; we consider a start in these directions to be an important part of the emergency programme.

Action must commence or be intensified on certain other fronts also. The industrialized nations must give greater access to processed primary products from developing nations and take serious steps jointly with the developing nations to stabilize prices for commodities. The industrialized countries should also introduce measures to liberalize the international trading system, with a greater determination to restructure their industries towards higher levels of productivity, and allowing developing countries in the process of industrialization to expand their markets. The developing countries for their part must do their utmost to expand food production, take steps to decrease income inequalities within their own boundaries, increase cooperation amongst themselves, ensure that transferred financial resources are used efficiently and fairly, and encourage a positive international investment climate.

This emergency programme has been conceived as an integrated whole. Its implementation will do much to create confidence, stimulate trade and investment, and improve the prospects for growth in the world economy. Conducted in partnership between North and South, it would amount to a major step towards a new international order, and the development of a true world community.

A Summit of World Leaders

The global agreement we envisage, with the understanding that must lie behind it, will call for a joint effort of political will and a high degree of trust between the partners, with a common conviction in their mutual interest. We believe that an essential step towards achieving this would be a summit meeting with leaders from both industrialized and developing nations. Such a summit should be limited to some twenty-five world leaders who could ensure fair representation of major world groupings, to enable initiatives and concessions to be thrashed out with candour and boldness. There have already been many important discussions involving the OPEC countries and other countries of the South with the industrialized nations. The United Nations and its agencies continue to provide the means for discussion and negotiation on these global economic problems, for which no meeting of world leaders can or should provide a substitute. And we recognize that leaders at a summit cannot commit those not present. But they could change the international climate and enlarge the prospects for global agreement.

A summit meeting would be able to provide a new focus, and a new concentration on current world problems and their possible solutions; it could provide guidelines and a new impetus for future negotiations; it could launch ideas for a world economic recovery programme. But it should in our view concentrate mainly on the emergency programme. It should not deflect from the other long-term actions to turn round the world economy; in fact, the immediate programme would establish the basis for cooperation and shared responsibility on which the more fundamental changes would rest. But we believe the present deadlock is so serious, and the need to break through is so evident, that nothing should delay discussion and negotiation at the highest level. We hope that a summit could enable political leaders to take the first steps towards committing themselves and their people to a global agreement for the benefit of the whole world.

Whatever their differences and however profound, there is a mutuality of interest between North and South. The fate of both is intimately connected. The search for solutions is not an act of benevolence but a condition of mutual survival. We believe it is dramatically urgent today to start taking concrete steps, without which the world situation can only deteriorate still further, even leading to conflict and catastrophe. It is in a spirit of concern but also of hope that we have formulated the proposals contained in this Report.

Annexe 1
Summary of Recommendations

The Poorest Countries

An action programme must be launched comprising emergency and longer-term measures, to assist the poverty belts of Africa and Asia and particularly the least developed countries. Measures would include large regional projects of water and soil management; the provision of health care and the eradication of such diseases as river-blindness, malaria, sleeping sickness and bilharzia; afforestation projects; solar energy development; mineral and petroleum exploration; and support for industrialization, transport and other infrastructural investment.

Such a programme would require additional financial assistance of at least $4 billion per year for the next two decades, at grant or special concessional terms, assured over long periods and available in flexibly usable forms. New machinery is required on a regional basis to coordinate funding and to prepare plans in cooperation with lending and borrowing countries. Greater technical assistance should be provided to assist such countries with the preparation of programmes and projects.

Hunger and Food

There must be an end to mass hunger and malnutrition. The capacity of food-importing developing countries, particularly the low-income countries, to meet their food requirements should be expanded and their mounting food import bill reduced through their own efforts and through expanded financial flows for agricultural development. Special attention should be given to irrigation, agricultural research, storage and increased use of fertilizer and other inputs, and to fisheries development.

Agrarian reform is of great importance in many countries both to increase agricultural productivity and to put higher incomes into the hands of the poor.

International food security should be assured through the early establishment of an International Grains Arrangement, larger international emergency reserves, and the establishment of a food financing facility.

Food aid should be increased and linked to employment promotion and agricultural programmes and projects without weakening incentives to food production.

Liberalization of trade in food and other agricultural products within and between North and South would contribute to the stabilization of food supplies.

Support for international agricultural research institutions should be expanded with greater emphasis given to regional cooperation.

Population: Growth, Movement and the Environment

In view of the vicious circle between poverty and high birth rates, the rapid population growth in developing countries gives added urgency to the need to fight hunger, disease, malnutrition and illiteracy.

We also believe that development policies should include national population programmes aiming at a satisfactory balance between population and resources and making family planning freely available. International assistance and support of population programmes must be increased to meet the unmet needs for such aid.

The many migrant workers in the world should be assured fair treatment, and the interests of their home countries and the countries of immigration must be better reconciled. Governments should seek bilateral and multilateral cooperation to harmonize their policies of emigration and immigration, to protect the rights of migrant workers, to make remittances more stable and to mitigate the hardships of unanticipated return migration.

The rights of refugees to asylum and legal protection should be strengthened. We also believe that commitments to international cooperation in the resettlement of refugees in the future will be necessary to protect countries of first asylum from unfair burdens.

The strain on the global environment derives mainly from the growth of the industrial economies, but also from that of the world's population. It threatens the survival and development opportunities of future generations. All nations have to cooperate more urgently in international management of the atmosphere and other global commons, and in the prevention of irreversible ecological damage.

Ocean resources outside the 'exclusive economic zones' of 200 miles should be developed under international rules in the balanced interests of the whole world community.

Disarmament and Development

The public must be made more aware of the terrible danger to world stability caused by the arms race, of the burden it imposes on national economies, and of the resources it diverts from peaceful development.

The mutal distrust which stimulates the arms race between East and West calls for continuing the process of *détente* through agreements on confidence-building measures. All sides should be prepared for negotiations (including those on the regional level) to get the arms race under control at a time before new weapons systems have been established.

The world needs a more comprehensive understanding of security which would be less restricted to the purely military aspects.

Every effort must be made to secure international agreements preventing the proliferation of nuclear weapons.

A globally respected peace-keeping mechanism should be built up – strengthening the role of the United Nations. In securing the integrity of states such peace-keeping machinery might free resources for development through a sharing of military expenditures, a reduction in areas of conflict and of the arms race which they imply.

Military expenditure and arms exports might be one element entering into a new principle for international taxation for development purposes. A tax on arms trade should be at a higher rate than that on other trade.

Increased efforts should be made to reach agreements on the disclosure of arms exports and exports of arms-producing facilities. The international community should become more seriously concerned about the consequences of arms-transfers or of exports of arms-producing facilities and reach agreement to restrain such deliveries to areas of conflict or tension.

More research is necessary on the means of converting arms production to civilian production which could make use of the highly skilled scientific and technical manpower currently employed in arms industries.

The Task of the South

In any assault on international poverty, social and economic reforms within developing countries must complement the critical role to be played by the international environment for development, which itself needs to be made more favourable.

In countries where essential reforms have not yet taken place, redistribution of productive resources and incomes is necessary. A broader package of policy improvements would include expansion of social services to the poor, agrarian reform, increased development expenditures in rural areas, stimulation of small-scale enterprises and better tax administration. Such measures are important both for satisfying elementary needs and for increasing productivity, particularly in rural areas.

The full potential of the informal sector to contribute to economic development requires the provision of increased resources in the form of easier access to credit, and expanded training and extension services.

The strengthening of indigenous technological capacity often requires a more scientific bias in education, the encouragement of a domestic engineering industry, increased emphasis on intermediate technology and the sharing of experience.

Improved economic management and the increased mobilization of domestic resources are essential to the promotion of development. In many countries there is scope for improvements in such fields as taxation policies, public administration and the operation of the pricing system.

Wider participation in the development process should be encouraged; measures to achieve this could include decentralized governmental administrative systems and support for relevant voluntary organizations.

Regional and sub-regional integration, or other forms of close cooperation, still offer a viable strategy for accelerated economic development and structural transformation among developing countries especially the smaller ones. It supports industrialization and trade expansion and provides opportunities for multi-country ventures.

Developing countries should take steps to expand preferential trade schemes among themselves. This could be encouraged by such measures as the untying of aid.

Developing countries should give special attention to the establishment and extension of payments and credit arrangements among themselves to facilitate trade and to ease balance of payments problems.

The emergence of capital-surplus developing countries provides special scope for the establishment of projects on the basis of tripartite arrangements involving developing countries alone or in partnership with industrialized countries. Such arrangements should be supported by both developed and developing countries. Tripartite projects – including, when appropriate, industrialized countries – should be encouraged by nations with complementary resources such as capital and technology.

Developing countries should consider what forms of mutual assistance organization might help them to participate more effectively in negotiations and in the work of international organizations and to promote economic cooperation among themselves.

Commodity Trade and Development

The commodity sector of developing countries should contribute more to economic development through the greater participation of these countries in the processing, marketing and distribution of their commodities. Action for the stabilization of commodity prices at remunerative levels should be undertaken as a matter of urgency.

Measures to facilitate the participation of developing countries in processing and marketing should include the removal of tariff and other trade barriers against developing countries' processed products, the establishment of fair and equitable international transport rates, the abolition of restrictive business practices, and improved financial arrangements for facilitating processing and marketing.

Adequate resources should be provided to enable the Common Fund to encourage and finance effective International Commodity Agreements which would stabilize prices at remunerative levels; to finance national stocking outside ICAs; and to facilitate the carrying out of Second Window activities such as storage, processing, marketing, productivity improvement and diversification.

Greater efforts should be made to bring to a rapid and successful conclusion negotiations on individual commodity agreements wherever these are feasible.

Compensatory financing facilities should be expanded and improved to provide more adequately for shortfalls in real commodity export earnings.

The mutual interest of producing and consuming countries in

the development of mineral resources requires the creation of new financial arrangements leading to more equitable and stable mineral development agreements, greater assurance of world mineral supplies and increased developing-country participation in their resource development. A new financing facility, whose primary function will be to provide concessional finance for mineral exploration, should be established on the basis of a global responsibility for investment in mineral development.

Energy

An orderly transition is required from high dependence on increasingly scarce non-renewable energy sources.

Immediate steps towards an international strategy on energy should be taken as part of the Emergency Programme recommended in the final chapter of the Report.

Prices which reflect long-term scarcities will play an important role in this transition; orderly and predictable price changes are important to facilitate a smooth development of the world economy.

Special arrangements including financial assistance should be made to ensure supplies to the poorer developing countries.

International and regional financial agencies must increase substantially their financing of exploration and development of energy sources including the development of renewable energy resources.

A global energy research centre should be created under UN auspices to coordinate information and projections and to support research on new energy resources.

Industrialization and World Trade

The industrialization of developing countries, as a means of their overall development efforts, will provide increasing opportunities for world trade and need not conflict with the long-term interests of developed countries. It should be facilitated as a matter of international policy.

Protectionism threatens the future of the world economy and is inimical to the long-term interests of developing and developed countries alike. Protectionism by industrialized countries against the exports of developing countries should be rolled back; this should be facilitated by improved institutional machinery and new trading rules and principles.

Adjustment to new patterns of world industrial production

should be accepted as a necessary and desirable process. Industrialized countries should vigorously pursue positive and time-bound adjustment programmes developed through international consultation and subject to international surveillance.

Safeguard measures must be internationally negotiated and should be taken only on the basis of established need. They should be non-discriminatory, of limited duration and subject to international surveillance.

The Generalized System of Preferences should be eased in respect of its rules of origin, its exceptions and its limits. It should be extended beyond its present expiration and not be liable to unilateral termination.

Financial support and technical assistance should be given to the poorer countries to facilitate their establishment of improved commercial infrastructure and their participation in international trade negotiations.

Fair labour standards should be internationally agreed in order to prevent unfair competition and to facilitate trade liberalization.

An international trade organization incorporating both GATT and UNCTAD is the objective towards which the international community should work. Meanwhile, there is need for improvement in existing arrangements including wider development of trade cooperation in such matters as the establishment and administration of rules, principles and codes covering restrictive business practices and technology transfer.

Transnational Corporations, Investment and the Sharing of Technology

Effective national laws and international codes of conduct are needed to govern the sharing of technology, to control restrictive business practices, and to provide a framework for the activities of transnational corporations.

The investment regime we propose would include:

1 Reciprocal obligations on the part of host and home countries covering foreign investment, transfer of technology, and repatriation of profits, royalties and dividends.
2 Legislation, coordinated in home and host countries, to regulate transnational corporation activities in matters such as ethical behaviour, disclosure of information, restrictive business practices and labour standards.
3 Intergovernmental cooperation in regard to tax policies and the monitoring of transfer pricing.

4 Harmonization of fiscal and other incentives among host developing countries.

In addition to improved access to international development finance the bargaining capacity of developing countries, particularly of the smaller and least developed countries, *vis-à-vis* the transnational corporations should be strengthened with the technical assistance now increasingly available from the UN and other agencies.

Permanent sovereignty over natural resources is the right of all countries. It is necessary, however, that nationalization be accompanied by appropriate and effective compensation, under internationally comparable principles which should be embodied in national laws. Increasing use should also be made of international mechanisms for settling disputes.

Greater international, regional and national efforts are needed to support the development of technology in developing countries and the transfer of appropriate technology to them at reasonable cost.

There should be increased efforts in both rich and poor countries to develop appropriate technology in the light of changing constraints regarding energy and ecology; the flow of information about such technology should be improved. The international aid agencies should change those of their practices which restrict the recipients' freedom to choose technology, and should make more use of local capacities in preparing projects.

The World Monetary Order

The reform of the international monetary system should be urgently undertaken by all interested parties building on the large measure of consensus which emerged in the Committee of Twenty, and taking account of current difficulties and dangers. Reform involves improvements in the exchange rate regime, the reserve system, the balance of payments adjustment process, and the overall management of the system which should permit the participation of the whole international community.

Mechanisms should be agreed for creating and distributing an international currency to be used for clearing and settling outstanding balances between central banks. Such a currency would replace the use of national currencies as international reserves. It could take the form of an improved Special Drawing Right, and could be facilitated by an appropriately designed 'substitution account'.

New SDRs should be created to the extent called for by the need for non-inflationary increases in world liquidity. The distribution of such unconditional liquidity should favour the developing countries who presently bear high adjustment burdens. Such a distribution – often referred to as an SDR link – would also assist the adjustment process of the international monetary system.

There should be agreement on an adjustment process which will not increase contractionist pressures in the world economy. The adjustment process of developing countries should be placed in the context of maintaining long-term economic and social development. The IMF should avoid inappropriate or excessive regulation of their economies, and should not impose highly deflationary measures as standard adjustment policy. It should also improve and greatly extend the scope of its compensatory financing facility, for example by relaxing quota limits, measuring shortfalls in real terms and making repayment terms more flexible. Surplus countries should accept greater responsibility for payments adjustments, and IMF measures to encourage this should be considered.

Increased stability of international exchange rates, particularly among key currencies, should be sought through domestic discipline and coordination of appropriate national policies.

The participation of developing countries in the staffing, management and decision-making of the IMF should be enlarged.

In furthering the demonetization of gold, the bulk of the IMF gold stock should, after the completion of the present sales arrangements, be used as collateral against which the IMF can borrow from the market for onward lending particularly to middle-income developing countries. Staggered sales should also be undertaken and accruing profits of such sales should be used as interest subsidy on loans to low-income developing countries.

A New Approach to Development Finance

There must be a substantial increase in the transfer of resources to developing countries in order to finance:

1 Projects and programmes to alleviate poverty and to expand food production, especially in the least developed countries.
2 Exploration and development of energy and mineral resources.
3 Stabilization of the prices and earnings of commodity exports and expanded domestic processing of commodities.

The flow of official development finance should be enlarged by:

1 An international system of universal revenue mobilization, based on a sliding scale related to national income, in which East European and developing countries – except the poorest countries – would participate.

2 The adoption of timetables to increase Official Development Assistance from industrialized countries to the level of 0.7 per cent of GNP by 1985, and to one per cent before the end of the century.

3 Introduction of automatic revenue transfers through international levies on some of the following: international trade, arms production or exports; international travel; the global commons, especially sea-bed minerals.

Lending through international financial institutions should be improved through:

1 Effective utilization of the increased borrowing capacity of the World Bank resulting from the recent decision to double its capital to $80 billion

2 Doubling the borrowing-to-capital ratio of the World Bank from its present gearing of 1:1 to 2:1, and similar action by Regional Development Banks.

3 Abstaining from the imposition of political conditions on the operations of multilateral financial institutions.

4 Channelling an increasing share of development finance through regional institutions.

5 A substantial increase in programme lending.

6 The use of IMF gold reserves either for further sales, whose profits would subsidize interest on development lending, or as collateral to borrow for on-lending to developing countries.

7 Giving borrowing countries a greater role in decision making and management.

Resource transfers should be made more predictable by long-term commitments to provide ODA, increasing use of automatically mobilized revenues, and the lengthening of the IDA replenishment period.

Consideration should be given to the creation of a new international financial institution – a World Development Fund – with universal membership, and in which decision-making is more evenly shared between lenders and borrowers, to supplement existing institutions and diversify lending policies and practices. The World Development Fund would seek to satisfy the unmet needs in the financing structure, in particular that of programme lending. Ultimately it could serve as a channel for such resources as may be raised on a universal and automatic basis.

291

There is need for major additional multilateral finance to support mineral and energy exploration and development in developing countries. Some of this will come from existing institutions, but we believe there is a case for a new facility for this purpose.

The flow of lending from commercial banks and other private financial bodies to developing countries must be strengthened. Middle-income countries need special measures to lengthen the maturity of their debt structures and poorer developing countries should be enabled to borrow more easily in the market. The World Bank and other international financial institutions should assist this process by co-financing, by the provision of guarantees, and by using concessional funds to improve lending terms and reduce interest rates.

Measures should be adopted to facilitate the placing of bonds by developing countries in international markets. These should include the removal of restrictions and the provision of guarantees and adequate arrangements for the assessment of risks.

International Organizations and Negotiations

Policies, agreements and institutions in the field of international economic, financial and monetary cooperation should be guided by the principle of universality.

The UN system, which faces ever-expanding tasks, needs to be strengthened and made more efficient. This calls for more coordination of budgets, programmes and personnel policies, to avoid duplication of tasks and wasteful overlapping.

The performance of the various multilateral organizations in the field of international development should be regularly monitored by a high-level advisory body.

There needs to be a review of the present system of negotiations to see whether more flexible, expeditious and result-oriented procedures can be introduced without detracting from cooperation within established groups.

Increased attention should be paid to educating public opinion and the younger generation about the importance of international cooperation.

The occasional use of limited summit meetings should be considered to advance the cause of consensus and change.

Annexe 2
The Commission and Its Work

On 28 September 1977 Willy Brandt, former Chancellor of the Federal Republic of Germany, announced at a press conference in New York that he was ready to launch and chair an 'Independent Commission on International Development Issues'. This announcement had been preceded by a large number of private consultations and discussions. The Chairman made a point of emphasizing that the Commission would not interfere in any way with governmental negotiations nor with the ongoing work of international organizations. Rather, such a group would have a supplementary function, to present recommendations which could improve the climate for further deliberations on North–South relations.

UN Secretary-General Kurt Waldheim showed great interest in the formation of this Independent Commission, and agreed that he would receive the first copy of the Commission's Report.

The suggestion of creating such a Commission under the chairmanship of Mr Brandt had first been advanced by Robert S McNamara, President of the World Bank, in a speech in Boston, early in 1977, and he reverted to it in his address to the Annual Meeting of the IMF and World Bank in Washington in the autumn of that year.

This Commission has been independent. Its members were invited to serve in a private capacity, not under governmental instructions. In addition, its Chairman was anxious that the Third World members should not be in a minority position.

The Commissioners

Chairman
Willy Brandt   Bonn, Federal Republic of Germany.
Chairman of the Social Democratic Party, Federal Chancellor 1969–74, Minister of Foreign Affairs 1966–9, Mayor of Berlin 1957–66, Nobel Peace Prize 1971.

Members
Abdlatif Y. Al-Hamad Kuwait. Member of Governing Body, Institute of Development Studies, Sussex, Member of Visiting Committee, Center for Middle East Studies, Harvard University, Director-General of Kuwait Fund for Arabic Economic Development, Trustee, Kuwait Institute of Economic and Social Planning in the Middle East.

Rodrigo Botero Montoya   Bogotá, Colombia, Economist, Editor and Publisher of *Estrategia Económica y Financiera,* Minister of Finance 1974–6, Executive Director, Foundation for Higher Education and Development (FEDESARROLLO) 1970–74, Special Presidential Assistant for Economic Affairs in Bogotá 1966–70.

Antoine Kipsa Dakouré   Ouagadougou, Upper Volta. Adviser to the President of Upper Volta since 1976, Coordinating Minister for Drought

Control in the Sahel 1973–5, Minister of Planning 1970–76, Minister of Agriculture 1966–70.

Eduardo Frei Montalva Santiago, Chile. Lawyer and Politician, President of the Parliament 1973, Former Chairman of the Christian Democratic Party, President of Chile 1964–70, Minister of Public Works and Transport 1944–5, Author of various books, including most recently *America Latina – Opción y Esperanza* ('Latin America – The Best Hope').

Katharine Graham Washington DC, USA. Chairman of the Board, Washington Post Co. since 1963, Publisher, *Washington Post* 1969–79.

Edward Heath London, United Kingdom. Politician, MP, Prime Minister 1970–74, Leader of the Conservative Party 1965–75, Secretary of State for Industry, Trade and Regional Development 1963–4, Leader of the British Delegation to UNCTAD 1964, Lord Privy Seal at the Foreign Office 1960–63, Minister of Labour 1959–60.

Amir H. Jamal Dar-es-Salaam, Tanzania. Politician, Minister of Finance, Minister of Communications and Transport 1977–9, Minister of Finance and Economic Planning 1975–7, Minister for Commerce and Industries 1972–5, Minister of Finance 1965–72, Minister of Economic Planning 1964–5, Minister of Communications and Power 1962–4.

Lakshmi Kant Jha Srinagar, India. Governor of Jammu and Kashmir, Chairman of UN Group of Eminent Persons on Multinational Corporations 1973–5, Ambassador to the USA 1970–73, Governor of Reserve Bank of India 1967–70.

Khatijah Ahmad Kuala Lumpur, Malaysia. Economist and banker, Managing Director of KAF Discounts Ltd since 1974, Director of Administration and Secretary of National Paddy and Rice Authority 1971–3.

Adam Malik Jakarta, Indonesia. Vice-President, President of National Assembly 1977–8, Minister of Foreign Affairs 1966–77, President of UN General Assembly 1971–2, Minister of Commerce 1963–5, Ambassador to the USSR 1959–63.

Haruki Mori Tokyo, Japan. Ambassador to the United Kingdom 1972–5, Vice-Minister in the Ministry of Foreign Affairs 1970–72, Ambassador to the OECD 1964–7.

Joe Morris Victoria, Canada. President-Emeritus of Canadian Labour Congress and Vice-Chairman of International Labour Organization's Governing Body 1970–77, 1978–9, Chairman, ILO Governing Body 1977–8, Vice-President ICFTU 1976–8.

Olof Palme Stockholm, Sweden, Chairman of the Social Democratic Party, Prime Minister 1969–76, Minister of Education and Culture 1967–9, Minister of Communications 1965–7, Minister without Portfolio 1963–5.

Peter G. Peterson New York, USA. Chairman of the Board of Lehman Bros. Kuhn Loeb, Secretary of Commerce 1972–3, Assistant to the

President of USA for International Economic Affairs and Executive Director of the Council on International Economic Policy 1971–2.

Edgard Pisani* Paris, France. Senator, Member of European Parliament, Minister of National Equipment 1966–7, Minister of Agriculture 1961–5, Author: *Défi du monde – campagne d'Europe, La France dans l'affrontement économique international.*
*Mr Pisani replaced Mr Pierre Mendès-France, former Prime Minister of France, who had originally been a member and participated in the Commission's work but had to resign for personal reasons in summer 1978.

Shridath Ramphal Georgetown, Guyana. Commonwealth Secretary-General, Minister of Foreign Affairs and Justice 1972–5, Attorney-General and Minister of State for External Affairs 1966–72.

Layachi Yaker Algiers, Algeria. Ambassador to the USSR, Member of the Central Committee of the Party of the National Liberation Front, Member of Parliament and Vice-President, National People's Assembly 1977–9, Minister of Commerce 1969–77, Minister Plenipotentiary, Director of Economic, Cultural and Social Affairs, Ministry of Foreign Affairs 1962–9.

Honorary Treasurer

Jan P. Pronk The Hague, Netherlands. Member of Parliament 1971–3 and since 1978, Minister for Development Cooperation 1973–7, Research Assistant to Professor Jan Tinbergen 1965–71.

Executive Secretary

Goran Ohlin Stockholm, Sweden. Professor of Economics at Uppsala University since 1969, Staff Member of the Pearson Commission 1968–9, Fellow of the Development Centre of OECD, Paris 1962–6, Consultant to various international organizations.

Director of the Secretariat

Dragoslav Avramović Belgrade, Yugoslavia. Senior economic staff positions in World Bank 1965–77, Director, Economics Department, Industrialization Studies, Commodity Studies, Debt Studies, Special Adviser to UNCTAD on Commodity Stabilization 1974–5, before 1953, senior posts Government of Yugoslavia and teaching, University of Belgrade.

Mr Goran Ohlin, Mr Jan Pronk and Mr Dragoslav Avramović became *ex-officio* members of the Commission. Mr Fritz Fischer assisted the Chairman in the preparations to launch the Commission and was responsible for his liaison office in Bonn.
At several meetings Mr Brandt asked Governor Jha to take over the chair temporarily; due to the Chairman's illness, L. K. Jha presided over the whole of the fifth meeting in Kuala Lumpur. He also chaired the New Delhi round-table on Economic Cooperation between Developing Countries.

Opening Session in Gymnich, Germany, 9-11 December 1977

At an opening ceremony in the presence of the media, statements were made by the Chairman, President Walter Scheel and Commission member Shridath Ramphal.

William Clark, a Vice-President of the World Bank, was present. The Commission was received by Chancellor Helmut Schmidt for a discussion. It also met with Egon Bahr, a former Federal Minister, who discussed questions of *détente* and disarmament, and subsequently continued to advise the Chairman on these issues.

In its closed session the Commission had a first overall discussion, adopted its Terms of Reference and set the basis for a frank exchange of views, without detailed minutes and without giving meetings the character of conferences.

Terms of Reference

The task of the Independent Commission on International Development Issues is to study the grave global issues arising from the economic and social disparities of the world community and to suggest ways of promoting adequate solutions to the problems involved in development and in attacking absolute poverty. As an independent commission it is free to raise any aspects of the world situation which the Commission considers pertinent and to recommend any measures it finds in the interest of the world economy.

The Commission should pay careful attention to the UN resolutions on development problems and other issues explored in international fora in recent years. It should seek to identify desirable and realistic directions for international development policy in the next decade, giving attention to what in their mutual interest both the developed and the developing countries should do.

In pursuit of those objectives the Commission's work will encompass the following:

1 *The record of development*
The Commission will examine the record of development in the Third World and the influences on it of the international political and economic environment. It will review, firstly, the outcome of past economic growth and the widening disparities of *per capita* income; secondly, the results of that growth within developed and developing countries in terms of employment, inflation, international trade, and other important respects; thirdly, the effects of the recent recession in the industrialized countries on the world economy. Against this background it will examine international action to change the context for development: the record on international trade, including access to markets, terms of trade, and commodity policies, financial cooperation, other capital flows, debt, and the activities of multinational corporations. The need for a new international economic order will be at the centre of the Commission's concern.

2 Prospects for the world economy

The Commission will examine relevant trends in the world economy, particularly for the 1980s but also looking further into the future. It will consider the various projections which have been made, concentrating on the likely prospects for the developing and developed countries under different assumptions about measures adopted by the international community. It will refer to a number of aspects of those prospects including: food and agriculture; industrializaton; population growth; development and transfer of technology; problems of exhaustible resources and energy; water supply, environmental and ecological problems. The Commission will pay attention to the question of expenditures on armaments and the political conditions which affect them.

3 Roads to a new international economic order

The Commission will strive above all to carry conviction with decision makers and with public opinion that profound changes are required in international relations, particularly international economic relations. It will consider firstly the restructuring of international trade, including improved commercial and industrial policies, access to markets, commodity policies and economic cooperation among developing countries; secondly, international finance, including private and public sources of credit, and financial cooperation especially in favour of the least developed countries, the international monetary system, debt problems, the role of the International Monetary Fund, the World Bank and Regional Banks; thirdly, the regulation of the activities of multinational corporations; fourthly, the framework within which bilateral and multilateral economic negotiations are carried out, with special attention to North–South relations; and fifthly, the prospects for a greater involvement of all countries in international development efforts. The Commission will pay attention to the responsibilities of developing countries in their domestic policies, to match the effort for international economic and social justice with efforts to promote the same ends among their own populations. The Commission will devote particular attention to exploring the interdependence of all countries in the world economy and to the need for solutions for world employment problems. Finally the Commission will attempt to shift the framework of debate so that public opinion will be led to see the problem of international development not in terms of 'the rich helping the poor' but of the developing countries achieving a just return for their own productive efforts, and the developed countries working in cooperation with them for the economic and social development of all nations.

Eminent Persons

At the Gymnich meeting a roster of Eminent Persons was discussed to be invited to testify or submit their views:

Angelos Angelopoulos, Greece	Harlan Cleveland, USA
Roberto Campos, Brazil	John Crawford, Australia
Guido Carli, Italy	Luis Echeverria, Mexico
Claude Cheysson, France	Erhard Eppler, Germany (FR)

Robert Gardiner, Ghana
Mahbub ul Haq, Pakistan
Crown Prince Hassan, Jordan
Enrique Iglesias, Uruguay
Lal Jayawardena, Sri Lanka
Henry Kissinger, USA
W. Arthur Lewis, Jamaica
Donald Macdonald, Canada
Takeo Miki, Japan

Raul Prebisch, Argentina
Ibrahim Abdul Rahman Hilmy, Egypt
Maurice Strong, Canada
Inga Thorsson, Sweden
Jan Tinbergen, Netherlands
Joop den Uyl, Netherlands
Barbara Ward, United Kingdom
Takeshi Watanabe, Japan

Secretariat

In January 1978 a Secretariat took up its work in Geneva. The Executive Secretary of the Commission and the Director of the Secretariat became co-responsible for draft proposals and other documentation prepared by the Secretariat for the use of the Commission.

Staff of the Commission

Goran Ohlin, Executive Secretary, Dragoslav Avramović, Director of the Secretariat, Liaqat Ali, Robert H. Cassen, S. Guhan, Javad Khalilzadeh-Shirazi, Martha F. Loutfi, Justinian F. Rweyemamu, Gerhard G. Thiebach, Fritz Fischer, Special Assistant to the Chairman, Michael Hofmann (Bonn), Anthony Sampson, Editorial Adviser, Nicholas Harman, Press Consultant. Interpreters: Norman Edwards, Irène Testot-Ferry, Claire Tolnay-Gaucheron, André Gaucheron, Marie-France Skuncke. Research Assistants: Eshetou Mengesha, Nimala Perera, Mary Ann Knotts. Administration and General Services: Jagge Andersen, Samuel Amalemba, Judy Barnes, Jeanne Berkeley, Christa Bigler, Annie Degraeve, Margaret Ducommun, Susan Evans, Janette Ferguson, Rosa Ganose, Oonagh Guyonnet, Philippa Heale, Ernest Kurt, Jelka de Marsano, Jean-Pierre Ruchti, Christel Siebel-Wolters, Ulla Tabatabay, Nuria Tarre-Cancellieri, Jennifer Weeks.

Talks in India and Japan

Together with Commission members L. K. Jha and Shridath Ramphal the Chairman released an extensive press statement about the start of the Commission on the occasion of a visit to New Delhi in December 1977, which he made a few days after the first meeting in Gymnich. The Indian authorities were informed and consulted.

Prior to the Delhi visit, the Chairman had been to Tokyo and discussed problems with the Prime Minister and othe Japanese leaders. A visit was also paid to the UN University.

Second Meeting, Mont-Pèlerin, Switzerland, 10-12 March 1978

The Commission's main discussion focused on its work programme and on the notion of 'mutuality of interests' as the underlying concept for the Report; the latter would not cover all economic subjects presently under negotiation, but it would also examine other areas, such as disarmament and development, as well as a greater universality of global efforts through increased participation by eastern countries.

At the beginning of this meeting, Messrs Claude Cheysson, Mahbub ul Haq and Jan Tinbergen as Eminent Persons presented their views on major

298

North–South problems. The Commission also met with the Swiss Minister of Foreign Affairs, M Pierre Aubert, and had informal discussions with the Prime Ministers of Turkey and Portugal.

Third Meeting in Bamako, Mali, 14-17 May 1978

Prior to this meeting most Commission members took part in a round-table discussion with experts on commodities, held in London at the premises of the Commonwealth Secretariat, which assisted with arrangements for the round-table.

In its plenary session in Mali the Commission focused on the problems of Least Developed Countries and established a Working Group for this purpose, chaired by M Antoine Dakouré from Upper Volta. It also discussed commodity issues, and the problem of 'basic needs'.

The Commission was received by President Traoré. It also heard the views of members of the Government. The Zambian Minister of Education, Mr L. K. H. Goma, and a Director of the African Development Bank made presentations.

Other African contacts

Prior to the Mali meeting the Chairman was the guest of the President of Senegal.

Towards the end of 1977 the Chairman was the guest of the Presidents of Tanzania and of Zambia. He also met with other leaders in the region. And in Bonn, he met with the President of Sudan.

Mr Dakouré had consultations about the specific problems of the least developed countries with political leaders and representatives of youth organizations and of the public and private sector in Upper Volta, with prominent West African personalities, with experts and officials of sub-regional African organizations and African diplomats.

Arab and other Middle Eastern contacts

After the Mali meeting, the Chairman and some Commissioners met Mr Boumedienne, the late President of Algeria.

In Bonn and elsewhere he had meetings with the Presidents of Egypt, Syria, the Prime Minister of Saudi Arabia and the King of Jordan.

High-ranking Arab guests addressed the Commission at its Vienna meeting (see below).

In December 1979, before the tenth meeting, the Chairman and Commissioners visited Kuwait and Saudi Arabia at the invitation of their Governments. They met with: HH the Emir of Kuwait and HRH Crown Prince Fahd and government representatives.

Contacts were also made with representatives from Israel.

The EEC and European capitals

In July 1978 Mr Brandt had high-level talks with governments in EEC countries (Italy, France, United Kingdom, Ireland, Belgium, Luxembourg, the Netherlands, Denmark) as well as with the President and members of the Community's Commission.

Austria was included in that 'tour' while meetings with the Prime

Ministers of Sweden and Norway, the President of Finland, and the Prime Minister of Spain had been arranged earlier in 1977. In October 1979 Mr Brandt met with both the President and the Prime Minister of Portugal.

Soviet Union and Eastern Europe

The Pearson Report while emphasizing the future importance of Centrally Planned Economies nonetheless refrained from dealing with them in any detail. This Commission felt that it was necessary to devote more attention to these aspects – and not only in the context of disarmament problems.

The Chairman met with Secretary-General Brezhnev in May 1978 and arranged for a meeting of Secretariat members with representatives from the Institute of World Economy and International Relations and colleagues from other research bodies in Moscow, which took place in July 1978.

The Chairman met political leaders from Poland, Hungary, Czechoslovakia, Romania and Bulgaria. The government of the German Democratic Republic was also informed at an expert level.

Fourth Meeting in Tarrytown, USA, 25-28 August 1978

In accordance with its agreed work programme, the Commission discussed the topic of 'mutual interests' and had an exchange of views on migration and brain drain, on debt, and on food and agriculture.

It listened to three of its Eminent Persons as invited guests: Raul Prebisch, Harlan Cleveland and Henry Kissinger. The Commission also heard statements by Mr Kenneth Dadzie, UN Director-General for Development and International Economic Cooperation; Mr Idriss Jazairy, Chairman of the UN Committee of the Whole; Ambassador Donald Mills, Chairman of the Group of 77; and Mr Jacques de Larosière, Managing Director of the International Monetary Fund. The Chairman met with Mr Bradford Morse, Administrator of UNDP.

Views of the United States Government were presented by Mr Richard Cooper, Under-Secretary for Economic Affairs in the Department of State. Senator Jacob Javits and Mr Orville Freeman, President of the Business International Corporation, also addressed the Commission, and its members met informally with the late former Vice-President Nelson Rockefeller.

Other North American contacts

Prior to the launching of the Commission, the Chairman had met with President Carter and Secretary of State Vance. A continuation of these contacts was envisaged in October 1978 but could not be realized because the Chairman fell ill while in Washington.

Other Commission members, especially Mrs Graham, Mr Peterson and Mr Botero, had talks with representatives from the US Administration.

Further, in September 1979 a seminar was held in Ottawa upon the invitation of the Canadian Government with representatives from Canadian business and finance.

Fifth Meeting in Kuala Lumpur, Malaysia, 24-27 November 1978
The Commission discussed economic cooperation among developing countries and access for their manufactures to markets in the industrialized countries. Also on the agenda were: non-renewable resources, energy and environment, technology, foreign investment and transnational corporations, and prospects for the 1980s.

As invited guests, the Deputy Prime Minister of Korea, Mr Duck-Woo Nam, the Minister of Trade of Sri Lanka, Mr Lalith Athulathmudali, as well as the President of the Asian Development Bank, Mr Taroichi Yoshida, addressed the Commission, and the discussion focused on national development strategies and on possibilities of increased regional cooperation.

Following a meeting with Prime Minister Datuk Hussein Onn, these questions were also discussed in a working session with members of the Malaysian Government.

Other contacts in the Asian and Pacific region
Prior to the Kuala Lumpur meeting most Commission members took part in a round-table discussion in Delhi devoted to the question of greater cooperation among developing countries. The Working Group on Least Developed Countries also met on that occasion.

Upon conclusion of the meeting in Malaysia, groups of Commissioners conducted high-level talks in Singapore, Indonesia, the Republic of Korea, Sri Lanka and Japan.

The Commission's Executive Secretary discussed North–South issues with experts in Canberra and Sydney, and the Chairman met with the Australian Prime Minister in Bonn.

Discussions in China
At the invitation of the People's Republic of China, the Honorary Treasurer and Secretariat members held discussions in Peking in August 1979. Mr Peterson had paid a visit to China in April 1979. In September 1979 Commission member Mr Heath conducted high-level talks there. The Chairman also met with Prime Minister Hua who was in Bonn in October 1979.

Modifications of venues and contacts
Due to his illness, which ruled out air travel for a period, Mr Brandt to his regret had to limit himself to holding discussions in Europe rather than continuing to visit other parts of the world. The envisaged plenary meeting in Latin America could not be held; but the Latin American members of the Commission maintained contacts in this area and personalities from Latin America were invited to other venues.

In December 1979 a delegation of the Commission visited Kuwait and Saudi Arabia where a plenary meeting had originally been envisaged.

Sixth Meeting, Mont-Pèlerin, Switzerland, 22-26 February 1979
With the participation of Mrs Inga Thorsson, the Commission discussed the relationship between disarmament and development. It had an

301

exchange of views on the international financial and monetary system, as well as on the coordination of multilateral aid agencies.

The Commission also met with two other Eminent Persons, Messrs Lal Jayawardena and Angelos Angelopoulos and had discussions with the Secretary-General of UNCTAD, Mr Gamani Corea, as well as the Director-General of GATT, Mr Olivier Long.

Contacts with heads of international and regional organizations
In April 1979 as a guest of a joint meeting with UN Secretary-General Waldheim and the Heads of the Administrative Committee on Coordination (ACC) in Geneva, the Chairman continued his previous contacts in this domain. In the course of the Commission's work, Mr Brandt had a chance to talk to many of them individually and he met with high-level representatives from regional organizations such as OECD and EEC.

Other Commission members also exchanged views with representatives of international and regional organizations including the heads of the World Bank and of the IMF.

Several Commission members took part in meetings of the Non-Aligned Movement. The Chairman maintained relations with this Movement and met twice with President Tito.

He also met with the late Pope Paul VI, as well as the Reverend Potter from the World Council of Churches and was encouraged by their sympathy and support as well as by similar convictions shared by other world religious leaders.

Seventh Meeting in Annecy, France, 2-6 May 1979
In continuation of earlier discussions, the Commission examined the international financial and monetary system and institutions. Urgent development objectives, including ecological restoration and conservation were studied. Other items of discussion included the question of women in development, of population, as well as the reform of international institutions.

As invited guests two Eminent Persons, Dame Barbara Ward (Lady Jackson) and Mr Maurice Strong, addressed the Commission. From Latin America, President Ortiz Mena of the Inter-American Development Bank, as well as Mr Carlos Massad, Adviser to the UN Economic Commission for Latin America, addressed the Commission.

Other contacts with Latin America and the Caribbean
The Chairman met with the Presidents of Mexico and Brazil as well as the Prime Minister of Jamaica and had an exchange of views also with political leaders from Venezuela.

Commissioners Eduardo Frei and Rodrigo Botero established high-level contacts with representatives of the Interamerican Development Bank, the Organization of American States and the United Nations Economic Commission for Latin America, ECLA. Mr Frei maintained contact with ECLA headquarters in Santiago during the time of the Commission's work.

Mr Botero met with government representatives in Argentina, Brazil, Colombia, Ecuador, Jamaica, Mexico, Peru and Venezuela, as well as in Portugal and Spain.

The Honorary Treasurer of the Commission had an occasion in 1978 to inform the President of Cuba about the Commission's goals and activities.

Eighth Meeting in Vienna, Austria, 4-9 July 1979
On the basis of draft material for its Report, the Commission substantially concluded its discussions and focused on the various aspects of energy problems as well as on the problems of the poorest countries, and the discussion on previous subjects was also resumed.

The Commission received two of its Eminent Persons, Crown Prince Hassan of Jordan, and the former Prime Minister of the Netherlands, Mr Joop den Uyl. It also met with the Executive Director of the United Nations Industrial Development Organization, Dr Abd-El Rahman Khane, as well as the following Arab personalities: the Secretary-General of the Organization of Arab Petroleum Exporting Countries (OAPEC), Dr Ali Attiga, the Deputy Secretary-General of OPEC, Dr Fadhil Al-Chalabi, and the Director-General of the OPEC Special Fund, Dr Ibrahim Shihata.

The Commission was received by Chancellor Kreisky and met with members of his cabinet as well as representatives of the international community in Vienna.

First editing session (Ninth Meeting) in Brussels, Belgium, 5-9 October 1979
The Commission discussed the draft text of its Report. The Chairman and some Commissioners had prepared the discussion of the draft papers for the final Report at a preceding meeting in Bonn. In Brussels a concluding discussion was also held on a strategy for long-term, permanent reforms to redress the imbalance between the rich and the poor nations of the world.

The Commission was received by the Belgian Prime Minister.

Second editing session (Tenth Meeting) in Leeds Castle, Kent, 14-16 December 1979
An Editorial Group advised by experts was set up under the leadership of Mr Heath and Mr Ramphal, in consultation with the Chairman, to work in London and prepare a complete draft of the Report for submission to the Tenth Meeting.

In a concentrated two days' debate the Commission adopted the final text of the Report and its recommendations. The Chairman informed the public at a press conference in London on 17 December 1979.

Special volume by the Secretariat
In addition to the Commission's Report the Secretariat will publish selected papers which formed part of the background to the Commission's deliberations.

Acknowledgements
The Commission has drawn encouragement, support and advice from many political leaders, national and international organizations, trade unions, youth organizations, institutes and interested citizens, many of whom offered their advice spontaneously. A word of sincere gratitude is owed to them all. Commission members themselves have contributed many valuable papers and have established fruitful working contacts through

contribution of their assistants and

Financial contributions

With a generous pledge to guaranteee the total costs, the Dutch Government enabled the Commission's work to start; it financed about half of the total expenditure.

The governments of Denmark, Finland, India, Japan, Republic of Korea, Norway, Saudi Arabia, Sweden and the United Kingdom joined in with substantial untied contributions. Regional organizations and Funds, such as the Commission of the European Communities and the OPEC Special Fund assisted. So did Foundations and Research Centres such as the German Marshall Fund of the United States, the Ford Foundation, the Friedrich-Ebert and the Friedrich-Naumann Foundations, Germany (FR), and the International Development Research Center, Canada. Private sources from Germany (FR) and France also contributed smaller amounts.

Other contributions

The Swiss Government kindly covered the costs of office rent and equipment of the Secretariat in Geneva. Local costs of four Commission meetings were met by the Governments of Germany (Federal Republic), Malaysia, Austria and Belgium. Similarly, the Governments of India, Canada and Germany met the costs of the round-table discussions and preparatory sessions in their capitals. Equally, the costs of the stay of Commission delegations in Singapore, Indonesia, USSR, Republic of Korea, Kuwait and Saudi Arabia were met by the host governments. The Commonwealth Secretariat provided office accommodation for the work of the Editorial Group in London.

This wide variety of funds and contributions strengthened the Commission's independence.

Auditing of ICIDI's accounts was carried out by Ernest Kurt, Finance Inspector, Geneva.

Follow-up

While there will be no formal follow-up after the publication of the Commission's Report, it was nonetheless found to be advisable to have an office where comments, requests, etc. can be dealt with. It was therefore, very much appreciated that – with the assistance of the Dutch Government – the possibility was created to take care of these tasks. The address will be:

Independent Bureau for International Development Issues (IBIDI)
Institute of Social Studies
251 Badhuisweg
PO Box 90733
NL-2509 LS The Hague
Netherlands

Tel: 57 22 01
Cables: SOCINST